KU-303-990

WWW.

Visit the Waterstone's bookshop on the internet
for the very latest reviews, comment and special offers
at www.waterstones.co.uk/granta.htm

WATERSTONE'S

READ ON

GRANTA

GRANTA 63, AUTUMN 1998

EDITOR *Ian Jack*
DEPUTY EDITOR *Robert Winder*
MANAGING EDITOR *Karen Whitfield*
EDITORIAL ASSISTANT *Sophie Harrison*

CONTRIBUTING EDITORS *Neil Belton, Pete de Bolla, Frances Coady, Ursula Doyle, Will Hobson, Liz Jobey, Blake Morrison, Andrew O'Hagan*

FINANCE *Geoffrey Gordon*
ASSOCIATE PUBLISHER *Sally Lewis*
SALES *David Hooper*
PUBLICITY *Gail Lynch, Rebecca Linsley*
SUBSCRIPTIONS *John Kirkby, Darryl Wilks*
PUBLISHING ASSISTANT *Mark Williams*
TO ADVERTISE CONTACT *Jenny Shramenko* 0171 274 0600

PUBLISHER *Rea S. Hederman*

Granta, 2-3 Hanover Yard, Noel Road, London N1 8BE
Tel 0171 704 9776 Fax 0171 704 0474
e-mail for editorial: editorial@grantamag.co.uk

Granta US, 1755 Broadway, 5th Floor, New York, NY 10019-3780, USA
Website: www.granta.com

TO SUBSCRIBE call 0171 704 0470 or e-mail subs@grantamag.co.uk
A one-year subscription (four issues) costs £24.95 (UK), £32.95 (rest of Europe) and £39.95 (rest of the world).

Granta is printed in the United States of America. The paper used in this publication meets the minimum requirements of American National Standard for Information Sciences—Permanence of Paper for Printed Library Materials, ANSI Z39.48-1984. ♾

Granta is published by Granta Publications and distributed in the United Kingdom by Bloomsbury, 38 Soho Square, London W1V 5DF, and in the United States by Penguin Books USA Inc, 375 Hudson Street, New York, NY 10014, USA. This selection copyright © 1998 Granta Publications.

Design: The Senate
Front cover photograph: Richard Lewisohn, The Special Photographers Library

ISBN 0 903141 20 5

ROBERT
STONE

A passionate, humorous and wise book
about the search for God, power,
salvation and apocalypse.

'A stunning novel by a great
American author'
Washington Post

'This year's *Mason & Dixon*
or *Underworld*. Not to
be missed'
Kirkus Reviews

DAMASCUS
GATE

PICADOR

On sale from 23 October 1998
£16.99

Looking for something new?
Something to stimulate?

Try a literary magazine.

But to get it regularly you
must subscribe.

London Review
OF BOOKS

Alan Bennett calls the *London Review of Books* 'the liveliest, the most serious and also the most radical literary magazine we have'.

To subscribe at a discount of 50% AND get six free trial issues: call FREE on 0500 345 789 (24 hrs, UK only).

Details also available by:
Telephone: 0171 209 1141
or FAX: 0171 209 1151
or e-mail: subs@lrb.co.uk
or visit our website: www.lrb.co.uk

the NORTH

Poetry, reviews, critical articles, interviews and features.

Recent issues include poems by Paul Farley, Dorothy Nimmo, Ruth Padel and Dennis O'Driscoll; articles on Derek Mahon and Roy Fisher; and interviews with Edwin Morgan and Michael Schmidt.

'Excellent' – The Guardian

UK subscription £10 for 2 issues
The Poetry Business,
The Studio, Byram Arcade,
Huddersfield HD1 1ND

Literary magazines offer the newest short fiction, poetry and essays to stimulate the mind and feed the soul. They provide glimpses of work in progress, reviews and news to keep you aware of the latest literary issues, and offer a forum for world literature in translation.

Only in literary magazines will you find such a rich mix - supplying a vital platform for writers and a window on contemporary literature highly valued by discerning readers.

But such pleasures are not easily found. Subscription ensures you won't miss out on a regular literary treasure-trove from established writers and the hottest new talent.

There are literary magazines to suit all tastes – take out a subscription now.

MPT MODERN POETRY in TRANSLATION

Over 250 pages of poems from around the world, with essays and reviews.

1998:
No 13 – **Modern Greece**
No 14 – **Arabic and Hebrew** poetry

Subscription (2 issues post free):
£20 UK/EU; £24 foreign

Write to: Norma Rinsler, *MPT*
King's College London, Strand,
London WC2R 2LS

Cheques payable to:
King's College London

THE **ARTS COUNCIL** OF ENGLAND

GRANTA 63

Beasts

NATIVE NATIONS

Journeys in American photography

10 September – 13 December 1998
Barbican Art Gallery
Barbican Centre, London EC2
⊖ Barbican, Moorgate

Edward S Curtis *A Tewa Girl* Vol XII The North American Indian, published 1992 Photogravure
Courtesy of Guildhall Library, Corporation of London
Barbican Art Gallery is owned, funded and managed by the Corporation of London.

INTRODUCTION

We can be sentimental about animals (they are almost human, aren't they?) but we have little idea what, or even if, they think. We do know that their senses are more finely honed than ours: a human being has only five million olfactory cells to smell with, while a German sheepdog has 220 million. We know that bats and butterflies can perform amazing feats of navigation and air traffic control; and that dolphins are capable of something we usually call altruism. We also know that animals do suffer on a physical level: pigs that undergo excessive 'pre-slaughter stress' produce bad quality pork. But their mental states, their inner lives, the things that keep them awake at night? These matters remain as mysterious as they were when Darwin watched the orang-utans in London Zoo toying with their reflections in a mirror. In 1986 the British government added the octopus to the elite group of creatures deemed to be sentient (and therefore not eligible for surgery without anaesthetic). This was not because there was any evidence that an octopus could be conscious (in the way we understand the term) of pain. It was just in case.

We are quick to attribute aspects of our own behaviour to our kinship with the animal kingdom. We can be foxy or dogged, sheepish or venomous, mulish or bovine. We can wolf down our lunch, hare home, and ape the mannerisms of our colleagues. We can be hawks or doves, bulls or bears. We fight the temptation, however, to allow the reverse to be true. To attribute too many human characteristics to our pets would, we know, be unscientific.

Animals do play a busy role in the human imagination, however, and this issue of *Granta* includes several pieces in which they play a central part. Nothing new here. In the myths of the ancient world the lines between *Homo sapiens* and the animal kingdom were blurred: a man might become a bull; a woman could find herself a swan. The woods swarmed with gods disguised in fur or feathers. Later, in Aesop and Ovid, animals were deployed as sweet emblems of human urges—ravenous wolves, timid rabbits—in fables of vanity and greed. The fairy tales and folk myths related by La Fontaine and the Brothers Grimm envisaged wildlife in a similar way. And children's literature, channelled through the Disney Corporation (*Dumbo*, *Bambi*, *The Jungle Book*, *The Lion King* and so on) has been constructed almost wholly along anthropomorphic lines—even if we do call it 'animation'.

There is a conservative, almost propagandizing quality to this: no one finds it odd that, in nature, the boy animals hunt and gambol, while the girl animals flutter their colourful eyelashes and look after the little ones; so our children grow up in a world where such divisions seem utterly and unarguably 'natural'. The creatures in classic children's books (Peter Rabbit, the Cat in the Hat) inspire a poignant but narrow palette of emotions and attitudes. The aim is not to tell us anything about animals as such—these are little humans in disguise, just like their friends the talkative railway engines, helicopters and tug-boats.

Victorian literature, when it noticed the wilder beasts, noticed them for the most part as wall-mountings or hearthrugs. When Virginia Woolf narrated the life of Robert and Elizabeth Browning from the point of view of their dog, she was exploiting little more than the vantage point of someone who was, after all, in the room at the time. But in this century literature has once again been busy dissolving and even questioning the imaginative boundaries that divide us from the so-called lower species. Kafka, in 'The Metamorphosis', spoke as an insect to dramatize the oppressive horror and comedy of living in an incomprehensible universe. Italo Calvino's Mr Palomar listened to the blackbirds in his garden and wondered whether the eloquent sighs and groans that passed between himself and his wife sounded as mysterious to the birds as their song did to him. Orwell, in *Animal Farm*, spun farmyard rivalries into a parable of totalitarian hierarchy.

There are several more recent examples, enough almost to constitute a vogue. Art Spiegelman, in *Maus*, depicted the Holocaust as a Tom and Jerry cartoon—horrible Nazi cats pouncing on cowering Jewish mice. Julian Barnes began his *History of the World in 10½ Chapters* with a description of Noah's ark, narrated by a stowaway who turned out to be a woodworm. The heroine of Marie Darrieussecq's *Pig Tales* was a woman who turned into a sow. And Peter Høeg and Will Self have both built fictions around apes.

As science begins to explore animal cognition, and as the animal rights culture continues to erode our once blithe attitude to wild things, it is not surprising if the old cartoon simplicities are fading. New research into the complexities of animal intelligence—the memory feats of elephants and birds, the loyalty of dogs, the broken hearts of whales and so on—might easily inspire a new species of fiction, always greedy for new lives to inhabit. This issue of *Granta* imagines a world in which the edges of what we think of as civilization are soft.

RW

GRANTA

MR BONES

Paul Auster

Mr Bones

Mr Bones knew that Willy wasn't long for this world. The cough had been inside him for over six months, and by now there wasn't a chance in hell that he would ever get rid of it. Slowly and inexorably, without once taking a turn for the better, the thing had assumed a life of its own, advancing from a faint, phlegm-filled rattle in the lungs on February third to the wheezy sputum-jigs and gobby convulsions of high summer. All that was bad enough, but in the past two weeks a new tonality had crept into the bronchial music—something tight and flinty and percussive—and the attacks came so often now as to be almost constant. Every time one of them started, Mr Bones half expected Willy's body to explode from the rockets of pressure bursting against his ribcage. He figured that blood would be the next step, and when that fatal moment finally occurred on Saturday afternoon, it was as if all the angels in heaven had opened their mouths and started to sing. Mr Bones saw it happen with his own eyes, standing by the edge of the road between Washington and Baltimore as Willy hawked up a few miserable clots of red matter into his handkerchief, and right then and there he knew that every ounce of hope was gone. The smell of death had settled upon Willy G. Christmas, and as surely as the sun was a lamp in the clouds that went off and on every day, the end was drawing near.

What was a poor dog to do? Mr Bones had been with Willy since his earliest days as a pup, and by now it was next to impossible for him to imagine a world that did not have his master in it. Every thought, every memory, every particle of the earth and air was saturated with Willy's presence. Habits die hard, and no doubt there's some truth to the adage about old dogs and new tricks, but it was more than just love or devotion that caused Mr Bones to dread what was coming. It was pure ontological terror. Subtract Willy from the world, and the odds were that the world itself would cease to exist.

Such was the quandary Mr Bones faced that August morning as he shuffled through the streets of Baltimore with his ailing master. A dog alone was no better than a dead dog, and once Willy breathed his last, he'd have nothing to look forward to but his own immanent demise. Willy had been cautioning him about this for many days now, and Mr Bones knew the drill by heart: how to avoid the dogcatchers and constables, the paddy wagons and unmarked cars, the hypocrites

RICHARD KALVAR/MAGNUM

11

from the so-called humane societies. No matter how sweetly they talked to you, the word *shelter* meant trouble. It would begin with nets and tranquillizer guns, devolve into a nightmare of cages and fluorescent lights, and end with a lethal injection or a dose of poison gas. If Mr Bones had belonged to some recognizable breed, he might have stood a chance in the daily beauty contests for prospective owners, but Willy's sidekick was a hodgepodge of genetic strains— part collie, part Labrador, part spaniel, part canine puzzle—and to make matters worse, there were burrs protruding from his ragged coat, bad smells emanating from his mouth, and a perpetual, bloodshot sadness lurking in his eyes. No one was going to want to rescue him. As the homeless bard was fond of putting it, the outcome was written in stone. Unless Mr Bones found another master in one quick hurry, he was a pooch primed for oblivion.

'And if the stun guns don't get you,' Willy continued, clinging to a lamp-post that foggy morning in Baltimore to prevent himself from falling, 'there's a thousand other things that will. I'm warning you, keemosabe. You get yourself some new gig, or your days are numbered. Just look around this dreary burg. There's a Chinese restaurant on every block, and if you think mouths won't water when you come strolling by, then you don't know squat about Oriental cuisine. They prize the taste of dog, friend. The chefs round up strays and slaughter them in the alley right behind the kitchen—ten, twenty, thirty dogs a week. They might pass them off as ducks and pigs on the menu, but the in-crowd knows what's what, the gourmets aren't fooled for a second. Unless you want to wind up in a platter of moo goo gai pan, you'll think twice before you wag your tail in front of one of those Chink beaneries. Do you catch my drift, Mr Bones? Know thine enemy—and then keep a wide berth.'

Mr Bones understood. He always understood what Willy said to him. This had been the case for as long as he could remember, and by now his grasp of Ingloosh was as good as that of any other immigrant who had spent seven years on American soil. It was his second language, of course, and quite different from the one his mother had taught him, but even though his pronunciation left something to be desired, he had thoroughly mastered the ins and outs of its syntax and grammar. None of this should be seen as strange or unusual for an animal of Mr Bones's intelligence. Most dogs acquire a good working knowledge of two-legged speech, but in Mr Bones's case there was the advantage of being blessed with a master who did not treat him as an inferior. They had been boon companions from the start, and when you added in the fact that Mr Bones was not just Willy's best friend but his only friend, and then further considered that Willy was a man in love with the sound of his own voice, a genuine, dyed-in-the-wool logomaniac who scarcely stopped talking from the instant he opened his eyes in the morning until he passed out drunk at night, it made perfect sense that Mr Bones should have felt so at home in the native lingo. When all was said and done, the only surprise was that he hadn't learned to talk better himself. It wasn't for lack of earnest effort, but biology was against him, and what with the configuration of muzzle, teeth and tongue that fate had saddled him with, the best he could do was emit a series of yaps and yawns and yowls, a mooning, muddled sort of discourse. He was painfully aware of how far from fluency these noises fell, but Willy always let him have his say, and in the end that was all that mattered. Mr Bones was free to put in his two cents, and whenever he did so his master would give him his full attention, and to look at Willy's face as he watched his friend struggle to make like a member of the human tribe, you would have sworn that he was hanging on every word.

That gloomy Sunday in Baltimore, however, Mr Bones kept his mouth shut. They were down to their last days together, perhaps even their last hours, and this was no time to indulge in long speeches and loopy contortions, no time for the old shenanigans. Certain situations called for tact and discipline, and in their present dire straits it would be far better to hold his tongue and behave like a good, loyal dog. He let Willy snap the leash on to his collar without protest. He didn't whine about not having eaten in the past thirty-six hours; he didn't sniff the air for female scents; he didn't stop to pee on every lamp-post and fire hydrant. He simply ambled along beside Willy, following his master as they searched the empty avenues for 316 Calvert Street.

Mr Bones had nothing against Baltimore per se. It smelled no worse than any other city they'd camped in over the years, but even though he understood the purpose of the trip, it grieved him to think that a man could choose to spend his last moments on earth in a place he'd never been to before. A dog would never commit such a blunder. He would make his peace with the world and then see to it that he gave up the ghost on familiar ground. But Willy still had two things to accomplish before he died, and with characteristic stubbornness he'd gotten it into his head that there was only one person who could help him. The name of that person was Bea Swanson, and since said Bea Swanson was last known to be living in Baltimore, they had come to Baltimore to find her. All well and good, but unless Willy's plan did what it was supposed to do, Mr Bones would be marooned in this city of crab cakes and marble steps, and what was he going to do then? A phone call would have done the job in half a minute, but Willy had a philosophical aversion to using the telephone for important business. He would rather walk for days on end than pick up one of those contraptions and talk to someone he couldn't see. So here they were 200 miles later, wandering around the streets of Baltimore without a map, looking for an address that might or might not exist.

Of the two things Willy still hoped to accomplish before he died, neither one took precedence over the other. Each was all-important to him, and since time had grown too short to think of tackling them separately, he had come up with what he referred to as the Chesapeake Gambit: an eleventh-hour ploy to kill both birds with one stone. The first has already been discussed in the previous paragraphs: to find new digs for his furry companion. The second was to wrap up his own affairs and make sure that his manuscripts were left in good hands. At that moment, his life's work was crammed into a rental locker at the Greyhound Bus terminal on Fayette Street, two and a half blocks north of where he and Mr Bones were standing. The key was in his pocket, and unless he found someone worthy enough to entrust with that key, every word he had ever written would be destroyed, disposed of as so much unclaimed baggage.

In the twenty-three years since he'd taken on the surname of Christmas, Willy had filled the pages of seventy-four notebooks with his writings. These included poems, stories, essays, diary entries, epigrams, autobiographical musings, and the first 1,800 lines of an epic-in-progress, *Vagabond Days*. The majority of these works had been composed at the kitchen table of his mother's apartment in Brooklyn, but since her death four years ago he'd been forced to write in the open air, often battling the elements in public parks and dusty alleyways as he struggled to get his thoughts down on paper. In his secret heart of hearts, Willy had no delusions about himself. He knew that he was a troubled soul and not fit for this world, but he also knew that much good work was buried in those notebooks, and on that score at least he could hold his head high. Maybe if he had been more scrupulous about taking his medication, or maybe if his body had been a bit stronger, or maybe if he hadn't been so fond of malts and spirits and the hubbub of bars, he might have done even more good work. That was perfectly possible, but it was too late to dwell on regrets and errors now. Willy had written the last sentence he would ever write, and there were no more than a few ticks left in the clock. The words in the locker were all he had to show for himself. If the words vanished, it would be as if he had never lived.

That was where Bea Swanson entered the picture. Willy knew it was a stab in the dark, but if and when he managed to find her, he was convinced that she would move heaven and earth to help him. Once upon a time, back when the world was still young, Mrs Swanson had been his high school English teacher, and if not for her it was doubtful that he ever would have found the courage to think of himself as a writer. He was still William Gurevitch in those days, a scrawny sixteen-year-old boy with a passion for books and bebop jazz, and she had taken him under her wing and lavished his early work with praise that was so excessive, so far out of proportion to its true merit, that he began to think of himself as the next great hope of American literature. Whether she was right or wrong to do so is not the question, for results are less important at that stage than promise, and Mrs Swanson had recognized his talent, she'd seen the spark in his fledgling soul, and no one can ever amount to anything in this life without someone else to believe in him. That's a proven fact, and while the rest of the junior class at Midwood High saw Mrs Swanson as a squat, fortyish woman with blubbery arms that bounced and wiggled whenever she wrote on the blackboard, Willy thought she was beautiful, an angel who had come down from heaven and taken on a human form.

By the time school started again in the fall, however, Mrs Swanson was gone. Her husband had been offered a new job in Baltimore, and since Mrs Swanson was not only a teacher but a wife, what choice did she have but to leave Brooklyn and go where Mr Swanson went? It was a tough blow for Willy to absorb, but it could have been worse, for even though his mentor was far away, she did not forget him. Over the next several years, Mrs Swanson kept up a lively correspondence with her young friend, continuing to read and comment on the manuscripts he sent her, to remember his birthday with gifts of old Charlie Parker records, and to suggest little magazines where he could begin submitting his work. The gushing, rhapsodic letter of recommendation she wrote for him in his senior year helped clinch a full scholarship for Willy at Columbia. Mrs Swanson was his muse, his protector and his good luck charm all rolled into one, and at that point in Willy's life, the sky was definitely the limit. But then came the schizo flip-out of 1968, the mad fandango of truth or consequences on a high-voltage tension wire. They shut him up in a hospital, and after six months of shock treatment and psycho-pharmacological therapy, he was never quite the same again. Willy had joined the ranks of the walking wounded, and even though he continued to churn out his poems and stories, to go on writing both in sickness and in health, he rarely got around to answering Mrs Swanson's letters. The reasons were unimportant. Perhaps Willy was embarrassed to stay in touch with her. Perhaps he was distracted, preoccupied with other business. Perhaps he had lost faith in the US Postal Service and no longer trusted the mail carriers not to snoop inside the letters they delivered. One way or the other, his once voluminous exchanges with Mrs Swanson dwindled to almost nothing. For a year or two, they consisted of the odd, desultory postcard, then the store-bought Christmas greeting, and then, by 1976, they had stopped altogether. Since that time, not one syllable of communication had passed between them.

Mr Bones knew all this, and that was precisely what worried him. Seventeen years had gone by. Gerald Ford had been President back then, for Chrissakes, and he himself would not be whelped for another decade. Who was Willy trying to kid? Think of all the things that can happen in that time. Think of the changes that can occur in seventeen hours or seventeen minutes—let alone in seventeen years. At the very least, Mrs Swanson had probably moved to another address. The old girl would be pushing seventy by now, and if she wasn't senile or living in a trailer park in Florida, there was a better than even chance that she was dead. Willy had admitted as much when they hit the streets of Baltimore that morning, but what the fuck, he'd said, it was their one and only shot, and since life was a gamble anyway, why not go for broke?

Ah, Willy. He had told so many stories, had talked in so many different voices, had spoken out of so many sides of his mouth at once that Mr Bones had no idea what to believe anymore. What was true, what was false? It was difficult to know when dealing with a character as complex and fanciful as Willy G. Christmas. Mr Bones could vouch for the things he'd seen with his own eyes, the events he'd experienced in his own flesh, but he and Willy had been together for only seven years, and the facts concerning the previous thirty-eight were more or less up for grabs. If Mr Bones hadn't spent his puppyhood living under the same roof with Willy's mother, the whole story would have been shrouded in darkness, but by listening to Mrs Gurevitch and measuring her statements against her son's, Mr Bones had managed to stitch together a reasonably coherent portrait of what Willy's world had looked like before he came into it. A thousand details were lacking. A thousand others were muddled in confusion, but Mr Bones had a sense of the drift, a feeling for what its shape both was and wasn't.

It wasn't rich, for example, and it wasn't cheerful, and more often than not the air in the apartment had been tinged with sourness and desperation. Considering what the family had been through before it landed in America, it was probably a miracle that David Gurevitch and Ida Perlmutter managed to produce a son in the first place. Of the seven children born to Willy's grandparents in Warsaw and Lodz between 1910 and 1921, they were the only two to survive the war. They alone did not have numbers tattooed on their forearms, they alone were granted the luck to escape. But that didn't mean they had an easy time of it, and Mr Bones had heard enough stories to make his fur tingle. There were the ten days they spent hiding in an attic crawl space in Warsaw. There was the month-long walk from Paris to the Free Zone in the south, sleeping in haylofts and stealing eggs to stay alive. There was the refugee internment camp in Mende, the money spent on bribes for safe conducts, the four months of bureaucratic hell in Marseilles as they waited for their Spanish transit visas. Then came the long coma of immobility in Lisbon, the stillborn son Ida delivered in 1944, the two years of looking out at the Atlantic as the war dragged on and their money ebbed away. By the time Willy's parents arrived in Brooklyn in 1946, it wasn't a new life they were starting so much as a posthumous life, an interval between two deaths. Willy's father, once a clever young lawyer in Poland, begged a job from a distant cousin and spent the next thirteen years riding the Seventh Avenue IRT to a button-manufacturing firm on West Twenty-eighth Street. For the first year, Willy's mother supplemented their income by giving piano lessons to young Jewish brats in the apartment, but that ended one morning in November of 1947 when Willy poked his little face out from between her legs and unexpectedly refused to stop breathing.

He grew up American, a Brooklyn boy who played stickball in the streets, read *Mad* magazine under the covers at night, and listened to Buddy Holly and the Big Bopper. Neither one of his parents could fathom such things, but that was just as well as far as Willy was concerned, since his great goal in life at that stage was to convince himself that his mother and father were not his real parents. He found them alien, wholly embarrassing creatures, a pair of sore thumbs with their Polish accents and stilted foreign ways, and without really having to think about it, he understood that his only hope of survival lay in resisting them at every turn. When his father dropped dead from a heart attack at forty-nine, Willy's sorrow was mitigated by a secret sense of relief. Already, at twelve, just barely on the brink of adolescence, he had formulated his lifelong philosophy of embracing trouble wherever he could find it. The more wretched your life was, the closer you were to the truth, to the gritty nub of existence, and what could be more terrible than losing your old man six weeks after your twelfth birthday? It marked you as a tragic figure, disqualified you from the rat race of vain hopes and sentimental illusions, bestowed on you an aura of legitimate suffering. But the fact was that Willy didn't suffer much. His father had always been a riddle to him, a man prone to week-long silences and sudden outbursts of rage, and more than once he had slapped down Willy for the smallest, most trifling infraction. No, it wasn't hard to adjust to life without that bag of explosives. It didn't take any effort at all.

Or so reckoned the good Herr Doktor Bones. Ignore his opinion if you will, but who else are you prepared to trust? After listening to these stories for the past seven years, had he not earned the right to be called the world's leading authority on the subject?

That left Willy alone with his mother. She was hardly anyone's idea of a good time, but at least she kept her hands to herself and showed him considerable amounts of affection, enough warmth of heart to counterbalance the periods when she nagged him and harangued him and got on his nerves. By and large, Willy tried to be a good son. At those rare moments when he was able to stop thinking about himself, he even made a conscious effort to be nice to her. If they had their differences, they were less a result of personal animosity than of starkly opposing world-views. From hard-won experience, Mrs Gurevitch knew that the world was out to get her, and she lived her life accordingly, doing everything in her power to stay clear of harm's way. Willy also knew that the world was out to get him, but unlike his mother he had no qualms about fighting back. The difference was not that one was a pessimist and the other an optimist, it was that one's pessimism had led to an ethos of fear, and the other's pessimism had led to a noisy, fractious disdain for Everything-That-Was. One shrank, the other flailed. One toed the line, the other crossed it out. Much of the time they were at loggerheads, and because Willy found it so easy to shock his mother, he rarely wasted an opportunity to provoke an argument. If only she'd had the wit to back off a little, he probably wouldn't have been so insistent about making his points. Her antagonism inspired him, pushed him into ever more extreme positions, and by the time he was ready to leave the house and go off to college, he had indelibly cast himself in his chosen role: as malcontent, as rebel, as outlaw poet prowling the gutters of a ruined world.

Lord knows how many drugs that boy ingested in the two

and a half years he spent on Morningside Heights. Name an illegal substance, and Willy either smoked it or snorted it or shot it into his veins. It's one thing to walk around pretending you're the second coming of François Villon, but feed an unstable young man enough toxic confections to fill a dump site in the Jersey Meadowlands, and his body chemistry is bound to be altered. Sooner or later, Willy might have cracked up anyway, but who would argue that the psychedelic free-for-all of his student days didn't accelerate the process? When his room-mate walked in on him one afternoon in the middle of his junior year and found Willy buck naked on the floor—chanting names from the Manhattan phone book and eating a bowl of his own excrement—the academic career of Mr Bones's future master came to an abrupt and permanent end.

The loony-bin followed, and then Willy returned to his mother's apartment on Glenwood Avenue. It wasn't the ideal place for him to live, perhaps, but where else could a burn-out like poor Willy go? For the first six months, not much good came of the arrangement. Other than Willy's switch from drugs to alcohol, things were essentially the same as they had been. The same tensions, the same conflicts, the same misunderstandings. Then, out of the blue, in late December 1969, Willy had the vision that changed everything, the mystical encounter with blessedness that turned him inside out and set his life on an entirely different course.

It was two-thirty in the morning. His mother had gone to bed several hours before, and Willy was parked on the living-room sofa with a pack of Luckies and a bottle of bourbon, watching television out of the corner of one eye. Television was a new habit for him, a by-product of his recent stay in the hospital. He wasn't particularly interested in the images on the screen (in fact, he seldom bothered to look at them), but he enjoyed having the hum and glow of the tube in the background and found comfort in the grey-blue shadows it cast on the walls. *The Late Late Show* was on just then (something to do with gigantic grasshoppers devouring the citizens of Sacramento, California), but most of the airtime had been given over to chintzy exhortations on behalf of miracle breakthrough products: knives that never went dull, light bulbs that never burned out, secret-formula lotions that removed the curse of baldness. Yak yak yak, Willy muttered to himself, it's the same old suds and blather. Just as he was about to stand up and turn off the television, however, a new commercial came on, and there was Santa Claus popping out of someone's fireplace in what looked like a suburban living-room in Massapequa, Long Island. Given that Christmas was just around the corner, Willy had grown used to commercials that featured actors dressed up as Santa Claus. But this one was better than most—a roly-poly guy with rosy cheeks and an honest-to-goodness white beard. Willy paused to watch the beginning of the spiel, fully expecting to hear something about rug shampoos or burglar alarms, when all of a sudden Santa uttered the words that would change his destiny.

'William Gurevitch,' Santa said. 'Yes, William Gurevitch of Brooklyn, New York, I'm talking to you.'

Willy had drunk only half a bottle that night, and it had been eight months since his last full-blown hallucination. Nobody was going to trick him into swallowing this garbage. He knew the difference between reality and make-believe, and if Santa Claus was talking to him from his mother's television set, that could only mean he was a lot drunker than he supposed.

'Fuck you, mister,' Willy said, and without giving the matter another thought, he clicked off the machine.

Unfortunately, he wasn't able to leave things as they were. Because he was curious, or because he wanted to make sure he wasn't having another breakdown, Willy decided it would be all right if he turned the television back on—just for a peek, a last little peek. It wasn't going to hurt anyone, was it? Better to learn the truth now than to walk around with that sack of Yuletide shit preying on his mind for the next forty years.

And lo and behold, there he was again. There was Santa bloody Claus, wagging his finger at Willy and shaking his head with a sad, disappointed look in his eyes. When he opened his mouth and started to talk (picking up precisely where he had left off ten seconds earlier), Willy didn't know whether he should burst out laughing or jump through the window. It was happening, folks. What could not happen was happening, and right then and there Willy knew that nothing in the world would ever look the same to him again.

'That wasn't nice, William,' Santa said. 'I'm here to help you, but we're never going to get anywhere if you don't give me a chance to talk. Do you follow me, son?'

The question seemed to call for a response, but Willy hesitated. Listening to this clown was bad enough. Did he really want to make things worse by talking back to him?

'William!' Santa said. His voice was stern and reproachful, and it contained the power of a personality that was not to be trifled with. If Willy was ever going to squirm out of this nightmare, his only hope would be to play along.

'Yeah, boss,' he mumbled, 'I read you loud and clear.'

The fat man smiled. Then, very slowly, the camera moved in on him for a close-up. For the next several seconds Santa stood there stroking his beard, apparently lost in thought.

'Do you know who I am?' he finally said.

'I know who you look like,' Willy said, 'but that doesn't mean I know who you are. At first I thought you were some asshole actor. Then I thought maybe you were that genie in the bottle. Now I don't have a clue.'

'The thing I look like is the thing I am.'

'Sure, pal, and I'm Haile Selassie's brother-in-law.'

'Santa Claus, William. A.k.a. Saint Nick. Father Christmas himself. The only force for good left in the world.'

'Santa, huh? And you wouldn't happen to spell that S-A-N-T-A, would you?'

'Yes, I would. That's exactly how I'd spell it.'

'That's what I figured. Now rearrange the letters a little bit, and what do you have? S-A-T-A-N, that's what. You're the goddamn devil, grandpa, and the only place you exist is in my mind.'

Notice how Willy struggled against the apparition, how determined he was to thwart its charms. He wasn't some pea-brained psycho who let figments and spectres push him around. He wanted no part of this one, and the disgust he felt, the downright hostility he expressed whenever he recalled the first moments of the encounter, was precisely what convinced Mr Bones that it was true, that Willy had experienced an authentic vision and was not making the story up. To hear him tell it, the situation was a scandal, an insult to his intelligence, and merely having to look at that bovine lump of clichés brought his blood to a boil. Let someone else make with the ho-ho stuff. Christmas was a fraud, a season for quick bucks and ringing cash registers, and as the symbol of that season, as the very essence of the whole consumerist shebang, Santa was the biggest fake of them all.

But this Santa was no fake, and he was no devil in disguise. He was the true Father Christmas, the one and only Lord of the Elves and Spirits, and the message he'd come to preach was one of goodness, generosity and self-sacrifice. This unlikeliest of fictions, this contradiction of everything Willy stood for, this absurd display of hokum in the red jacket and the fur-fringed boots—yes, Santa Claus in all his Madison Avenue glory—had sprung forth from the depths of Television Land to debunk the certitudes of Willy's scepticism and put his soul back together again. It was as simple as that. If anyone was a fraud, Santa said, it was Willy, and then he let him have it in no uncertain terms, lecturing the frightened and bewildered boy for the better part of an hour. He called him a sham, a poseur and a no-talent hack. Then he upped the ante and called him a zero, a douche bag, a dunderhead, and little by little he broke down the wall of Willy's defences and made him see the light. Willy was on the floor by then, weeping his eyes out as he begged for mercy and promised to mend his ways. Christmas was real, he learned, and there would be no truth or happiness for him until he began to embrace its spirit. That would be his mission in life from now on: to embody the message of Christmas every day of the year, to ask nothing from the world and give it only love in return.

In other words, Willy decided to turn himself into a saint.

And so it happened that William Gurevitch concluded his business on this earth, and from his flesh a new man named Willy G. Christmas was born. To celebrate the event, Willy scuttled off to Manhattan the next morning and had himself tattooed with a picture of Santa Claus on his right arm. It was a painful ordeal, but Willy suffered the needles gladly, triumphant in the knowledge that he now bore a visible sign of his transformation and would carry its mark with him for ever.

Alas, when he returned to Brooklyn and proudly showed his mother this new ornament, Mrs Gurevitch went wild, erupting in a tantrum of tears and angry disbelief. It wasn't just the idea of the tattoo that bent her out of shape (although that was part of it, given that tattooing was proscribed by Jewish law—and given what role the tattooing of Jewish skin had played in her lifetime), it was what *this particular tattoo* represented, and in that Mrs Gurevitch saw the three-colour Santa Claus on Willy's arm as a token of betrayal and incurable madness, her outburst at that moment was perhaps understandable. Until then, she had managed to delude herself into thinking that her son would make a full recovery. She blamed his condition on the drugs, and once the noxious residues were flushed out of his system and his blood count returned to normal, she felt it would only be a matter of time before he turned off the television set and went back to college. But not anymore. One glance at the tattoo, and all those vain hopes and false expectations shattered at her feet like so much glass. Santa Claus was from the other side. He belonged to the Presbyterians and the Roman Catholics, to the Jesus-worshippers and Jew-haters, to Hitler and all the rest of them. The goyim had taken hold of Willy's brain, and once they crawled inside you, they never let go. Christmas was only the first step. Easter was just a few months down the road, and then they'd drag out those crosses of theirs and start talking about murder, and before long the storm troopers would be breaking down the door. She saw the picture of Santa Claus emblazoned on her son's arm, but as far as she was concerned, it might just as well have been a swastika.

Willy was frankly perplexed. He hadn't meant any harm, and in his present blissful state of remorse and conversion, the last thing he wanted was to offend his mother. But talk and explain as he did, she refused to listen. She shrieked at him and called him a Nazi, and when he persisted in trying to make her understand that Santa Claus was an incarnation of the Buddha, a holy being whose message to the world was one of merciful love and compassion, she threatened to send him back to the hospital that very afternoon. This brought to mind a sentence that Willy had heard from a fellow patient at Saint Luke's—'I'd rather have a bottle in front of me than a frontal lobotomy'—and suddenly he knew what was in store for him if he let his mother have her way. So, rather than go on beating a dead horse, he climbed into his overcoat and left the apartment, heading in a beeline for God knows where.

Thus began a pattern that continued for the next umpteen years. Willy would stay with his mother for several months, then leave for several months, then come back. The first departure was probably the most dramatic, if only because Willy still had everything to learn about the wandering life. He was gone for just a short spell, and although Mr Bones was never quite certain what Willy meant by *short*, whatever happened to his master during the weeks or months he was away proved to him that he had found his true calling. 'Don't tell me that two and two is four,' Willy said to his mother when he returned to Brooklyn. 'How do we know that two is two? That's the real question.'

The next day, he sat down and started writing again. It was the first time he'd picked up a pen since before the hospital, and the words poured out of him like water gushing from a broken pipe. Willy G. Christmas proved to be a better and more inspired poet than William Gurevitch had ever been, and what his early efforts lacked in originality, they made up for in hell-bent enthusiasm. 'Thirty-three Rules to Live By' was a good example. Its opening lines read as follows:

> Throw yourself into the arms of the world
> And the air will hold you. Hold back
> And the world will jump you from behind.
> Go for broke down the highway of bones.
> Follow the music of your steps, and when the lights go out
> Don't whistle—sing.
> If you keep your eyes open, you'll always be lost.
> Give away your shirt, give away your gold,
> Give away your shoes to the first stranger you see.
> Much will come of nothing
> If you dance the jitterbug waltz...

Literary pursuits were one thing, but how you conducted yourself in the world was quite another. Willy's poems might have changed, but that still didn't answer the question about whether Willy himself had changed. Did he actually become a new person, or was the plunge into sainthood no more than a passing impulse? Had he boondoggled himself into an untenable position, or was there something more to be said about his rebirth than the tattoo on his right bicep and the ridiculous moniker he took such pleasure in using? An honest answer would be yes and no, perhaps, a little of both. For Willy was weak, and Willy was often belligerent, and Willy was prone to forget things. Mental mishaps dogged him, and whenever the pinball machine in his head speeded up and went tilt, all bets were off. How could a man of his ilk propose to don the mantle of purity? Not only was he an incipient lush, and not only was he a bred-in-the-bone liar with a strong paranoiac bent, he was too damn funny for his own good. Once Willy started in with the jokes, Santa Claus burst into flames, and the whole hearts-and-flowers act burned to the ground with him. Still and all, it would be wrong to say that he didn't try, and in that trying hung a large part of the story. Even if Willy didn't always live up to his expectations for himself, at least he had a model for how he wanted to behave. At those rare moments when he was able to focus his thoughts and curb his excesses in the beverage department, Willy demonstrated that no act of courage or generosity was beyond him. In 1972, for example, at no small risk to himself, he rescued a four-year-old girl from drowning. In 1976, he came to the defence of an eighty-one-year-old man who was being mugged on West Forty-third Street in New York—and for his pains received a knife wound in his shoulder and a bullet in his leg. More than once he gave his last dollar to a friend down on his luck, he let the lovelorn and the heartsick cry on his shoulder, and over the years he talked one man and two women out of suicide. There were fine things in Willy's soul, and whenever he let them come out, you forgot the other things that were in there as well. Yes, he was a bedraggled, demented pain in the ass, but when all was right in his head, Willy was one in a million, and everyone who crossed paths with him knew it.

Whenever he talked to Mr Bones about those early years, Willy tended to dwell on the good memories and ignore the bad. But who could blame him for sentimentalizing the past? We all do it, dogs and people alike, and in 1970 Willy had been nowhere if not in the pink of youth. His health was as robust as it would ever be, his teeth were intact, and to top it off he had money in the bank. A small sum had been set aside for him from his father's life insurance policy, and when he came into this money on his twenty-first birthday, he was kept in pocket change for close to a decade. But above and beyond the boon of money and youth, there was the historical moment, the times themselves, the spirit abroad in the land when Willy set forth on his career of vagabondage. The country was crawling with drop-outs and runaway children, with long-haired neo-visionaries, dysfunctional anarchists and doped-up misfits. For all the oddness he demonstrated in his own right, Willy hardly stood out among them. He was just one more weirdo on the Amerikan scene, and wherever his travels happened to take him—be it Pittsburgh or Plattsburgh, Pacatello or Boca Raton—he managed to latch on to like-minded souls for company. Or so he said, and in the long run Mr Bones saw no reason to doubt him.

Not that it would have made any difference if he had. The dog had lived long enough to know that good stories were not necessarily true stories, and whether he chose to believe the stories Willy told about himself or not was less important than the fact that Willy had done what he had done, and the years had passed. That was the essential thing, wasn't it? The years, the number of years it took to go from being young to not-so-young, and all the while to watch the world change around you. By the time Mr Bones crept forth from his mother's womb, Willy's salad days were but a dim memory, a pile of compost mouldering in a vacant lot. The runaways had crawled back home to mom and dad; the potheads had traded in their love beads for paisley ties; the war was over. But Willy was still Willy, the boffo rhymester and self-appointed bearer of Santa's message, your basic sorry excuse rigged out in the filthy duds of tramphood. The passage of time had not treated the poet kindly, and he didn't blend in so well anymore. He stank and drooled, he rubbed people the wrong way, and what with the bullet wounds and the knife wounds and the general deterioration of his physical self, he'd lost his quickness, his heretofore astonishing knack for slithering out of trouble. Strangers robbed him and beat him up. They kicked him while he slept, they set his books on fire, they took advantage of his aches and pains. After one such encounter landed him in the hospital with blurred vision and a fractured arm, he realized that he couldn't go on without some kind of protection. He thought of a gun, but weapons were abhorrent to him, and so he settled on the next best thing known to man: a bodyguard with four legs.

Mrs Gurevitch was less than thrilled, but Willy put his foot down and got his way. So the young Mr Bones was torn from his mother and five siblings at the North Shore Animal Shelter and moved to Glenwood Avenue in Brooklyn. To be perfectly honest, he didn't remember much about those early days. Ingloosh was still virgin territory to him back then, and what with Mrs Gurevitch's bizarrely mangled locutions and Willy's penchant for talking in different voices (Gabby Hayes one minute, Louis Armstrong the next; Groucho Marx in the morning, Maurice Chevalier at night), it took several months before he got the hang of it. In the meantime, there were the agonies of puppyhood: the struggles with bladder and bowel control, the newspapers on the kitchen floor, the snout-whacks from Mrs Gurevitch every time the pee dribbled out of him. She was a crotchety old complainer that one, and if not for Willy's gentle hands and soothing endearments, life in that apartment would have been no picnic. Winter was upon them, and with everything ice and stinging salt pellets on the streets below, he spent ninety-eight per cent of his time indoors, either sitting at Willy's feet as the poet cranked out his latest masterpiece or exploring the nooks and crevices of his new home. The apartment consisted of four and a half rooms, and by the time spring came Mr Bones was familiar with every stick of furniture, every blot on the rugs, every gash in the linoleum. He knew the smell of Mrs Gurevitch's slippers and the smell of Willy's underpants. He knew the difference between the doorbell and the telephone, could distinguish between the sound of jangling keys and the clatter of pills in a plastic vial, and before long he was on a first-name basis with every cockroach who lived in the cupboard under the kitchen sink. It was a dull, circumscribed routine, but how was Mr Bones to know that? He was no more than a lamebrained pup, a nincompoop with floppy paws who ran after his own tail and chomped on his own shit, and if this was the only life he'd ever tasted, who was he to judge whether it was rich or poor in the stuff that makes life worth living?

Was that little mutt in for a surprise! When the weather at last turned warm and the flowers unfurled their buds, he learned that

Willy was more than just a pencil-pushing homebody and professional jerk-off artist. His master was a man with the heart of a dog. He was a rambler, a rough-and-ready soldier of fortune, a one-of-a-kind two-leg who improvised the rules as he went along. They simply upped and left one morning in the middle of April, launched out into the great beyond, and saw neither hide nor hair of Brooklyn until the day before Hallowe'en. Could a dog ask for more than that? As far as Mr Bones was concerned, he was the luckiest creature on the face of the earth.

There were the winter hibernations, of course, the returns to the ancestral home, and with them the inevitable drawbacks of life indoors: the long months of hissing steam radiators, the infernal ruckus of vacuum cleaners and Waring blenders, the tedium of canned food. Once Mr Bones caught on to the rhythm, however, he had little cause for complaint. It was cold out there, after all, and the apartment had Willy in it, and how bad could life be if he and his master were together? Even Mrs Gurevitch eventually seemed to come round. Once the housebreaking issue was resolved, he noticed a distinct softening in her attitude toward him, and though she continued to grumble about the hairs he deposited throughout her domain, he understood that her heart was not fully in it. Sometimes, she would even let him sit beside her on the living-room sofa, softly stroking his head with one hand as she flipped through her magazine with the other, and more than once she actually confided in him, unburdening herself of assorted worries in regard to her wayward, benighted son. What a sorrow he was to her, and what a sad thing it was that such a fine boy should be so screwed up in the head. But half a son was better than no son, *farshtaist?*, and what choice did she have but to go on loving him and hope that things turned out for the best? They'd never allow him to be buried in a Jewish cemetery—not with that funny business on his arm they wouldn't—and just knowing that he wouldn't be laid to rest beside his mother and father was another sorrow, another torment that preyed on her mind, but life was for the living, wasn't it, and thank God they were both in good health—touch wood—or at least not so bad, all things considered, and that in itself was a blessing, something to be thankful for, and you couldn't buy that at the five-and-dime, could you, they didn't have commercials for that on TV. Colour, black-and-white, it didn't matter what kind of set you had. Life wasn't for sale, and once you found yourself at death's door, all the noodles in China weren't going to stop that door from opening.

As Mr Bones discovered, the differences between Mrs Gurevitch and her son were much smaller than he had at first supposed. It was true that they often disagreed, and it was true that their smells had nothing in common—the one being all dirt and male sweat, the other a mélange of lilac soap, Pond's facial cream, and spearmint denture paste—but when it came to talking, this sixty-eight-year-old *Mom-san* could hold her own with anyone, and once she let fly with one of her interminable monologues, you quickly understood why her offspring had turned into such a champion chatterbox. The subjects they talked about might have been different, but their styles were essentially the same: lurching, non-stop runs of free association, numerous asides and parenthetical remarks, and a full repertoire of extra-verbal effects, including everything from clicks to chortles to deep glottal gasps. From Willy, Mr Bones learned about humour, irony, and metaphorical abundance. From Mom-san, he learned important lessons about what it meant to be alive. She taught him about anxiety and *tsouris*, about bearing the weight of the world on your shoulders, and—most important of all—about the benefits of an occasional good cry.

As he trudged along beside his master that dreary Sunday in Baltimore, Mr Bones found it odd that he should be thinking about these things now. Why hark back to Mrs Gurevitch? he wondered. Why recall the tedium of the Brooklyn winters when there were so many fuller and more buoyant memories to contemplate? Albuquerque, for example, and their blissful sojourn in that abandoned bed factory two years ago. Or Greta, the voluptuous she-hound he'd romped with for ten nights running in a cornfield outside of Iowa City. Or that nutty afternoon in Berkeley four summers ago when Willy had sold eighty-six xeroxed copies of a single poem on Telegraph Avenue for a dollar apiece. It would have done him a world of good to be able to relive some of those things now, to be back somewhere with his master before the cough began—even last year, even nine or ten months ago, yes, maybe even hanging out with that tubby broad Willy had shacked up with for a while—Wanda, Wendy, whatever her name was—the girl who lived out of the back of her station wagon in Denver and liked to feed him hard-boiled eggs. She was a pistol, that one, a bawdy sack of blubber and booze, always laughing too much, always tickling him on the soft part of his belly and then, whenever his pink doggy dick came popping out of its sheath (not that Mr Bones objected, mind you), roaring with even more laughter, so much laughter that her face would turn fifteen shades of purple, and so often was this little comedy repeated during the short time they spent with her that he had only to hear the word 'Denver' now for Wanda's laugh to start ringing in his ears again. That was 'Denver' for him, just as 'Chicago' was a bus splashing through a rain puddle on Michigan Avenue. Just as 'Tampa' was a wall of light shimmering up from the asphalt one August afternoon. Just as 'Tucson' was a hot wind blowing off the desert, bearing with it the scent of juniper leaves and sagebrush, the sudden, unearthly plenitude of the vacant air.

One by one, he tried to attach himself to these memories, to inhabit them for a few more moments as they flitted past him, but it was no use. He kept going back to the Brooklyn apartment, to the languors of those cold-weather confinements, to Mom-san padding around the rooms in her fluffy white slippers. There was nothing to be done but to stay there, he realized, and as he finally gave in to the force of those endless days and nights, he understood that he had returned to Glenwood Avenue because Mrs Gurevitch was dead. She had left this world, just as her son was about to leave it, and by rehearsing that earlier death, he was no doubt preparing himself for the next one, the death of deaths, which was destined to turn the world upside down, perhaps even destroy it entirely.

Winter had always been the season of poetic labour. Willy kept nocturnal hours when he was at home, and most often he would start his day's work just after his mother went to bed. Life on the road did not allow for the rigours of composition. The pace was too hurried, the spirit too peripatetic, the distractions too continuous for anything but an infrequent jotting, the odd note or phrase dashed

Paul Auster

off on a paper napkin. During the months he spent in Brooklyn, however, Willy generally put in three or four hours a night at the kitchen table, scratching out his verses into 8½ by 11 inch spiral notebooks. At least that was the case when he wasn't off on a binge somewhere, or too down in the dumps, or stymied by a lack of inspiration. He sometimes muttered to himself as he wrote, sounding out the words as he put them down on paper, and sometimes he even went so far as to laugh or growl or pound his fist on the table. At first, Mr Bones assumed these noises were directed at him, but once he learned that carryings-on of this sort were part of the creative process, he would content himself with curling up under the table and dozing at his master's feet, waiting for the moment when the night's work was done and he would be taken outside to empty his bladder.

Still, it hadn't been all slump and torpor, had it? Even in Brooklyn there had been some bright spots, some deviations from the literary grind. Go back thirty-eight years on the dog calendar, for example, and there was the Symphony of Smells, that unique and shining chapter in the annals of Willydom, when for one whole winter there were no words at all. Yes, that surely was a time, Mr Bones said to himself, a most beautiful and crazy time, and to recollect it now sent a warm glow of nostalgia coursing through his blood. Had he been capable of smiling, he would have smiled at that moment. Had he been capable of shedding tears, he would have shed tears. Indeed, if such a thing were possible, he would have been laughing and crying at the same time—both celebrating and mourning his beloved master, who was soon to be no more.

The Symphony went back to the early days of their life together. They had left Brooklyn twice, had returned to Brooklyn twice, and in that time Willy had developed the keenest, most ardent affection for his four-legged friend. Not only did he feel protected now, and not only was he glad to have someone to talk to, and not only did it comfort him to have a warm body to curl up against at night, but after living with the dog at such close quarters for so many months, Willy had judged him to be wholly and incorruptibly good. It wasn't just that he knew that Mr Bones had a soul. He knew that soul to be better than other souls, and the more he saw of it, the more refinement and nobility of spirit he found there. Was Mr Bones an angel trapped in the flesh of a dog? Willy thought so. After eighteen months of the most intimate, clear-eyed observations, he felt certain of it. How else to interpret the celestial pun that echoed in his mind night and day? To decode the message, all you had to do was hold it up to a mirror. Could anything be more obvious? Just turn around the letters of the word 'dog', and what did you have? The truth, that's what. The lowest being contained within his name the power of the highest being, the almighty artificer of all things. Was that why the dog had been sent to him? Was Mr Bones, in fact, the second coming of the force that had delivered Santa Claus to him on that December night in 1969? Perhaps. And then again, perhaps not. To anyone else, the matter would have been open to debate. To Willy—precisely because he was Willy—it wasn't.

Still and all, Mr Bones was a dog. From the tip of his tail to the end of his snout, he was a pure example of *Canis familiaris*, and whatever divine presence he might have harboured within his skin, he was first and foremost the thing he appeared to be. Mr Bow Wow, Monsieur Woof Woof, Sir Cur. As one wag neatly put it to Willy in a Chicago bar four or five summers back: 'You want to know what a dog's philosophy of life is, pal? I'll tell you what it is. Just one short sentence: "If you can't eat it or screw it, piss on it."'

Willy had no problem with that. Who knew what theological mysteries were at work in a case like this? If God had sent his son down to earth in the form of a man, why shouldn't an angel come down to earth in the form of a dog? Mr Bones was a dog, and the truth was that Willy took pleasure in that dogness, found no end of delight in watching the spectacle of his confrère's canine habits. Willy had never kept company with an animal before. As a boy, his parents had turned him down every time he'd asked for a pet. Cats, turtles, parakeets, hamsters, goldfish—they would have nothing to do with them. The apartment was too small, they said, or animals stank, or they cost money, or Willy wasn't responsible enough. As a result, until Mr Bones came into his life, he had never had the opportunity to observe a dog's behaviour at close hand, had never even bothered to give the subject much thought. Dogs were no more than dim presences to him, shadowy figures hovering at the edge of consciousness. You avoided the ones who barked at you, you patted the ones who licked you. That was the extent of his knowledge. Two months after his thirty-eighth birthday, all that suddenly changed.

There was so much to absorb, so much evidence to assimilate, decipher, and make sense of that Willy hardly knew where to begin. The wagging tail as opposed to the tail between the legs. The pricked ears as opposed to the flaccid ears. The rolling on to the back, the running in circles, the anus-sniffs and growls, the kangaroo-hops and mid-air turns, the stalking crouch, the bared teeth, the cocked head, and a hundred other minute particulars, each one an expression of a thought, a feeling, a plan, an urge. It was like learning how to speak a new language, Willy found, like stumbling on a long-lost tribe of primitive men and having to figure out their impenetrable mores and customs. Once he had surmounted the initial barriers, what intrigued him most was the conundrum he referred to as the Eye-Nose Paradox, or the Senses Census. Willy was a man, and therefore he relied chiefly on sight to form his understanding of the world. Mr Bones was a dog, and therefore he was next to blind. His eyes were useful to him only in that they helped to distinguish shapes, to make out the broad outlines of things, to tell him whether the object or being that loomed up before him was a hazard to be shunned or an ally to be kissed. For true knowledge, for a genuine grasp of reality in all its manifold configurations, only the nose was of any value. Whatever Mr Bones knew of the world, whatever he had discovered in the way of insights or passions or ideas, he had been led to by his sense of smell. At first, Willy could scarcely believe his eyes. The dog's avidity for smells seemed boundless, and once he had found an odour that interested him, he would clamp his nose over it with such determination, such whole-hog enthusiasm, that everything else in the world would cease to exist. His nostrils were turned into suction tubes, sniffing up scents in the way a vacuum cleaner inhales bits of broken glass, and there were times, many times in fact, when Willy marvelled that the sidewalk did not crack apart from the force and fury of Mr Bones's snout work. Normally the most obliging of creatures, the dog would grow stubborn, distracted, seem to forget his master entirely, and if Willy happened to tug on the leash before Mr Bones was ready to move on, before he had ingested the full savour of the turd or urine puddle under scrutiny, he would plant his legs to resist the yank, and so unbudgeable did he become, so firmly did he anchor himself to the spot, that Willy often wondered if there wasn't a sac hidden somewhere in his paws that could secrete glue on command.

How not to be fascinated by all this? A dog had roughly 220 million scent receptors, whereas a man had but five million, and with a disparity as great as that, it was logical to assume that the world perceived by a dog was quite different from the one perceived by a man. Logic had never been Willy's strength, but in this case he was driven by love as much as by intellectual curiosity, and therefore he stuck with the question with more persistence than usual. What did Mr Bones experience when he smelled something? And, just as important, why did he smell what he smelled? Close observation had led Willy to conclude that there were essentially three categories of interest to Mr Bones: food, sex, and information about other dogs. A man opens the morning paper to find out what his fellow creatures have been up to; a dog does the same thing with his nose, sniffing trees and lamp-posts and fireboxes to learn about the doings of the local dog population. Rex, the sharp-fanged Rottweiler, has left his mark on that bush; Polly, the cute Cocker Spaniel, is in heat; Roger the mutt ate something that didn't agree with him. That much was clear to Willy, a matter beyond dispute. Where things grew complicated was when you tried to understand what the dog was feeling. Was he merely looking out for himself, digesting information in order to keep a leg up on the other dogs, or was there something more to these frantic sniff-fests than simple military tactics? Could pleasure be involved as well? Could a dog with his head buried in a garbage can experience something akin, say, to the heady swoon that comes over a man when he presses his nose against a woman's neck and breathes in a whiff of fifty-dollar-an-ounce French perfume?

It was impossible to know for sure, but Willy tended to think that he did. Why else would it have been so difficult to wrench Mr Bones away from the sites of certain smells? The dog was enjoying himself, that's why. He was in a state of intoxication, lost in a nasal paradise he could not bear to leave. And if, as has already been established, Willy was convinced that Mr Bones had a soul, did it not stand to reason that a dog of such spiritual inclinations would aspire to loftier things—things not necessarily related to the needs and urgencies of his body, but spiritual things, artistic things, the immaterial hungers of the soul? And if, as all philosophers on the subject have noted, art is a human activity that relies on the senses to reach that soul, did it not also stand to reason that dogs—at least dogs of Mr Bones's calibre—would have it in them to feel a similar aesthetic impulse? Would they not, in other words, be able to appreciate art? As far as Willy knew, no one had ever thought of this before. Did that make him the first man in recorded history to believe that such a thing was possible? No matter. It was an idea whose time had come. If dogs were beyond the pull of oil paintings and string quartets, who was to say they wouldn't respond to an art based on the sense of smell? Why not an olfactory art? Why not an art for dogs that dealt with the world as dogs knew it?

Thus began the lunatic winter of 1988. Mr Bones had never seen Willy so excited, so calm, so filled with steadfast energy. For three and a half months he worked on the project to the exclusion of everything else, scarcely bothering to smoke or drink anymore, sleeping only when absolutely compelled to, all but forgetting to write, read, or pick his nose. He drew up plans, made lists, experimented with smells, traced diagrams, built structures out of wood, canvas, cardboard and plastic. There were so many calculations to be made, so many tests to be run, so many daunting questions to be answered. What was the ideal sequence of smells? How long should a symphony last, and how many smells should it contain? What was the proper shape of the symphony hall? Should it be constructed as a labyrinth, or was a progression of boxes within boxes better suited to a dog's sensibility? Should the dog do the work alone, or should the dog's owner be there to guide him from one stage of the performance to the next? Should each symphony revolve around a single subject—food, for example, or female scents—or should various elements be mixed together? One by one, Willy talked out these problems with Mr Bones, asked for his opinions, solicited his advice, and begged his indulgence to serve as guinea pig for the numerous trials and errors that followed. The dog had rarely felt so honoured, so implicated in the throb of human affairs. Not only did Willy need him, but that need had been inspired by Mr Bones himself.

From his humble origins as a mutt of no particular worth or distinction, he had been turned into the dog of dogs, an exemplar of the whole canine race. Of course he was happy to do his bit, to play along with whatever Willy asked of him. What difference did it make if he didn't fully understand? He was a dog, wasn't he, and why should he object to sniffing a pile of urine-soaked rags, to pushing his body through a narrow trapdoor, or to crawling through a tunnel whose walls had been smeared with the traces of a meatball-and-spaghetti dinner? It might not have served any purpose, but the truth was that it was fun.

That was what came back to him now: the fun of it, the ongoing rush of Willy's excitement. Forget Mom-san and her sarcastic comments. Forget the fact that their laboratory was in the sub-basement of the building, next to the furnace and the sewage pipes, and that they worked on a cold dirt floor. They were collaborating on something important, enduring hardships together in the name of scientific progress. If there was anything to regret sometimes, it was simply the depth of Willy's commitment to what they were doing. He was so consumed by it, so wrapped up in the nuts and bolts of the project, that it became increasingly hard for him to keep things in perspective. One day, he would talk about his invention as if it were a major discovery, a breakthrough on a par with the light bulb, the airplane, or the computer chip. It would rake in bags of money, he said, turn them into millionaires many times over, and they would never have to worry about anything again. On other days, however, suddenly filled with doubt and uncertainties, he would present arguments to Mr Bones that were so finely parsed, so hair-splitting in their exactitude, that the dog began to fear for his master's health. Was it perhaps pushing things too far, Willy asked one evening, to include female scents in the orchestration of the symphonies? Wouldn't those smells induce lust in the dog who inhaled them, and wouldn't that undermine their aesthetic aspirations, turning the piece into something pornographic, a kind of smut for dogs? Immediately following that statement, Willy started bending words again, which happened whenever his mind was working at top speed. 'Cure porn with corn,' he muttered to himself, pacing back and forth across the dirt floor, 'pure corn will cure porn.' Once Mr Bones had untangled the knots of the spoonerism, he understood Willy to mean that sentimentality was preferable to sex, at least as far as the symphonies were concerned, and that to remain faithful to the endeavour of bringing aesthetic pleasure to dogs, spiritual longings would have to be emphasized over physical ones. So, after two straight weeks of rubbing his nose in towels and sponges saturated with the aromas of bitches in heat, Mr Bones was offered a whole new set of instruments: Willy himself, in all his vaporous guises. Dirty socks, undershirts, shoes, handkerchiefs, pants, scarves, hats—anything and everything that bore the scent of his master. Mr Bones enjoyed these things, just as he had enjoyed the other things. For the fact was that Mr Bones was a dog, and dogs enjoyed smelling whatever they were given to smell. It was in their nature; it was what they were born to do; it was, as Willy had correctly observed, their calling in life. For once, Mr Bones was glad that he had not been endowed with the power of human speech. If he had, he would have been forced to tell Willy the truth, and that would have caused him much pain. For a dog, he would have said, for a dog, dear master, the fact is that the whole world is a symphony of smells. Every hour, every minute, every second of his waking life is at once a physical and a spiritual experience. There is no difference between the inner and the outer, nothing to separate the high from the low. It's as if, as if…

Just as Mr Bones was beginning to unfurl this imaginary speech in his head, he was interrupted by the sound of Willy's voice. *Damn*, he heard him say. *Damn, damn*, and *double damn*. Mr Bones jerked up his head to see what the trouble was. A light rain had begun to fall, a drizzle so faint that Mr Bones hadn't even felt it landing on his fluffy coat. But little beads of wetness were glistening in Willy's beard, and the master's black T-shirt had already absorbed enough moisture to be showing a fine polka-dotted pattern. This wasn't good. The last thing Willy needed was to get drenched, but if the sky delivered what it seemed to have promised, that's exactly what was going to happen. Mr Bones perused the clouds overhead. Barring a sudden change of wind, in less than an hour the present feeble raindrops would develop into a full-blown, lusty downpour. Damn, he thought. How much farther to go before they found Calvert Street? They had been stumbling around for the past twenty or thirty minutes, and Bea Swanson's house was still nowhere in sight. If they didn't get there soon, they weren't going to make it. They weren't going to make it, because Willy wouldn't have the strength to go on.

Given their predicament, the last thing Mr Bones was expecting just then was that his master would start to laugh. But there it was, rumbling up from the depths of his stomach and bursting forth into the Sunday stillness: the old familiar *haw*. For a moment he thought that maybe Willy was trying to clear his throat, but when the first *haw* was followed by another *haw*, and then another, and still another after that, he could no longer doubt what his ears were telling him.

'Lookee here, ol' bud,' Willy said, launching into his best cowboy twang. This was a voice reserved for special occasions, an accent that Willy called upon only when he found himself in the presence of life's grandest, most dizzying ironies. Baffled though he was to hear it now, Mr Bones tried to take heart from this sudden shift in the emotional weather.

Willy had come to a full stop on the sidewalk. The neighbourhood all around them stank of poverty and uncollected garbage, and yet where should they be standing but in front of the loveliest little house Mr Bones had ever seen, a toy-sized edifice made of red bricks and adorned with slatted green shutters, three green steps, and a brightly painted white door? A plaque was affixed to the wall, and Willy was squinting forward to read what it said, sounding more and more like a Texas ranch hand with each passing second.

'Two-oh-three North Amity Street,' he recited. 'Residence of Edgar Allan Poe, eighteen-thirty-two to eighteen-thirty-five. Open to the public April to December, Wednesday through Saturday, noon to three-forty-five p.m.'

It sounded like pretty dull stuff to Mr Bones, but who was he to grumble about his master's enthusiasms? Willy sounded more inspired than at any moment in the past two weeks, and even though his recitation was followed by another brutal coughing fit (more sputum, more gasping, more foot-stomping as he clung to the downspout for dear life), he quickly rebounded once the spasm was over.

'We done hit pay dirt, little pard,' Willy said, spitting out the last bits of mucus and pulmonary tissue. 'It ain't Miss Bea's house, that's for sure, but give me my druthers, and there's no place on earth I'd rather be than here. This Poe fella was my grandpa, the great forebear and daddy of all us Yankee scribes. Without him, there wouldn't have been no me, no them, no nobody. We've wound up in Poe-Land, and if you say it quick enough, that's the same country my own dead ma was born in. An angel's led us to this spot, and I aim to sit here awhile and pay my respects. Seein' as how I can't take another step anyway, I'd be much obliged if you joined me, Mr Bones. That's right, take a seat beside me while I rest my pins. Never mind the rain. It's just a few drops is all, and it don't mean us no harm.'

Willy let out a long, labouring grunt and then eased himself to the ground. It was a painful thing for Mr Bones to observe—all that effort to travel just a few inches—and the dog's heart welled up with pity to see his master in such a sorrowful state. He could never be certain exactly how he knew it, but as he watched Willy lower himself to the sidewalk and lean his back against the wall, he knew that he would never get up again. This was the end of their life together. The last moments were upon them, and there was nothing to do now but sit there until the light faded from Willy's eyes.

Still, the trip hadn't worked out so badly. They'd come here looking for one thing and had found another, and in the end Mr Bones much preferred the thing they'd found to the thing they hadn't. They weren't in Baltimore, they were in Poland. By some miracle of luck or fate or divine justice, Willy had managed to get himself home again. He had returned to the place of his ancestors, and now he could die in peace.

Mr Bones raised his left hind paw and began working on an itch behind his ear. In the distance, he saw a man and a little girl walking slowly in the opposite direction, but he didn't trouble himself about them. They would come, they would go, and it made no difference who they were. The rain was coming down harder now, and a small breeze was beginning to kick around the candy wrappers and paper bags in the street. He sniffed the air once, twice, then yawned for no particular reason. After a moment, he curled up on the ground beside Willy, exhaled deeply, and waited for whatever was going to happen next.

☐

GRANTA

DESTROYED
Hilary Mantel

LAURIE SPARHAM/NETWORK

When I was very small, small enough to trip every time on the raised kerbstone outside the back door, the dog Victor used to take me for a walk. We would proceed at caution across the yard, my hand plunged deep into the ruff of bristly fur at the back of his neck. He was an elderly dog, and the leather of his collar had worn supple and thin. My fingers curled around it, while sunlight struck stone and slate, dandelions opened in the cracks between flags, and old ladies aired themselves in doorways, nodding on kitchen chairs and smoothing their skirts over their knees. Somewhere else, in factories, fields and coal mines, England went dully on.

My mother always said that there is no such thing as a substitute. Everything is intrinsically itself, and unlike any other thing. Everything is just once, and happiness can't be repeated. Children should be named for themselves. They shouldn't be named after other people. I don't agree with that, she said.

Then why did she do it, why did she break her own law? I'm trying to work it out, so meanwhile I have a different story, about some dogs, which perhaps relates to it. If I offer some evidence, will you be the judge?

My mother held her strong views, there's no doubt, because she herself was named after her cousin Clara, who died in an accident. If Clara had lived she would have been 107 now. It wasn't anything in her character that made my mother angry about the substitution, because Clara was not known to have had any character. No, what upset her was the way the name was pronounced by the people in our village. Cl-air-airra: it came sticky and prolonged out of their mouths, like an extruded rope of glue.

In those days we were all cousins and aunts and great-aunts who lived in rows of houses. We went in and out of each others' doors the whole time. My mother said that in the civilized world people would knock, but though she made this observation over and over, people just gave her a glassy-eyed stare and went on the way they always had. There was a great disjunction between the effect she thought she had on the world, and the effect she actually achieved. I only thought this later. When I was seven I thought she was Sun and Moon. That she was like God, everywhere and always. That she was reading your thoughts, when you were still a poor reader yourself, because you were only up to *Far & Wide Readers, Green Book III.*

Next door to us in the row lived my aunt Pauline. She was really my cousin, but I called her aunt because of her age. All the relationships were mixed up, and you don't need to know about them; only that the dog Victor lived with Pauline, and mostly under her kitchen table. He ate a meat pie every day, which Pauline bought him specially, walking up the street to buy it. He ate fruit, anything he could get. My mother said dogs should have proper food, in tins.

Victor had died by the time I was seven. I don't remember the day of his death, just a dull sense of cataclysm. Pauline was a widow. I thought she always had been.

When I was seven I was given a watch, but for my eighth birthday I had a puppy. When the idea of getting a dog was first proposed, my mother said that she wanted a Pekinese.

People gave her the look that they gave her when she suggested that civilized people would knock at the door. The idea of anyone in our village owning a Pekinese was simply preposterous; I knew this already. The inhabitants would have plucked and roasted it.

I said, 'It's my birthday, and I would like a dog like Victor.'

She said, 'Victor was just a mongrel.'

'Then I'll have just a mongrel,' I said.

I thought, you see, that a mongrel was a breed. Aunt Pauline had once told me, 'Mongrels are very faithful.'

I liked the idea of fidelity. Though I had no idea what it implied.

A mongrel, after all, was the cheap option. When the morning of my birthday came I suppose I felt excitement, I don't know. A young boy fetched the puppy from Godber's Farm. It stood blinking and shivering on the rug before the fire. Its tiny legs were like chicken bones. I am a winter-born person and there was frost on the roads that day. The puppy was white, like Victor, and had a curly tail like Victor, and a brown saddle on his back which made him look useful and domestic. I put my hand into the fur at the back of his neck and

I judged that one day it would be long enough to hang on to.

The boy from Godber's Farm was in the kitchen, talking to my stepfather, who I was told to call Dad these days. I heard the boy say it was a right shame, but I didn't listen to find out what the shame was. The boy went out, my stepfather with him. They were chatting as if they were familiar.

I didn't understand in those days how people knew each other. They'd say, you know *her, her* who married *him. Constant was her name before she married him*, or, *her name was Reilly*. There was a time when I didn't understand how names got changed, or how anything happened, really. When somebody went out of the door I always wondered who or what they'd come back as, and whether they'd come back at all. I don't mean to make me sound simple, my infant self. I could pick out reasons for everything I did. I thought it was other people who were the sport of fortune, and the children of whim. One day about a year back, my father had gone out of the front door, looking so happy that I thought he was off to the corner for twenty cigarettes. If he had luggage, I didn't notice it. An hour had scarcely passed when the back door flew open and another man dumped a case down. He occupied a bed and tried to thieve a name.

So, when my stepfather had gone out, I found myself alone in our front room, before the slumbering and low-burning fire; and I started talking to the puppy Victor. I had read manuals of dog training in preparation for his arrival. They said that dogs liked a low, calm, soothing tone, but they didn't suggest what to say in it. He didn't look as if he had many interests yet so I told him about the things that interested me. I squatted on the floor next to him, so my great size wouldn't intimidate him. I looked into his face. Know my face, I prayed. After a certain amount of boredom from me, Victor fell to the floor as if his legs had been snapped, and slept like the dead. I sat down beside him to watch him. I had a book open on my knees but I didn't read it. I watched him, and I had never been so still. I knew that fidgeting was a vice, and I had tried to combat it, but I did not know stillness like that was in me, or calm like in the half-hour I first watched Victor.

When my stepfather came back he appeared to be himself, and

no other; you could say that at least. He had a worried frown on his face, and something under his overcoat. A foxy muzzle poked out, noisily snuffling the air. 'This is Mike,' my stepfather said. 'He was going to be destroyed.' He put the new puppy on the ground. It was a bouncing skewbald made of rubber. It ran to the fire. It ran to Victor and sniffed him. It raced in a circle and bit chunks out of the air. Its tongue panted. It jumped on Victor and began to pulverize him.

Mike—let it be understood—was not an extra present for me. Victor was my dog and my responsibility. Mike was the *other* dog: he was everyone's, and no one's responsibility. Victor, as it proved, was of sedate, genteel character. When he was first put on his lead, he walked daintily, at heel, as if he had been trained in a former life. But when the lead was first clipped on to Mike's collar, he panicked. He ran to the end of it and yelped and spun into the air, and hurtled out into space, and turned head over heels. Then he flopped down on his side, and thrashed around as if he were in danger of a heart attack. I fumbled at his collar, desperate to set him free; his eye rolled, the fur of his throat was damp.

Try him again, when he's a bit older, my mother suggested.

Everybody said that it was nice that Victor had got his brother with him, that they would be faithful to each other, etc. I didn't think so, but what I didn't think I kept to myself.

The puppies had a pretty good life, except at night when the ghosts that lived in our house came out of the stone-floored pantry, and down from the big cupboard to the left of the chimney breast. Depend upon it, they were not dripping or ladies or genteel; they were nothing like the ghost that drowned Clara would have been, her sodden blouse frilled to the neck. These were ghosts with filed teeth. You couldn't see them, but you could sense their presence when you saw the dogs' bristling necks, and saw the shudders run down their backbones. The ruff on Victor's neck was growing long now. Despite everything my mother had vowed, the dogs did not get food out of tins. They got scraps of anything that was going. Substitutions were constantly made, in our house. Though it was said that no one thing was like any other.

'Try the dog on his lead again,' my mother said. If a person said, 'the dog', you knew Mike was the dog meant. Victor sat in the corner.

He did not impose his presence. His brown eyes blinked.

I tried the dog on his lead again. He bolted across the room, taking me with him. I borrowed a book from the public library, *101 Hints on Dog Care*. Mike took it in the night and chewed it up, all but the last four hints. Mike would pull you in a hedge, he would pull you in a canal, he would pull you in a boating lake so you drowned like cousin Clara, when her careless beau tipped her out of the rowing boat. When I was nine I used to think quite a lot about Clara, her straw hat skimming among the lily pads.

It was when my brother P. G. Pig was born that my mother broke her own rule. I heard the cousins and aunts talking in lowered voices about the choice of name. They didn't take my views into account—no doubt they thought I'd recommend, Oh, call him Victor. Robert was mooted but my mother said Bob she could not abide. All those names were at first to be ruled out, that people naturally make into something else. But this left too few to draw on. At last my mother made up her mind on Peter, both syllables to be rigidly enforced. How did she think she would enforce them when he was a schoolboy, when he went to the football field, when he grew up to be a weaver or a soldier in a khaki blouson? I asked myself these things. And, mentally, I shrugged. I saw myself in my mind. 'Just asking?!!' I said. My fingers were spread and my eyes were round.

But there was something else about the baby's name, something that was going to be hidden. By listening at doors, by pasting myself against the wall and listening at doors, I found it was this: that the baby was to be given a second name, and it was to be George, which was the name of my aunt Pauline's dead husband. Oh, had Pauline a husband, I said to myself. I thought widow, like mongrel, was a category of its own.

Peter George, I said to myself, P.G., PG, PIG. He would have a name, and it would not be Peter, nor would it be Pete. But why so hushed? Why the averted shoulders and the voices dropped? *Because Pauline was not to be told.* It was going to be too much for her altogether, it would send her into a fit of the hysterics if she found out. It was my own mother's personal tribute to the long-destroyed George, who to my knowledge she had not mentioned before: a tribute, to pay which she was prepared to throw over one of her most characteristic notions. So strong, she said, were her feelings in the matter.

But wait. Wait a minute. Let logic peep in at the window here. This was Pauline, was it not? Aunt Pauline who lived next door? It was Pauline, who in three weeks' time would attend the christening? As Catholics we christen early, being very aware of the devil. I pictured the awful word 'George' weighting the priest's tongue, making him clutch his upper chest, reducing him to groans until it rolled out, crashing on the flags and processing down the aisle: and Pauline's arms flung up, the word 'Aa...gh!' flashing from her gaping mouth as she was mown down. What an awful death, I said to myself. Smirking, I said, what a destruction.

In the event, Pauline found out about the naming in very good time. My mother said—and thunder was on her brow—'They told her in the butcher's. And she'd only gone in, bless her, for her little bit of a slice of—'

I left her presence. In the kitchen, Victor was sitting in the corner, curling up an edge of liver-coloured lip. I wondered if something had provoked him. A ghost come out early? Perhaps, I thought, it's George.

Pauline was next door as usual, going about her tasks in her own kitchen. You could hear her through the thin wall; the metal colander knocking against the enamel sink, the squeak of chair legs across the linoleum. In the days following she showed no sign of hysterical grief, or even nostalgia. My mother watched her closely. 'They never should have told her,' my mother said. 'A shock such as that could do lasting harm.' For some reason, she looked disappointed.

I didn't know what it was about, and I don't now, and I doubt if I want to. You can say 'how strong are my feelings', but be smiling all the while; and pay back obscurely for some obscure injury inflicted, maybe before I was born. It blights my life, trying to fill these gaps: I'm glad if I can persuade other people to do it for me. As far as I could see then it was just some tactic one person was trying on another person and it was the reason I didn't like to play cat's cradle, patience, cutting out with scissors or any indoor games at all. Winter or not, I played outside with Victor and Mike.

It was spring when P. G. Pig was born. I went out into the field at the back, to get away from the screaming and puking and baby talk. Victor sat quivering at my heel. Mike raced in insane circles among the daisies. I pushed back my non-existent cowboy hat. I scratched my head like an old-timer and said, 'Loco.'

My brother was still a toddler when Victor's character took a turn for the worse. Always timid, he now became morose, and took to snapping. One day when I came to put on his lead he sprang into the air and nipped me on the cheek. Believing myself an incipient beauty and afraid of facial scarring, I washed the bite then rubbed raw Dettol on it. What resulted was worse than the bite and I rehearsed to the air the sentence 'Hurts like hell.' I tried not to tell my mother but she smelled the Dettol. Later he chased P. G. Pig, trying to get him on the calf. P. G. marched to the German goose-step. So, he escaped by inches, or even less. I plucked a ravelled thread of his towelling suit from between Victor's teeth.

Victor didn't attack grown people. He backed off from them. 'It's just the children he goes for,' my mother said. 'I find it very perplexing.'

So did I. I wondered why he included me with the children. If he could see into my heart, I thought, he would know I don't qualify.

By this time we had a new baby in the house. Victor was not to be trusted and my mother said a sorting-out was overdue. He went away under my stepfather's overcoat, wrapped tight, struggling. We said goodbye to him. He was pinioned while we patted his head. He growled at us, and the growl turned to a snarl, and he was hurried out of the front door, and away down the street. My mother said that she and my father had found a new home for him, with an elderly couple without children. How sad! I pictured them, their homely grieving faces softening at the sight of the white dog with his useful brown saddle. He would be a substitute child for them. Would they dip their old fingers into the ruff at his neck, and hold on tight?

It was strange, what I chose to believe in those days. P. G. Pig knew better. Sitting in the corner, he took a sideways swipe at his tower of blue bricks. 'Destroyed,' he said.

About a year after that, we moved to a new town. My surname was changed officially. Pig and the younger baby had the new name already, there was no need for them to change. My mother said that generally, the gossip and malice had got out of hand, and there were always those who were ready to do you a bad turn if they could contrive it. Pauline and the other aunts and cousins came to visit. But not too often. My mother said, we don't want *that* circus starting up again.

So the years began in which I pretended to be someone else's daughter. The word 'daughter' is long, pale, mournful; its hand is to its cheek. The word 'rueful' goes with 'daughter'. Sometimes I thought of Victor and I was rueful. I sat in my room with compass and square-ruled book, and bisected angles, while outside the children shrieked, frolicking with Mike. In truth I blamed Mike for alienating Victor's affections, but there is a limit to how much you can blame a dog.

With the move to the new house, a change had overtaken Mike, similar in magnitude though not in style to the one that had overtaken his brother x years before. I call it x years because I was beginning to lose track of that part of my life, and in the case of numbers it is allowable to make a substitution. I remembered the facts of things pretty well, but I had forgotten certain feelings, like how I felt on the day Victor arrived from Godber's Farm, and how I felt on the day he was taken away to his new home. I remembered his straitjacketed snarling, which hardly diminished as he was carried out of the door. If he could have bitten me that day, he would have drawn blood.

The trouble with Mike was this: we had become middle-class, but our dog had not. We had long ago ceased trying to take him for walks on a lead. Now he exercised himself, running away at all hours of the day and night. He could leap gates and make holes through hedges. He was seen in the vicinity of butcher's shops. Sometimes he went to the High Street and stole parcels and packets from baskets on wheels. He ate a white loaf, secretly, in the shadow of the privet. I saw that he looked dedicated and innocent as he chewed it, slice after slice, holding the dough carefully in paws that he turned inwards, as if praying.

When my mother saw the neighbours leaning over the larchlap, imparting gardening tips, she thought they were talking about Mike. Her face would become pinched. She believed he was letting the family down, betraying mongrel origins. I knew the meaning of the word now. I did not get involved in any controversy about Mike. I crouched in my room and traced the continent of South America. I stuck into my geography book a picture of Brasilia, the white shining city in the jungle. I placed my hands together and prayed, take me there. I did not believe in God so I prayed provisionally, to genies and ghosts, to dripping Clara and old dead George.

Mike was less than five years old when he began to show his age. He had lived hard, after all. One year, he could catch and snap in his jaws the windfalls our apple tree shook down. Those he did not catch as they fell, the babies would bowl for him, and he would hurtle after, tearing skidmarks in the turf as he cornered; then with a backward jerk of his neck he would toss the fruit up into the blue air, to give himself a challenge.

But a year later, he was on the blink. He couldn't catch the windfalls if they rained down on his head, and when old tennis balls were thrown for him he would trot vaguely, dutifully, away from the hue and cry, and then turn and plod back, his jaws empty. I said to my mother, I think Mike's eyes are failing. She said, I hadn't noticed.

The defect didn't seem to make him downhearted. He continued to lead his independent life; smelling his way, I supposed, through gaps in wire netting and through the open doors of vendors of fine foods and High Class Family Butchers. I thought, he could do with a guide-person really. Perhaps I could train up P. G. Pig? I tried the experiment we hadn't tried in years, clipping lead to collar. The dog lay down at my feet and whimpered. I noticed that the foxy patches of his coat had bleached out, as if he'd been in the sun and the rain too long. I unfastened the lead and wrapped it around my hand. Then I threw it at the back of the hall cupboard. I stood in the hall and practised swearing under my breath. I didn't know why.

On New Year's Day, a fortnight before my twelfth birthday, Mike went out in the morning and didn't come back. My stepfather said, 'Mike's not come in for his tea.'

I said, 'Mike's bloody blind.'

They all pretended not to have heard me. There was an edict against quarrelling anywhere near Christmas, and it was still near enough; we were lodged in the strange-menu days leading to the Feast of the Epiphany, when babies daub jelly in their hair and *The Great Escape* is on TV and no one notices what time it is. That's why we were less alarmed than we would usually have been, yawning off to bed.

But I woke up very early, and stood shivering by the window, the curtain wrapped around me, looking out over land that was imagined because there was no light: leafless, wet, warm for the time of year. If Mike were home I would feel it, I thought. He would whine and buffet the back door, and someone would hear if not me. But I didn't know. I couldn't trust that. I ran my hand through my hair and made it stand up in tufts. I crept back to bed.

I had no dreams. When I woke up it was nine o'clock. I was astonished at the leniency. My mother needs little sleep, and thinks it a moral failing in others, so usually she would have been bawling in my ear by eight, inventing tasks for me; the Christmas truce did not apply in the earlier hours of the morning. I went downstairs in my spotted pyjamas, the legs rolled up above the knee, in a *jeu d'esprit*.

'Oh, for God's sake,' my mother said. 'And what have you done with your hair?'

I said, 'Where's my dad?'

She said, 'He's gone to the police station, about Mike.'

'No,' I said. I shook my head. I rolled down my pyjama trousers to the ankle. Fuckit, I wanted to say. Why pretend I mean him? *Answer the question I put to you.*

The next day I went out calling, through the small woods that belted open fields, and along the banks of the canal. It rained part of the day, a benign and half-hearted precipitation. Everything seemed unseasonable, forward: the rotting wood of fences shimmered green. I took my redoubtable brother with me, and I kept my eye on the yellow bobble of his bobble hat. The minute he went out of sight, in undergrowth or copse, I called him, Peegie pig, Peegie pig! I felt him before I saw him, loping to my side.

I had penny chews in my pocket and I fed them to him to keep him going. 'Mike, Mike!' we called. It was Sunday, the end of an extended holiday which had added to the dislocation of Advent. We met no one on our quest. Peegie's nose began to run. After a time, when the dog didn't answer, he began to cry. He'd thought we were going to meet Mike, you see. At some place pre-arranged.

I just tugged Peegie along. It was all I could do. The word 'interloper' was rolling around my mind, and I thought what a beautiful word it was, and how well it described the dog Mike who loped and flapped his pink tongue in the open air, while Victor squatted in the house, thin like myself, and his skin leaking fear.

On the banks of the canal at last we met a man, not old, his jacket flapping and insufficient even for the mildness of the day; his hair cropped, his torn pocket drooping from his checked shirt, and his gym shoes caked in mud. Who was Mike, he wanted to know?

I told him my mother's theory, that Mike had been mowed down by a Drunken Driver. Peegie sawed his hand back and forth under his snuffling nose. The man promised he would call out for Mike, and take him if recovered to the police or the RSPCA. Beware of the police pounds, he said, for the dogs there are destroyed in twelve days.

I said, that within twelve days we would be sure to hear from them. I said, my step my step my father has been to the police: I managed the word in the end. I swear by Almighty God, the man said, that I will be calling for young Michael day and night. I felt alarmed for him. I felt sorry for his torn pocket, as if I should have been carrying needle and thread.

I walked away, and I had not gone a hundred yards before I felt there were misunderstandings that needed to be corrected. Mike is only my step-dog. Supposing I had misinformed this stranger? But if I went back to put the facts to him again, perhaps he would only forget them. He looked like a man who had forgotten almost everything. I had gone another hundred yards before it came to me that this was the very kind of stranger to whom you were warned not to speak.

I looked down at Peegie in second-hand alarm. I should have protected him. Peegie was learning to whistle that week, and now he was whistling and crying at the same time. He was whistling the tune from Laurel and Hardy, which I can't stand. I knew full well— 'full well' is one of my mother's expressions—that Mike was dead in a ditch, where he had limped or crawled away from the vehicle that had smashed him up before he saw it. All day I'd been searching, in defiance of this fact.

Oh, I'm tired, Peegie wailed. Carry me. Carry me. I looked down and knew I could not, and he knew it too, for he was such a big boy already that it could almost have been the other way around. I offered him a penny chew, and he smacked my hand away.

We came to a wall, and I hoisted him on to it. He could have hoisted me. We sat there, while the air darkened. It was four o'clock, and we had been walking and calling since early morning. I thought, I could drown Peegie Pig, and blame it on the man with the torn pocket. I could haul him across the towpath by the hood of his coat, and push him under the bright green weed; and keep pushing, a hand on his face, till the weight of his clothes pulled him under; and I saw myself, careless beau, other life, lily pad and floating hat. As far as I knew, no one had been hanged for Clara. 'What's for my tea?' Peegie said. Some words came to me, from the Shakespeare we were doing. *When the exigent is come, that now is come indeed.* The damp was making me ache, as if I were my own grandmother. I thought, nobody listens, nobody sees, nobody does any bloody fuckit thing. You go blind and savage and they carry on making Christmas trifles and frying eggs. Fuckit, I said to Peegie, experimentally. Fuckit, he repeated after me. Mike, Mike, we called, as we trod the towpath, and early night closed in on us. Peegie Pig slipped his hand into mine. We walked into the dark together, and our fused hands were cold. I said, to myself, I cannot kill him, he is fidelity itself; though it did occur to me that if he drowned, someone would be named after him. 'Come on, Peegie,' I said to him. 'But cut out the whistling.' I stood behind him, put my cold hands into the hood of his duffel coat, and began to steer him home.

There was a lot of blame flying in the air, about where had we been, up by the canal where vagrants live and anybody. My mother had already washed Mike's dishes out, and put them to drain. As she was not much of a housewife, we knew by this sign that he was not coming back, not through our door anyway. I cried a bit then, not out of the exhaustion of the day, but sudden scorching tears that leaped out of my eyes and scoured the pattern off the wallpaper. I saw Peegie gaping at me, open-mouthed, so I was sorry I'd bothered crying at all. I just wiped my fist across my face, and got on with the next thing. □

Mind   expanding

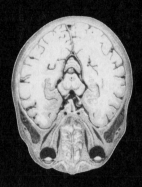 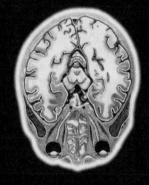

substance

The Times Literary Supplement has an unrivalled reputation for intelligent, incisive and sharp witted reviews of literature, theatre, broadcasting, opera and the arts. Subscribe today and you'll qualify for a substantial saving of up to 35% off the normal rates.

To take advantage of this special subscription offer call our hotline now on 01858 438805.

TLS

Seriously good reading

http://www.the-tls.co.uk

GRANTA

THE VENTRILOQUIST

Gary Enns

The Ventriloquist

It was the winter I turned thirteen and we taught the raven to speak. The winter Jerry Pierce and I were allowed to skip sixth-period Spanish to go to Mr Mullers' mobile home because we had speech impediments. Jerry wanted to be a mad bomber, a caballero crazy man of the West, and I wanted to be a falconer. We were training a raven that we had found in the spring, hungry and squeaking under a wall of budding grapevines. We raised him together, fed him chopped-up earthworms, made a nest for him out of rags and insulation in the loft of my dad's tractor barn. Mr Mullers gave us his name—Corvus, Latin for raven. When Corvus had grown, Jerry helped me fashion a falcon's hood for him out of old vinyl. Wearing the hood, perched tall and erect on one of our outstretched arms, Corvus looked like a tiny executioner.

Jerry had an exaggerated lisp, and I had a stutter. Two o'clock, Tuesdays and Thursdays, we would sit on Mullers' love seat and sound out phonemes.

'Fff, fr-, frame,' we would say. Or, 'Sss, sanc-, sanction.'

Mullers was a dark, smooth man with no hair on his arms and head except for a grey Fu Manchu that he trimmed with fingernail scissors. He was our speech therapist, but he also taught Latin and used it on us, made us sound out words like *segnitia* and *hiulcus*. Leaning back in a leather chair, face buried in *People* magazine, he would listen to the noises we made. 'Keep sounding, machines!' he would say if he heard us pause. He had a lisp of his own when he got angry or excited. 'Thtop it! Quit horthing around!' When he caught himself lisping, his eyes would close, and his lips would move as he counted backwards from ten to zero. Then, calmly, quietly, he would whisper, 'Stop.'

It was hard to concentrate, and I had reasons for my distraction: Columba Rodriguez, who was Mexican and who raced BMX bicycles. I couldn't stop dreaming of the purr of her *r*-sounds, of the hair like fine peach fuzz on the nape of her neck, of her little purple earrings that glistened like licked sweets in the light. We had been *going around* for two weeks, seeing each other on the sly so that no one noticed. Jerry knew nothing of this, of her riding her slick racing bike to my house, of her fondness for Corvus.

Jerry had his own dreams. On Mullers' couch he would close

W. EUGENE SMITH/MAGNUM

his eyes and snicker, or frown—even cry—at God-knows-what. And he would screw up his words on purpose:

'Jerry,' Mullers would say, 'say thumb.'

'...Fumb.' Jerry and I would giggle.

'No, goddamnit! Lithen! *Th-th-th-umb.*'

'...Fumb.'

I was Jerry's only friend. He had never told me this, but I knew it because the other kids were just plain scared of him. He made fun of people constantly and stared them down in the hallways. Once I saw him threaten a kid at the urinals with a sewing needle to the throat. The poor kid peed all over his pants and shoes. It was meanness. Posturing. Why Jerry had to do this, I don't know. But I wasn't scared. I understood. There were thoughts that he shared with no one, not even me. But there were things I did know: I knew that his dad had been killed years earlier over a money dispute—shot in the head while starting up his crop duster; I knew that Jerry had seen the blood splattered on the windshield of the yellow biplane. He told me once—and me alone—that the dried blood looked to him like crushed plums. Maybe on Mullers' love seat he was thinking of this.

Or maybe he was thinking of the plan he had created to get us out of the Valley: to take our bird on the road and make money by getting him to speak to passers-by. We had started training Corvus to sing 'Your Cheatin' Heart' in bits and pieces for the school talent show. In a tinny version of Jerry's out-of-tune voice, Corvus could already croon:

> *Your cheatin' heaaaaaart*
> *Will make you weeeeep*
> *You'll cry and crrrry*
> *And try to sleeeeep.*

The talent trophy would be our first step, Jerry said. Proof positive that we could *make* it in the world.

He talked about this dream often, of *making* it out of the San Joaquin, of proving our worth and joining the circus where they would like our kind of act, of travelling around the country in style, eating in dining cars on trains, sleeping in neat compartments and getting back rubs from scantily clad women. And not having to say a thing, not anything, just letting Corvus do the talking. Jerry had our future planned, and it was a plan I believed in when he told it just right. Once we had made our fortunes we would smuggle Corvus to Mexico, where everything was legal, and we would live on the beach at Guaymas and drink Cokes and fish for skate. Jerry had come up with some quarter sticks of dynamite, which he turned into huge firecrackers: we'd slingshot them across the Sea of Cortez to explode over the waves in the night.

I first saw Columba on a Thursday afternoon, a week after Christmas break. Her father was the new honcho for a large Mexican picking-and-pruning crew and had rented the little farm house across from my dad's vineyards. They pulled up in a rickety U-Haul with the insignia scratched off the sides and back.

'Wetbacks,' Jerry said. We were tying vines in the vineyard, slicing strips of wire with wire-cutters. Five dollars a row, compliments of my dad. Jerry had decided that with the money we should buy Corvus a wicker travelling box he had seen at a store in town.

Jerry rolled his wire down the row like a wheel. 'Prob'ly mudbogged right through the Rio Grande,' he said, but I didn't think so. Head honchos were usually legal.

A week later the little house was painted canary yellow, and Mr Rodriguez started building a tight cycling track in the field out back. At night, alone, he shovelled dirt into a wheelbarrow, lugged it across the yard and dumped it on to growing mounds. He watered down the dirt piles with a garden hose, smacked them with the flat of his shovel, shaped them into berms and jumps. He dragged metal bars and steel suspension springs around by a chain to smooth out the track. Finally, he mounted floodlights in the trees that surrounded the yard, and Columba, in full pads and helmet, began racing her bike around the track, careening round corners, ripping into fresh berms, flying over jumps.

Co-lum-ba. Co-lum-ba Rod-ri-guez. In class she looked bored, as if she didn't understand much. Every so often she would peek into her desk at a Spanish bicycle motocross magazine she kept there, sometimes even taking it out and hiding it within the pages of her textbook. Her lips would move silently to Spanish pronunciations. When she was called upon to read, we had to follow along closely, because 'guava' to her was 'wava', 'shoes' were 'shooss'. Once, in a book of flowers, when she came across the word 'chrysanthemum', she stopped reading, opened her mouth, tried different shapes, and said finally, slowly, articulately, as if pleased with herself: 'grrrease-ántimome.'

Every night, after homework, I would walk the fifth of a mile to the tractor barn; I would climb into Corvus's perch, open the door to the loft, and looking out over the dark vineyards I would watch Columba ride her bike. It was well known at school that she would be a champion some day. She had only been in town a week and had already won the junior trials in Fresno. I looked through my dad's old pair of binoculars, and she became huge, a streak of red and yellow and blue against the dark sky.

I started giving Corvus Spanish lessons. After the singing drills, and after Jerry had gone home, I would take up a phrase book and sound out *Hola, chica*, and *Pasa la mostaza, señorita*, and *Una preciosura*, words and phrases I thought Columba would like. I knew that Jerry would be pissed if he found out. To him everything—*everything*—was a distraction from the goal. So I was cautious about it, and always locked the door to guard against unexpected visits. I spoke the words quietly, close to Corvus's head, so that they wouldn't travel beyond the barn.

One month after the Rodriguezes moved in, I put Corvus in the wicker case Jerry and I had bought and carried it on my shoulder through the vineyard. The sky was dark; it was seven o'clock, early February. A thin white frost had begun to form on the bare vines.

Under the glow of the floodlights Columba was practising starts. She would stop at a pair of red and green flags and a series of four beeps would sound from a loudspeaker mounted on the side of the house. On the fourth, Columba would spring out, the bike whipping from side to side between her thighs. She would make a run around the track and stop with a slide at the line, digging her rear tyre into the oily dirt. Then she would make another run—beep, spring, slide, like clockwork.

I walked up to the edge of the track and stood in full view, wanting her to notice. But if she saw me, she didn't show it.

About a half hour later she laid her bike down on a berm, took her helmet off and sat looking up at the sky. Fog had begun to inch its way down from the hills, misting over the floodlights.

I walked across the track and squatted next to her. She was panting, sweaty. Her earrings glistened in the light.

'You're another Lars He-Hhhendersen,' I said. I had lifted the name out of a magazine at the 7–11 in town.

She smiled. 'You are reading,' she said.

Corvus shook inside the case. Columba glanced down at it. 'Bird inside?'

I nodded.

'I have seen it, uhh...*vuelo*...how you say, gliding.' She furrowed her brow, then looked at me. 'I have seen it on the road,' she said, 'eating a dead dog.'

I opened the box. Corvus quarked and looked up at us and tilted his head. He yawned. The white light shining on his back made him look purple. I lifted him out and set him on my shoulder.

'Ooo oosted—' I began, but Corvus, in his scratchy voice, finished what I wanted to say. He had my stutter:

'Ooo oosted es mmuy p-p-pronto en bicicleta.'

Columba's mouth dropped. '¡*Aiie!*' she said. '...¡*Habla Español!* ¡*Increíble!* ¡*Quánto tiempo!*'

The year before, in the seventh grade, Jerry had been busted carrying a little bomb and some martial arts truncheons at school. On Tuesdays and Thursdays, after our Mullers sessions, his mother had to drive him into town to perform community service, picking up trash in alleyways and around dumpsters. On those days Columba rode her bike over, and we fed Corvus together.

Jerry and I had a system of feeding worked out—anything we could shoot or trap in the fields was fair game. We had become creative. From the porch we would launch dead mice into the vineyards with our wrist-rocket slingshots, and Corvus would scoop them up with his beak, sometimes out of mid-air, and buzz us and fly around the house. Jerry said that once down south we would be able to trap pack rats, brown rodents so fat that we could survive off them ourselves. Just us and Corvus, living off the desert.

Sometimes we would throw a few of Jerry's larger explosives into the pools of the stagnant ditch, and mudsuckers, dead or stunned, would float to the surface on their sides. We would pound their heads on the ground and gut them with a couple of Jerry's knives. Then we would lay the dead fish and guts on the drive, and Corvus would pick at them and fly small scraps of meat up to the eaves of the house as a stash for future days.

But on Tuesdays and Thursdays it was Columba and me. Mostly we fed Corvus Alpo, because Columba felt sorry for the mice. Once, though, we rode our bikes into the foothills and collected tarantulas—scores of them—in mayonnaise jars. Columba said that in Mexico tarantulas were everywhere, and that the birds loved them. We brought them home in our backpacks, and Columba set them loose in the yard, letting them crawl from the back of her hand. Corvus plucked the huge spiders up with his beak, their hairy legs sticking out like cat's whiskers.

Columba's English improved quickly. She studied an hour each night. After Corvus's feeding time, we sat in the perch, and Columba took Corvus in her lap and taught him English—strange words nobody ever really said, like 'expeditious', and 'abscond'. Between us, she did most of the talking. She called me *callado chico*, and Corvus *la boca*. She told me that she was going to learn English well and then move east to Nevada, where they took bike racing seriously. She would win championships in all divisions, and then, when she was too old or her knees gave out, she would get married.

'My father, he thinks I am the boy he does not have. "You want to be a *pobre tonto?*" he says, "a poor fool in a dying Mexico with nothing to your name? That's why we left! ¡*Ingléz, Ingléz, Ingléz!*" he says. "Learn English and ride fast. If you do not you'll be just another *gandul Mexicano* with no place to go but the fields." *Gandul Mexicano*! As if I were a man! So I have to. He times me with his big stopwatch. Stands in the kitchen window, and if I do not get faster, he sends me to my room. I want to live *loco*, do it with men, be married and have *niños*. He says I will be good enough to *race* with males, and too good to sleep with them. He does not know he is hurting only himself. I do what he says. I be the best, then I leave and never see him again. He is giving me my ticket and not even knowing it.'

subscribe . . .

GRANTA

SAVE UP TO 30%

... and get a **serious** discount.

Subscribe to Granta and you will **save at least £7** and **up to £28** on the bookshop
price—and get Granta delivered to your home. See the prices on the order form belo'
You will get four fat issues a year of the most compelling new fiction, memoir,
reportage, argument and photography that Granta can commission, inspire or find.

So why not treat yourself now? (Or treat a friend? A subscription to Granta makes a
great gift.)

GRANTA

'**Essential.**' Observer
'**Indispensable.**' Glasgow Herald
'**Remarkable.**' Scotland on Sunday
'**Wonderful.**' The Times

Your details

Name _____

Address _____

_____

_____ Postcode _____

○ I'd like to subscribe for myself, for:
   ○ 1 year (4 issues) at £24.95 (22% off)
   ○ 2 years (8 issues) at £46.50 (27% off)
   ○ 3 years (12 issues) at £67.00 (30% off)
   starting with issue number _____

Details for a gift subscription

○ I'd like to give a subscription to the person
below, starting with issue number _____
   ○ 1 year ○ 2 years ○ 3 years.
   (My name and address are on the left.)

Name _____

Address _____

_____

_____ Postcode _____

TOTAL* £ _____ by ○ sterling cheque (to 'Granta') ○ Visa, Mastercard/Access, AmEx

card no /__/ __/ __/ __/ __/ __/ __/ __/ __/ __/ __/ __/ __/ __/ __/ __/ expires /__/ __/ __/ __/

signature _____

98H5S63B

*Postage.** The prices above include UK postage. Please add
£8 per year for the rest of Europe; £15 per year for overseas.

○ Please tick here if you would prefer not to receive occasional
promotional literature from other compatible organizations.

Return (free if in the UK) to: Granta, Freep'
2/3 Hanover Yard, Noel Rd, London N1 8BE,
Or phone/fax your order:
   UK: FreeCall 0500 004 033 (phone & '
   Outside the UK: Tel 44 171 704 0'
                      Fax 44 171 704 0'

Columba's bike was an Alacrán—or Scorpion—a top-of-the-line BMX imported from Spain. Aluminium alloy, red and white with racing pads, V-bar handlebars and all Shimano hardware. The name—Alacrán—was painted in delicate blue script across the lower frame. She loved that bike, called it her 'voleto', and maintained it herself. She was good with her hands.

I had an old bike I was too embarrassed to ride, a motorcycle lookalike, really heavy, with a fake plastic gas tank and a squishy seat, fenders and a kickstand. Columba ripped everything off the frame, stripped the bike down to its bare essentials and replaced its puny sprocket with a larger spare she had lying around. She painted the frame electric blue, greased the hubs and oiled the chain, and on her track, after school and into the evening, before her father returned from the fields, we would race. Sometimes we would alternate, time each other with her dad's stopwatch, and sometimes she would pretend she was slower than she really was. But most of the time we would just horse around, ride together, spray each other with rooster tails and mean slides. And all the while, Corvus circled in the sky, gliding on currents, watching, making his presence known with an occasional *quark*.

I had managed to keep Columba pretty much a secret. Jerry had seen me staring at her a few times in class, even asked me what was up with me and 'the spic', but he didn't seem to think much of it. Then one day he heard Corvus say:

'Columba esta c-c-caliente.'

'What the fuck was that?' Jerry said. We were sitting on the porch, feeding bits of dry dog food to Corvus as a reward for singing. Jerry had been trying to teach Corvus the line, *But sleep won't come*, for a half-hour; Corvus had kept silent—till now. I told Jerry I had been training the bird for Mexico.

'Then why the fuck is he saying "Co-*lum*-ba"?' He stared at me, waiting for an answer. I shrugged, as if the bird had simply learned the name himself. Corvus opened his beak wide for a chunk of food.

The talent show was two weeks off, and we kept training Corvus, but he couldn't seem to get past the first verse of the song. And what was worse, my Spanish phrases were muddling up the lines. Instead of singing *You'll cry and cry*, Corvus would crackle out a quiet 'Hola, ch-chica' or '¡Mmmmucho gusto!' Jerry said I had brainwashed our bird, fucked with his mind, crossed his wires. I stopped the Spanish lessons, but it was too late. It didn't matter how long or steady Jerry sang; my choppy Spanish was stuck in Corvus's vocal chords, programmed in, and there was nothing Jerry could do to force it out.

On the evening of the talent show, I turned up backstage with Corvus in the wicker case and found Jerry sitting on a choir platform behind the curtain. He was wearing a white button-down shirt with what looked to be old mud spots on the sleeves, and a large paisley tie that hung down well below his crotch. The Penner sisters were out on stage, kneeling in a little cardboard castle, practising a puppet skit.

'Llllet's d-drop out,' I said. I knew it was hopeless, that Corvus wasn't going to sing. And I think deep down Jerry felt it too. But he simply gazed at me as if I weren't even there.

'Oh, ya, so easy huh,' he mumbled. He lifted the lid of the travel case and scooped up Corvus in both hands, the falcon's hood pulled over the bird's head to keep him from spooking. 'Your cheatin' heaaaaart,' Jerry sang quietly, twice, three times, stroking Corvus's beak bristles with the back of a finger. The bird kept silent.

Then Columba showed up. I knew she would, and I tried to fool myself into feeling relaxed, into thinking that Jerry wouldn't pay her any mind. But when she walked through the stage door in full riding gear, the Alacrán cleaned and shined for her night's performance, I felt my stomach twist up.

She had prepared some special moves—bunny hops and wheelies—for the show. In her warm-up she did a few tyre steps up and down the risers Jerry had been sitting on. Then, in an effortless move, she braked her front wheel and swung the rear around into a quick 180, the tyre chirping to a stop on the wooden panel floor.

'*Buenas noches*, Corvus,' she said, smiling at the bird. '*¿Qué tal?*'

'¿K-k-kay tal?' Corvus said.

Jerry's face seemed to transform at that moment, seemed to fall in, painfully, like a salted snail.

'Fuck you, bitch,' he said, his mouth distorted. 'You're the one fucking with our bird. How 'bout I call immigration… Fuckin'

beaner.' Columba was still smiling, the words not yet sunken in.
'Fuckin' wetback. Should send you back to Tijuana.' Finally, her smile
disappeared, replaced by a blank stare. She looked to Corvus, then
to me.

'Fuckin' mute,' Jerry mumbled under his breath. He took
Corvus back behind some old gratings leaning against the wall.
Through the mesh, I could see patches of his white shirt.

Jerry sang the lines of that song, barely audible, over and over
again. And Corvus, quietly, in return: '¿K-k-kay tal?'

We never made it on to the stage. Before the twins had finished
their puppet act, Jerry walked out from behind the grating.
'Here,' he said, smirking. He handed Corvus over to me and walked
out the back door without another word.

Columba filled our time slot in the show with some extra moves.
She won first place.

That night, in Corvus's perch after the contest, with the bird on
her lap, she asked what was wrong between Jerry and me. I shook
my head, shrugged. Better than having to force out some lie.

She leaned toward me, started sucking on my neck. She kept it
up for five minutes it seemed, just hung there, sucking. *Like a leech*,
I thought. *Nice leech*. Corvus watched, cocking his head to one side.
The sucking hurt, but it was good. She told me she was giving me
a 'hickory'.

When Corvus jumped off her lap, she moved closer and put her
arm around me. She sucked some more in the same place, then kissed
me on the lips. She pulled her shirt up part-way, leaned back over
Corvus's nest and told me to give her one on the belly, right below
her navel so that her father wouldn't see. I had never touched a girl
before. I felt my body shaking all over from nervousness. I stilled
myself as much as I could and submitted, eased myself down, put
my lips to her skin. She was smooth, salty. I ran my lips across the
surface, then closed my eyes and sucked. I sucked and sucked, like
a good leech. I stopped from time to time and looked at the red mark
I was creating, at the tiny corpuscles bursting on the surface of her skin.

'Unbutton my pants,' she said. I reached over, pulled the first
button out. The second. I imagined sucking her thigh.

I was working on the third when a loud bang at the door echoed through the barn.

I put my finger to my lips. Columba buttoned her pants quickly. More banging, the whole barn shaking. Then silence.

'Is he gone?' Columba asked. Then, BLAMM!, like a gunshot near the ear. The rafters shook. Columba and I slapped our hands to our ears, and Corvus flew among the beams, karaaking.

'Open the goddamn door!' BLAMM!...BLAMM!...BLAMM! against the tin walls, against the roof.

'*¡Duele! ¡Duele!*' Columba screamed, and, still trying to hold her ears, nearly fell down the ladder. I followed, unlocked the door and stepped outside. Corvus swooped behind us and flew off, over the vineyard and into the ink-black sky.

From the light of the open door we could see Jerry, looming over our bikes like a statue, a firecracker in his hand. Over the shirt and tie he wore a dirty coat—the fluffy down jacket of a large man. The patch on the chest said *Pierce Crop Dusting*.

We said nothing, Jerry and I. We simply stared at each other for a long while. Finally, Columba broke the silence.

'You are a crazy!' she screamed at Jerry, her hands shaking. 'What, you are trying make us deaf?...*¡Loco!*'

I picked up both bikes and wheeled them to Columba.

'Mexico,' Jerry said quietly.

He put the cylinder back into his coat pocket and snapped the flap shut. 'Just remember who found that bird, quiet boy. You and me. Keep the facts straight.' Then he shrugged and turned as if he didn't care, and made his way into the vineyards. Standing there in the puddle of light from the door, we watched him leave. He was a tiny dot, a little dark cone moving off into the night.

The next day, in Mullers' mobile home, Jerry drummed his fingers on the arm of the love seat and gazed past me out the window.

'"Retrospective", machines,' Mullers said quietly, glancing at us over the top of *People* magazine.

'Retro-*thpec-thive*,' Jerry said, exaggerating his fake lisp.

'Rrrret-ret-ret-,' I said.

Jerry leaned in toward my ear, nearly touching it with his mouth.

'I don't forget,' he whispered. 'Corvuth ith our-th.'
'Cor*vussss*!' Mullers said behind his magazine.

Columba started coming over every day, and in the late afternoons I followed her home to ride on her track. Behind the berm, in the coldness, I became bold, pulling up her shirt, unsnapping her bra, moving my hands down into her pants, into her panties. When I sucked her belly, or kissed her small, perked breasts, she would close her eyes and whisper, '*Sí...sí, sí tal...sí tal...*' Jerry had stopped coming over. From time to time, in the trees beyond my father's vineyards, beyond where we could see, faint explosions echoed to our ears. We knew what they were, and were alarmed at first. But we soon learned to tune them out, like the distant barking of dogs, or the humming of sprayer rigs.

In early March, when the fog dissipated and the clouds started to sprinkle, Columba raced to her first loss in the Shimano Junior Classic. She placed second.

'It's OK,' she said. 'No big deal.' She shrugged it off as a small setback in her general upward trend. But then she lost another, and another, placing second again, then third, just a fraction of time behind the leaders. There was something in her voice, a slight quivering in her resignations, that told me she was bothered by something. Or scared. She stopped talking. Finally, one day, she started to cry.

'You should not come here anymore,' she said. 'Something is happening. My father talks quiet to people on the telephone. My mother smiles as if she is hiding something.' We were sitting behind the berm, our knees hugged against our chests. She looked out to the fields. I asked her what it was, but she wouldn't say.

'Go home,' she said. 'Go find something to do.' She turned to me, her eyes narrowed. 'And besides,' she said, 'my father, he is wondering about me. He saw me in the bath, the marks you gave on my belly.' I put my arm around her, but she didn't respond, didn't lean into me like she usually did. I sat there for a while longer, then rode my bike home.

But I didn't stop coming, and she kept losing. Week after week she travelled to Wasco, to Fresno, to Madera, to Hanford, and came in just behind the leaders, bringing home smaller trophies and red-and-white ribbons.

Then, two nights before the Fresno Regionals, the Alacrán disappeared. Vanished from its rack in the Rodriguez garage. No evidence. No tracks. Nothing. Mr Rodriguez refused to call the sheriff. He did not want them involved.

He drove to town and bought Columba a replacement bike from Bob's Cycles, but he had little money, and no credit, so he had to settle for a lesser bike, bright green, ten ounces heavier, with standard handlebars, low-end brakes and hardware. On the side of the frame, in bold white decals, were the words, GREEN MACHINE. I was sitting in the Rodriguez garage, watching Columba study the bike. I didn't know what to do, what to say. I watched her remove the kickstand and reflectors, tighten the chain around the sprockets, adjust the seat height and handlebars with a crescent wrench.

'My father, he is being investigated,' she said finally without looking up, a quiet harshness in her voice that I had never heard before. 'Somebody reported us.'

She flipped the bike over so that the tyres were in the air. She oiled the chain, spun the wheels to check their trueness. She picked up the crescent wrench and started in on the hub.

About a minute later, we heard footsteps outside, the squishy sound of waterlogged shoes. The noise made its way around the side of the garage. A shadow passed across a waxed-over window. Jerry walked through the doorway and stopped next to the workbench, his slingshot sticking out of the waist of his jeans. His sneakers were caked with a thick layer of mud.

'Been hunting out in the orchards,' he said to me. 'There's a big turkey buzzard in a peach tree. Thought maybe you'd wanna—'

The crescent wrench shot through the air, the sunlight glinting off its edges. Jerry pulled back and raised his arm just in time to deflect it from his head. The wrench jangled on the concrete, and suddenly Columba was at him.

'¡Pinche cabrón!' she screamed, throwing her tight fists at his chest. '¡Eres muy cabrón y desgraciado! ¡Malísimo comadreja!' She landed a blow to his left eye, smacked him hard on the arm, in the stomach. 'You terrible weasel!' she said. She shoved him back

toward the door, punching, kicking at his shins, knocking over jars
of bolts, of washers, and all the while, Jerry remained tight-lipped.
Over and over again she screamed, '¡Comadreja! You ugly weasel!
¡Malísimo comadreja!', beating him on the arm and shoving him
back until he turned and stormed out the door. His shadow passed
the window again. And then he was gone.

She turned and gazed at me as if I were next. 'He is the one!'
she said, pointing her finger toward the open door. 'He said it at the
talent show! I remember! He is the one!' She picked up the crescent
wrench, her hands shaking, and sat back down on the concrete next
to her bike. She started tightening the rear hub. I could tell she was
starting to cry.

I walked up behind her, put my hand on her shoulder. But she
didn't look up, just kept tightening, jerking that wrench.

'Go home, quiet boy,' she said, concentrating on the hub.

I left without a word.

Columba didn't come to school the next day, or the next. I rode
over to her house. I was expecting her to open the door, teary-eyed.
Instead, her father answered.

'Lo siento,' he said in a low voice. He wiped his hands on a frilly
apron around his waist. 'Columba esta ocupado. No mas frivolidad.'
He shut the door in my face.

At school, I learned she hadn't even placed.

I rode over to Jerry's. I knocked on the open door, then walked in,
through the dark living-room, through the hallway, past old family
pictures, to the door of his room. He was lying on his bed, his leg
raised on a pillow. The air reeked of dirty clothes and urine and
Campho-phenique.

'Grazed my knee doing a wheelie,' he said. 'Dried tractor-track.'

I looked around the room. Knives. A samurai sword. Junk. In
the corner, propped against the wall, was a bicycle. It was Columba's
bike. Only it wasn't Columba's bike. It had been spray-painted flat
black and brown and green camouflage—the frame, the rims, tyres,
racing pads, everything. Nothing was spared. The racing seat had
been replaced by a thin, black banana seat; it looked like a beak.

'F-ffuck you,' I said. I pointed at the bike.

He stared at me, bit his lip.

'I called immigration,' he said, and then quickly, to stress his seriousness: 'I didn't want to. They'll look at his green card... If he's legal, they'll be fine.'

I said nothing.

'You're as much a part of this as I am, compadre,' he said. 'Mexico, remember?'

I walked down the hall, out the door. I got on to my bike and rode home.

Two weeks later, the Rodriguezes packed up. From the vineyards, I watched Mr Rodriguez load furniture, watched Columba pack away her tools, wheel that cheap bike up the ramp of the old U-Haul. A sheriff's cruiser was parked in the drive, the deputy leaning against it, drinking from a steaming mug. I whispered *Columba*, loud enough so that she would hear. But she didn't look, just kept packing.

And then she was gone. Just as quickly as she had arrived. I walked around the track, the starting flags hanging limp, the lights still nailed to the trees. I looked down to the ground, to the stretches of thin tyre marks that wound themselves around the packed dirt.

At school, Jerry never talked to me, never looked at me, didn't ride the bus, just skulked off into the orchards after classes. On Friday, curious, I followed him. About twenty orchard rows from the edge of the school yard, he picked something up from behind a tree, then moved away as if levitating. The camouflaged bike was nearly invisible.

Jerry must have confessed about his lisp, because when I stepped into the mobile home on Tuesday, Mullers closed his magazine and smiled broadly, his lips shut.

'Your buddy Pierce thinks he's real funny, faking a lisp. I suppose you're faking too.'

'N-n-no—'

'Thit down!' he said. 'You're gonna thay cauliflower if I have to beat it outta you. Thay *cauliflower*... Thay it!... *Thay it!*...'

In the perch at night, trying to articulate my words as clearly as possible, I continued Corvus's lessons. I wanted him to say, 'I love you, Columba.' She was gone—I knew that. But it didn't matter.

Some voice in my head was telling me that she would be back. And when she arrived at my door, I would be ready, Corvus would be ready. Softly, nearly whispering, he would say it for her: *I love you, Columba.* And I would push her hair back, kiss the purple stone earrings of her lobes, and we would not have to say a word.

One day, as I sat in the rafters, speaking to Corvus, Jerry appeared. He was there suddenly, without a sound, standing in the doorway as if he had materialized from air. The pockets of the down jacket were full of something, ballooning out like stuffed squirrel cheeks.

'I got 'em in the mail,' he said, patting the pockets with his hands, 'a whole case. Come on.'

The sticks of dynamite had extra long, slow-burning fuses, and black stamps on their sides that said, *¡PELIGRO! ¡EXPLOSIVO!*

I went with him to the vineyards. It seemed beyond me to refuse. Under the grey sky, Jerry worked the slingshot, looping the leather sling around a firecracker and pulling back so hard that tiny cracks appeared in the rubber straps. I did what he told me to, flicked the Zippo open, lit the fuses. And *floosh*, the cylinders whirred through the air and landed in the dirt, or in the vines, and ten seconds later, BLAMM!, they would blow, ripping woody flesh from the trunks of vines.

After a while we made our way to the drop and killed some mudsuckers. We guided them to the bank with sticks and strung them on shaping twine. The last two fish came up messy, slime and blood drooling from their open mouths. They must have been sniffing and nibbling at the firecracker when it blew. I felt sorry for them. They were stupid and had no idea. Jerry put them in the pocket of the coat.

We walked back through the trees to the house. I carried the string of fish out away from my body to keep the blood and the slime from dripping on my clothing. Jerry's pocket was soaked through with water and blood, but he didn't seem to care. It was funny: after weeks of not talking, of not saying a word to each other, we were walking side by side with the fish we had killed together, as if nothing at all were wrong between us, as if Columba had never existed and I had never been in love.

I opened the door to the barn, said *quark quark*, and Corvus swooped out of the doorway and flew toward the house, ready for a meal.

We followed behind and sat down on the back steps, then unstrung the fish on the twine and sliced them in half so they would fit into the slingshot.

We slung two pieces out as far as we could. They warbled through the air and dropped on to the oiled drive, just short of the vineyard. Corvus pecked and pulled at the pieces, then took to the air again for another shot.

I went inside for some Cokes. I was only gone for a few seconds. A minute at most. I opened the refrigerator and pulled two sodas from behind the milk. From the cupboard I grabbed a bag of cookies. We were friends again, together, as it used to be. And for some reason, at that moment, I felt as if I no longer needed anything, as if my life could not have been better, as if Mexico, Guaymas and the Sea of Cortez really were possible, and we really *did* have the guts to take that leap.

I walked back through the kitchen to the porch and looked through the window of the door. Everything seemed normal: Corvus in mid-air, cumulus clouds beyond him to the south, floating east to the snowcapped Sierras, the ground in the vineyards dark brown from recent rain.

I looked down. There was Jerry, motionless, the slingshot pulled taut, fish blood and slime dripping from the lit firecracker in the sling.

'No!' I said and dropped the Cokes. But I was too late. The sling snapped. A quarter stick of dynamite hurtled through the air.

And Corvus swooped.

He caught it in his beak, flapped his wings hard and rose higher into the sky. There was nothing I could do but watch it happen.

The firecracker exploded. Corvus's body spun in mid-air, then fell, one wing extended, screwing toward the ground like a dried pea pod. He landed with a thump in a row of vines.

I ran to him, hoping he might still be alive. But when I crouched down, I realized that his head was gone. Black shimmering feathers floated through the wind.

I picked the body up and held it out in front of me with both hands. Blood from the open neck trickled down my arm.

I walked back to the porch and stood in front of Jerry. His mouth was slightly open, as if he were about to say something. But his lips didn't move.

'My bird,' I said to him, emphatically, without stuttering. Jerry shook his head.

'Ours,' he said. He got up, walked slowly down the drive, and disappeared around the corner.

Fish guts were at my feet.

I didn't know it then, but that summer would break heat records. One hundred and seventeen degrees, tape cassettes melting on dashboards of cars, bins full of fruit sunburned in the fields. I would get my first real job as a gofer at a packing shed down the road. Once the fruit had ripened, I would ride my bike to work each morning and run from roller to roller under the hot tin roof, stapling slats on to the tops of fruit boxes with an airgun and yelling, 'Ready!' Toward the end of the school year, Mr Mullers would tell me that I didn't need to see him anymore. To celebrate, we would take a peanut can lid out to the football field and play Frisbee and yell out words to each other, challenging ones like *xylophagous* and *zarzuela*. '*Bitte! Danke!*' Mullers would say, practising his new German hobby whenever he lunged for the lid.

But that night, after Corvus died, I knew nothing of the future. Alone and in the dark, I cried. I kept hearing something scratching in the eaves of the house outside, something small hunting for the rancid meat stuffed into the cracks. I opened my window and whispered *Corvus*, but I knew it was just a rat, looking for an easy meal. I closed the window and crawled back into bed. □

Cheltenham Festival
ᵒᶠLiterature

in association with

❤THE INDEPENDENT

9th - 18th October 1998

"I have always come to life after coming to books"

Jorge Luis Borges

Tariq Ali
Julian Barnes
Steven Berkoff
Raymond Blanc
William Boyd
Asa Briggs
Marilyn Butler
Alan Clark
Richard Dawkins
Judi Dench
Jenny Diski
Helen Dunmore
Sebastian Faulks
Helen Fielding
Orlando Figes
John Fowles
Stephen Fry
Linda Grant
Robert Harris
Edward Heath
Adrian Henri
Susan Hill
Richard Holmes
Douglas Hurd

Michael Ignatieff
Richard Ingrams
Jeremy Isaacs
John Keegan
Felicity Kendal
Frank Kermode
Hermione Lee
Hilary Mantel
Howard Marks
Blake Morrison
John Mortimer
Brian Patten
Jeremy Paxman
Nigel Planer
Terry Pratchett
Frederick Raphael
Michèle Roberts
John Simpson
Jane Smiley
Ralph Steadman
John Sutherland
Marina Warner
Lewis Wolpert
Philip Ziegler

These are just some of the exciting authors appearing at this year's Festival. In a packed programme, the Festival celebrates **Revolution** with an uprising of events featuring writers from all over the world. It explores the pains and pleasures of writing about family relationships in its **Family Ties** series, focuses on Shakespeare, and celebrates the revolutionary ethos of **The Sixties. Book It!**, the children's festival, has exciting events for readers of all ages, with visits from Quentin Blake, Michael Morpurgo and Helen Cresswell among many more.

For a free brochure ring the 24 hour Brochure Hotline or return the coupon below.

Tel: 01242 237377

To book tickets please call the Box Office

Tel: 01242 227979

Please return the form below to Festival Box Office, Town Hall, Imperial Square, Cheltenham, Glos GL50 1QA

Please send me the 1998 Cheltenham Festival of Literature brochure:
BLOCK CAPITALS PLEASE

NAME (Mr / Mrs / Ms / Miss): ....

ADDRESS: ....

.... POSTCODE: ....

HOME TEL: .... WORK TEL: ....

CODE: GR1

GRANTA

BAT COUNTRY
Gordon Grice

My first one: I was six years old. The thing clung to a cinder-block wall in my father's shop. It seemed feeble, rocking its head to dodge the light, tentative as a shivering newborn kitten. It looked nothing like the image I'd taken from vampire movies on television. Its blunt face terminated in a nose made of hideous convolutions of flesh. On TV the wings could have been cut from black velvet. The real ones were naked and veined, their grey hide suggesting both the delicacy of a child's skin and the desiccation of an old man's.

I wanted to catch it, but my father told me not to touch it, not even to approach. Months later two older boys brought a similar specimen to school in a fish tank. They brought it to all the classrooms, and we gazed at the creature from some other realm. When it died soon after, the two boys who'd handled it had to be vaccinated. The doctors stabbed long needles into their bellies.

It is a myth, of course, to say they're all rabid. Less than one per cent of them are. It's truer to say that one too slow and earthbound to stay out of human hands is dangerous—because it is near death, and a possible vector of death.

Having followed the directions in a press kit, I recently found myself standing in a landscape of eroded hills and red earth. This rugged country had risen abruptly as I drove across the plains of northern Oklahoma. An old couple met me as soon as I peeled myself out of the car. The man had a concavity of eyelid where his left eye had been, and the stump of his left forearm was encased in a leather sheath and held against his body by one of his suspenders. He said he was a farmer. The woman, who was dressed in yellow polyester and seemed impervious to the heat, asked brightly if I was a volunteer too. I said no, I'd only come to watch.

Soon we were piled, with a dozen others, into pick-up trucks and driven down a set of dirt roads crusted with caliche. We had vowed not to reveal the route to anyone else. The secrecy was meant to protect the biological treasure we'd come to see. We reached a valley of red cedar and tamarisk, yucca and sand plum, where a hot wind harried the black dragonflies. I gazed into the thin creek that crawled the valley floor and saw a peculiar abundance: minnows swimming in place against the current, sluggish catfish groping in the

GUNTER ZIESLER/BRUCE COLEMAN

mud with their tentacled faces. If I hadn't already known about the hidden life of this valley, the richness of fish might have been my first clue. The water trickles through gypsum caves before it gathers into the creek, and in the caves it becomes rich with the leavings of one million nocturnal predators.

I'd come here with workers in the wildlife business and conservation volunteers to witness these predators when they emerged at dusk. Meanwhile it was an arid ninety-five degrees and a fleshy cloud to the south was kneading itself into a tense knot as it approached, as if fretting that it had nothing to give us. We walked the trail, discussing plant life or the occasional reptile that revealed itself by rustling in its shaded bed of fallen cedar needles. The volunteers were here to learn about the ecosystem which lay before us, a cryptic web of relations connecting everything from the trees to the insects to the rabbits whose round pellets of scat betrayed their existence. The volunteers would have to answer questions from the tourists who would soon scuffle the trails of this park, each bus-load having first taken the vow of secrecy.

One of the black dragonflies buzzed into someone's face, prompting the woman to windmill ineffectually. Up close, each of the creature's wings seemed branded with blue thumbprints. The biologists reminisced about a monster insect of uncertain order that had terrorized them all for ten seconds the previous dusk. The volunteers offered helpful suggestions about what it might have been, all of which the professionals dismissed. It was, they said, an utter mystery.

A thorny tamarisk stood at an elbow of the path. 'Supposedly their roots go a hundred feet deep,' said Davis, a biologist. He said that was why this imported species can thrive among the dry valleys and buttes of northern Oklahoma. The twisted elms that tossed their heads in the wind were of the Siberian variety, another species imported for its deep-drilling roots.

At a turn of the path, everyone stopped. An unpleasant substance lay in the middle of the trail, its smell announcing its freshness. The professionals poked at the stuff with twigs and examined the pugmarks. A spirited debate erupted, one faction of biologists arguing that the substance was scat, another favouring vomitus. Because the prints showed no evidence of claw marks, Rena, the biologist leading the trail, ruled out coyote. Members of the canine clan can't retract their claws. This was the work of a cat. Since the smelly matter wasn't buried, it was probably vomitus rather than scat. Or else we had startled the cat away before it meant to leave.

'A neighbour of mine saw a mountain lion standing in the middle of the highway the other morning,' said the farmer. I followed the track off into the grass, where it disappeared. The pugmarks were small, surely the work of a bobcat rather than a mountain lion. I crouched to look along the path he might have taken. At that level I could see tunnels between the clumps of grass, roofed by the overarching stalks. These tunnels, Davis told me, are runways for killdeer and mice, paths for cottontail and roadrunner. And bobcat.

One of the volunteers mapped caves for a living. As we walked he told me about bat caves.

'You don't want to go into a cave that houses a big colony. You could die from it.'

The problem is a fungus that grows in the faeces. A large group of bats drops enormous quantities of guano, creating a heavy concentration of airborne histoplasm spores. The spores can infect human lungs, causing dense, fibrous knots of tissue to form there. On an X-ray, a victim's lungs look as if he's inhaled a handful of dimes. The infection can spread to other organs.

'The ironic thing,' the caver added, 'is that doctors used to think it was tuberculosis, and they'd send people into caverns to live in the cool and damp.'

I asked what it looks like in the cave.

'The guano is waist-deep. It's black and shiny, exactly like tar. I didn't take my mask off in there, of course, but before we went in we could smell the stink, like ammonia.' The odour is another sign of a concentrated bat population. Bat guano doesn't smell much until it's digested by a species of beetle that eats nothing else and thrives only where the deposits are deep.

The buttes rimming the valley jut like human molars. They're made of sandstone compacted in layers. Ages of water eroded the land around these relatively durable patches of sandstone, sculpting the rest of the landscape away to leave the buttes. Some of the less durable parts of the land are made of gypsum. Gypsum erodes into angular particles of sand that sting your face when the wind drives them. But, in an accumulation on the ground, gypsum sand takes on a peculiar fluidity, rippling along into drifts and dunes. It is softer to the touch than quartz sand.

Water eats greedily at gypsum, dismantling it faster than many other minerals. Because the buttes are riddled with gypsum, they are also riddled with caves. Rena explained this phenomenon as she made us stop and look west. The butte there was just going dark as the sunlight leaned towards the horizontal. 'What do you see?' she demanded.

'A butte,' someone said.

'A window,' someone else added.

'A window,' Rena confirmed. It looked a perfect rectangle punched high in the face of the butte. 'Just like everything else in this valley, it's a product of water erosion.' The desiccating wind slapped her hair around and into her face, as if mocking the idea of moisture.

The professionals, as it transpired, had discovered this hole only the night before. Davis had climbed the butte this very day to explore. He found a chimney in the top which seemed to connect with the horizontal shaft starting at the window. 'I could see about a dozen feet down,' he said. 'I wasn't going in.'

Everyone laughed. Everyone knew what he hadn't bothered to say: diamondback rattlesnakes live in holes like that. These reptiles grow thick as a man's leg, and they kill more human beings than any other snake in North America. After a pause, the stories about people bitten by diamondbacks started up. The peculiar thing about diamondbacks is that the tall tales you hear from fools and liars are never as horrible as the truths you hear from biologists and doctors. This day the best horror story described a bitten leg that swelled until it 'busted just like a ripe tomato.'

The diamondbacks in this region grow to more than seven feet long, and can weigh more than thirty pounds. These measurements are meagre compared to those of some tropical or marine reptiles, but they're substantial for a cold-blooded animal in a country of dry, boiling summers and ground-freezing winters. The secret of their survival here is the very wrinkling of the earth. In the eroded furrows that line the buttes, they can sulk through sunny days. In the gypsum caves, they can lie in a mass with hundreds of their brethren beneath the frost-line, sluggish through the winter. Occasionally a hunter sees a few of the reptiles basking on rocks on a clear winter day—then he knows he's near a den of them.

The diamondback survives by plugging itself like a sizzling power cord back into the earth. After travelling for miles in the summer, the snake finds its way back to the same den each winter. The young home in on an ancestral den they have never seen. The senses that guide this miraculous slithering journey are unknown. Rattlesnakes are known to have a heat-detecting sense and an extraordinarily acute chemical sense. Some think they can also navigate by the sun.

A researcher I knew spent a great deal of money on radio signalling devices. He captured rattlesnakes and operated on them to implant the devices. Then he tracked the snakes for a year, through their warm-weather wandering and hunting and mating, and their autumn return. On the maps where he plotted his data, the migrations of the snakes looked like a diagram of solid particles swirling into the mouth of a drain.

I asked the researcher what could explain such a feat of navigation.

'Nothing,' he said.

The bats are an ancient order of mammals, diversified into 900 species. Human beings have never quite known what to make of them. They've been classed as cousins of the monkeys and brothers of the rodent, though modern science claims they're no relation to either. Old myths explained them as symbols of luck or denizens of hell. When Cortés came to America and found a kind of bat that drank blood, his reports only echoed the European legends of winged succubi and soul-takers.

The strangest aspect of bats—their mastery of echolocation—is now common knowledge, but it was greeted as a fool's fantasy when a scientist first described it in 1938. The bat lives in a world painted in shades of its own voice. The various species speak in different ranges, so that a scientist with an ultrasound detector can tune his machine to read the species he's interested in. Individual bats have distinctive voices. In a maternity colony, the mothers return from their nightly hunts to find their young, and each mother detects her own pup among the multitudes by the sound of his voice. Some bats seem to read textures with sonar as well as a human can by touch. They can distinguish between a thrown pebble and a hard-shelled beetle. A bat knows whether insects are approaching or receding. It reads them as a meteorologist reads the track of a thunderstorm.

Some of a bat's sensory feats are beyond our grasp. No one knows, for example, how a bat finds its way on long journeys. A bat taken many kilometres from home can find its way back, as dogs are said to do. Some scientists think the bat navigates by the stars. Others think it is tuned to the magnetism of the earth.

A t dusk I sat with the professionals and the volunteers on wooden benches facing west. Our scattered party had gathered with the gloom. Another kind of party was about to disperse.

'The State's official estimate is one million bats in this colony,' said Davis. 'Personally, I think it's more.' He was whispering to me, because he didn't want to interrupt the discussion the other scientists were leading. They were bringing the volunteers to the climax of their indoctrination, formulating the larger meaning of the natural text they had explicated all day. Their message was one of conservation, under which, no longer disguised in the facts of biology, lay a sort of religious belief. Rena spoke of individual molecules cycling unchanged through stone, grass, herbivore, predator, larger predator, until they finally wash to the sea. Another biologist spoke of food chains and an 'energy flow' that binds every living thing.

One of the volunteers read out an essay on 'energy flow' which the professionals had recommended to him. As he read, attempting a certain dramatic flair, in the failing light, someone whispered urgently, 'They're out!'

Suddenly everyone was pointing and whispering, trying to locate the single bat the colony had sent out as a scout. The volunteer read on, unwilling, I suppose, to interrupt his sacred text. Despite the gloom, the buttes still looked red as sunburn. But the vegetation was greying towards darkness. The opening of the colony cave was somewhere in one of the buttes, though the professionals wouldn't say exactly where. Rena had admitted to me earlier that the nature walk wasn't merely educational. It was also meant to disorient the tourists so that they couldn't return to find the bat cave on their own and despoil it.

Everything was silent except for the voice of the reading volunteer and the quiet call of a wood duck. A power line ran behind the buttes, and on it sat a dark silhouette. 'There he is, same as usual,' someone whispered. It was a great horned owl. I'd seen them before, watching the night with eyes like fractured amber, eyes that seem to return your gaze. When they take off they often leave a stinking pile in which you can find undigested bones, if you have the stomach for such an enquiry. This one knew the schedule of the bats. It came to take one of the million every night.

We kept straining our eyes for the scout. Two nighthawks crossed the quiet air in front of the buttes, the white bands on their dark wings flashing each time they turned. They, too, had come to prey.

Suddenly a few bits of something were floating in the air between two buttes. They might have been shrapnel from a slow explosion. They rose. Everyone was whispering excitedly, and the eager volunteer finally finished his reading and watched with the rest of us. The bits of shrapnel became more numerous, forming a column which broadened at the top to resemble a silent tornado. The tornado moved towards us. Suddenly the twilight sky over our heads was pocked with uncountable marks, moving without a noise to the east. The silence was relative. To some of the insects and birds out that night, the conglomerate of sound must have been louder than nearby thunder. It was simply too high-pitched for human ears.

Occasionally one bat flew a little lower than the rest, and I could see the shape of the thing, its rapid wings appearing as short, sharp triangles cowled in the ghost of their own motion. Each of the professionals raised a hand and rubbed the fingers together as if contemplating a snap. They were making a little bug-noise to draw the bats down into better view.

A few moments before, I had been only subliminally aware of the insect life around me: moths popping out of the undergrowth, gnats venturing too close to my eyes, an occasional mosquito bite. Now I was acutely aware of the absence of insect life. This one colony of mother bats was said to scour tons of insects from the sky every night, each bat devouring half her body weight or more to maintain her flying heart-rate of 900 beats per minute.

At a distance you don't see the eating itself. Most people seem to visualize the process as a neat one, the bat gulping insects like a ramjet eats air. In fact, bats eat as messily as anyone else. If necessary, they snag insects with their wings or tails and toss them towards their mouths. They puncture insect husks with their canine teeth and grind down the shells with their molars. With luck, you may see a pair of butterfly wings wafting down, the butterfly body devoured from between them.

The birds of prey left, having silently taken their prey in the confusion of the emergence. The wind changed, and the bats turned to the south. They were still streaming out of the cave, and now, seen from a different angle, they looked like particles swept along in an invisible river. They wound into deepening dark, streaming beyond our sight. □

GRANTA

TARANTULA
Sam Toperoff

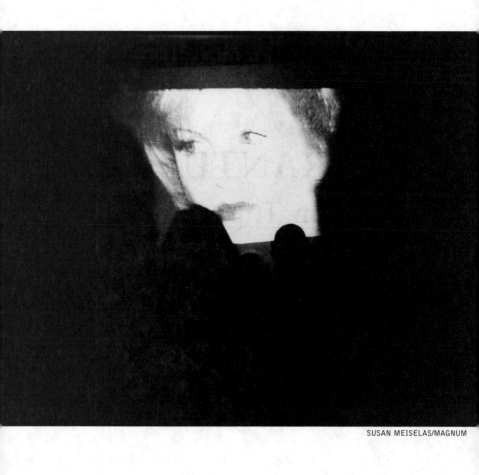

SUSAN MEISELAS/MAGNUM

I'm nocturnal. I love the moonlight, the shadows, the dark places, the dappled murk. I'm not being poetic. I'm simply being true to my nature, my nocturnal nature. Like all tarantulas.

I'm Texas to the core. Legs so bowed from behind I look like four hairy-legged cowhands walking behind each other. Amarillo. Been Lone Star all my life. Will be the rest of it, too. Hook 'em Horns! At the moment I'm in El Capitan, the only old-time theater left downtown.

I know the place well. Usually I saunter in under the Ladies' Room door from the dusty lot a little after dark, find my armrest along the wall, watch the feature, get a little hungry, and vamoose. Sometimes I don't even have to leave the theatre to find something tasty: an oversized roach or a kid mouse. There's nothing like a good snack when you're watching a movie.

I guess you can tell that behind my rough exterior I'm really a romantic kind of guy at heart. That's a line from *Wolf*, in case you don't know. Jack Nicholson. I love Jack. People say I look like him.

Anyway, I'm here watching *Kilimanjaro*, which I thought would be garbage, mostly because of all the hype about it and the fact that it came in about a billion dollars over budget. It's the remake, with Tom Cruise and Nicole Kidman. They're Scientologists in real life. This here is Baptist Country. But I don't judge, I just eat my snack and stare up at the screen.

I don't see real well. None of us do. We're better in the dark than in the light—we're nocturnal. If I squint, it's fine; fuzzy, but fine. And the music, unbelievable. One of those giant speakers is only a couple of rows up front. When the bass fiddles and the timpani come in, I vibrate. Every single cilia quivers. Maybe it's the music more than anything that draws me in. And the credits: I love to see names I know. Horst Rhein: he won an Oscar for *Two Wonders*. I like the way Juliette Taylor handled the casting, but there's no Oscar for that, even though it's important. The way the credits crawl up the screen is really a turn-on. It makes me dizzy, in a mellow way.

Did I tell you I've been here three days now, or what I take to be three days? It's hard to tell when it stays dark like it does in here. Usually, every time the theatre empties after the last show, I know that it's time to leave. But at the moment I can't get out.

They've boarded up the Ladies' Room. Repairs. Think what it means to be nocturnal and stuck in a movie theatre. Eternal nocturnal—too much of a good thing. I can't even sleep, though I am tired beyond belief.

So I'm watching *Kilimanjaro*. Seen it, seen it, and seen it. And let me tell you: no Oscars for this baby. Except there's this one scene. Maybe you remember it. It's the one where Tom Cruise, the great white hunter, goes into Nicole's tent at night with his lantern. He's sneaking around but doesn't want it to look that way—and that speaks to me, I also hate to look like I'm skulking. The scene has been lit by Raoul Flynn, but they won't give him another Oscar—it's too subtle.

Anyway, it's really hokey but I love it. Try as he might, Tom can't keep away from another man's wife, even though in real life she's his own. I loved that Nicole knew exactly how to tempt Tom without, you know, appearing to. She wasn't worth a damn as far as character was concerned and was sure to bring him down. But she was gorgeous, irresistibly gorgeous, and a little sad. It was such bad, beautiful karma.

I know. I'm a hopeless romantic.

So when he gets inside her tent she's sleeping, or pretending to be sleeping, underneath this mosquito netting. I think you can see her eyelashes flutter, but can't be absolutely sure. She's wearing a lacy nightgown, pink. On safari, a pink nightie? Oh sure. Nicole is pink and pleasing. Tom watches.

I'm wondering what he's feeling—not the character, but Tom himself, looking at his wife playing someone else's wife. He watches. She moves and makes a little sound, a sigh, still sleeping. Her hand slides up the pillow. And there—right there—coming down the pillow sideways is a black fist. The first time, I couldn't believe it. It was one of us—one of me. A young, really good-looking tarantula.

He moves like Baryshnikov, to the pizzicato strings of the Hollywood Bowl Orchestra. Two, two-and-a-half inches long. Tall, remarkably regular features, narrow white fangs, nice smile, sort of shy. You can see how he got the part. So he comes down the pillow—the violins stop—and steps on to her shoulder. How he lifts and curls his front legs. It's so graceful.

And they never see it. The audience. They don't see the grace, the elegance. They see... I don't know what they see. Usually they are disgusted, revolted, repelled, nauseated—any word of loathing you want to use. They don't even notice his lovely smile.

I've got to hand it to Cruise. He doesn't overreact; his eyes narrow a little, and that's all. It's tougher on Nicole: she has to keep still. And even though our boy has obviously had all the venom drained right out of him, those fangs are real enough.

He fans the air with a front leg and starts moving again. The violins buzz. He's across her shoulder, moving toward the hollow place. Her skin is flawless. Tom watches. He lifts the netting real slow. Her chest rises and falls. The lace on her nightgown rises and falls; the pulsing of her heart ripples that pale skin. When he approaches her cleavage his eyes narrow even more. It's time for the cellos.

Cruise leans in. He uses the back of his hand. One flick, and the spider's sent flying into the darkness. There's a quick middle shot of Tom raising his boot and smashing down on the dirt floor. There's a musical crescendo. Then silence. Close-up, we see his face: the great white hunter satisfied, the hint of a thoughtful smile. Nicole wakes, sees him, smiles. She doesn't have the faintest idea what has happened. She reaches out. They never speak. It's a Hemingway story.

And I'm wondering, is the spider still on his boot heel?

Why do they hate us? We have fangs, sure, and venom. But we do not—let me repeat: not—attack human beings. Certainly not a sleeping innocent—relatively speaking—like Nicole Kidman. Yet there's this attitude in Baptist West Texas: Tarantula equals terror. Like it was one of us back there in the Garden of Eden or something.

Wise old Nathan once told me that in Europe—especially in Italy—they still believe that a tarantula bite can be fatal. But tell me, why would we want to poison anything we weren't going to eat? In order to ward off death, they think, you have to dance like a dervish. The Tarantella. They whirl, they jump, they bounce, to fight off the lethargy, the paralysis. What can I tell you—Italians. Once, they even believed that a bite was communicable, so whole towns would dance for hours and hours, until the last dancer fell exhausted to the ground, bathed in sweat. When the last dancer goes down, the town is cured, apparently. I'd love to see something like that in Amarillo.

Want the truth? A man could hold us in the palm of his hand, and we'd never bite him. How'd you think they trained that guy for *Kilimanjaro*? And even if by some wild chance we did bite someone, what would it be like? No worse than a hornet's sting. And are they despised, as we are? Well, maybe, but loathed? I don't think so.

It's simple: if we're hungry, we eat—just like you. In *Kilimanjaro*, when the safari needed dinner they killed a wildebeest, and Tom had the natives roast it on a spit. No problem. But when I stun and numb a mouse, eat it in morsels, ingest it and leave the skin and skeleton, I'm disgusting. Come on.

I'm nine years old—early middle age; we live into our twenties. Mom laid 200 eggs. I didn't hang around, and neither did any of my brothers and sisters. I left the cocoon for a dark, peaceful burrow as soon as I could form this thought: Leave the cocoon for a dark, peaceful burrow.

As I already mentioned, we don't see or hear too well. But these faculties are not really necessary because, well, I'm tactile. Every living thing is tactile, but not Tarantula-tactile. We are to touch what an eagle is to sight. Brush my body wall in even the slightest way and I'll know almost everything about you. Believe me. Usually, I'll zip away, unless I'm hungry, in which case I might grab at whatever's tickling. And every once in a while, if I don't want to be bothered, I'll lean back, raise my front legs like Bruce Lee, and bare my fangs. It's a ferocious pose. It usually does the job.

It's the fine hairs—setae, cilia, call them what you will—that warn me of danger. They cover my entire body. Dark, dark hairs. Nathan tells me he's seen a film at the university where a cricket barely touches the body fuzz of a tarantula. The spider attacks, and even slowed to one sixty-fourth of a second you can't see the strike. You see only a blur, and then a dead cricket. I'd love to see that film. It's rare to see us in a starring role.

In Turkey, Nathan tells me, people use us to catch flies. I've always imagined an evening in Istanbul: tarantulas bouncing around a million bedroom walls like black tennis balls. Flies disappearing— thrrrippp, thrrrippp, thrrrippp. Advantage Tarantula.

I'm not your run-of-the-mill specimen. Certainly, when my

trichobothria—the especially sensitive hair on my legs—is riffled, I want to kill. I say 'want', but it's not a want: it's a—what's the word? There is no word exactly, it's just a Tarantula thing, and I can't control it. I just... But I can control lots of other things. That's why I'm not your run-of-the-mill. I don't know if it's a good thing to go against your deepest nature, but I've been doing it. I have an enquiring mind. I want to be, well, a little less Tarantula in some ways. Maybe it's because I can afford to be. I'm large and powerful. And it's like Nicholson said in *The Shining*: it's nice not to have to be afraid—gives a man plenty of slack. Then again, maybe I've seen too many movies.

I need a real day, I need a real night. I need to know that there's a natural cycle. So I had to try to escape from the El Capitan. The Ladies' Room, like I said, was blocked off, but there was this uncovered vent above the Men's Room. I gave it a go. It led to an air duct, and from there to a rusty grille in the outside wall—hell to get through—and then to a downspout full of withered leaves. By the time I got to the bottom, I sort of liked the prickly rub of them. The sun was coming up, and everything was in a morning haze. It took me a while, but I got my bearings and made my way over the asphalt, across the drainage ditch, into the stand of scrubby pines. Thirsty, tired, dull headache, *trichobothria* throbbing. Feeling cactus-mean and sort of loving it as I crawled up to my burrow. Home, but not quite. Some of the threads around the opening were torn, waving straight out in the morning air. I knew I had to repair them, right then—instinct, I guess. And silk doesn't come easy for me any time, but it's murder when you're bushed.

I was still at it twenty minutes later when I saw her. Shimmering blue, rust-coloured wings, hovering. She must have been watching me the whole time. And I mean she was gorgeous. Like-to-die-Nicole-Kidman-gorgeous. She landed on a branch close to the ground.

We just looked at each other. Never moved, never made a sound for maybe, what, half an hour? I'd say her wingspread must have been three inches or so, with these long antennae, curling, uncurling. I just stared, never even tried to figure out what she was, who she was, or what she had in mind.

But I knew her. I'd always known her. Nathan had told me all about her. And everywhere that tarantulas gather they always talk about her. The Digger Wasp. Genus *Pepsis*. Our mortal enemy. But oh, what a lovely nemesis. There were wild stories about *Pepsis* that could curl your hair, but the physical description was a constant: metallic-blue body, majestic russet wings, that incredible stinger in the abdomen—ah, I could see it now. Never more dangerous than when pregnant, they said. And this one was heavy with egg.

Nathan always poured scorn on the tales of enchantment and torture, but somehow or other the end result was always the same: tarantula skeletons at the bottom of deep, dark holes—an entombment right out of Edgar Allan Poe. The last time we talked about it, he told me that these creatures lived on nectar. Nectar: I thought that sounded poetic. Until he said that *we* were the nectar.

We stared. A breeze ruffled my body hair. My front legs flexed; I bared my fangs. I was feeling playful. We should begin to—what's the word?—interact. We didn't. We just carried on looking. I wanted to look away, get back to repairing the burrow; but I was damned if I was about to get stared down by a pregnant wasp. So we eyed each other up some more. Maybe for another twenty minutes. I had the feeling that someone was watching us, but I couldn't break my gaze. My stomach growled, *trichobothria* throbbing worse than ever.

I didn't even see her move. She was so fast. One moment she was in the air, darting, and then she was gone.

I turned around to see where she could be, but lost her. And then I felt her very close.

Very close? How about *on* my back?

I reached around with a front leg. She wasn't there. She was working her way under my stomach, probing the cilia with her stinger. Jesus, this gal was pushing me! Truth is, I kind of liked being able to hold back. What unbelievable restraint. Ascetic. And then— God, how did I stand it!—she wrapped those wings around me. I couldn't bear it. My fangs went for her flesh...and didn't even get close. She was Ali, moving like a butterfly, stinging like a...

I felt a pinch on my lower abdomen, right where it touches the rear leg joint. It was nothing, just a pinch.

She hopped right off as though nothing mattered, as though she didn't give a damn about me anymore. And she didn't. She began digging. With her jaws and legs, she dug right outside my burrow. I'd never seen such crazy digging in my life, dirt flying left and right and everywhere. She dug so deep that after a while she disappeared. I tried to look into the hole, but wobbled on my legs. I couldn't move. Well, not couldn't exactly—I just didn't want to badly enough. That hole was deep though, I could tell, and narrow, a tunnel really. I remember thinking that I'd hate to have to try and climb out of something like that.

It was early afternoon by the time she was done, and I was woozy as hell. My whole body was buzzing. I tried to show her that I didn't intend to hurt her. What with her pregnant and all. A cloud covered the sun and the air darkened. I could see her a little more clearly. She moved in jerks, like a wind-up toy, examining the hole, and then she came back to me. How could I let her know what I was, what I am? What I could do to her if I really wanted? It was hard not to be offended: she acted like I wasn't even there.

All right then. I struck the ferocious pose, or tried to. But she didn't even notice. Then she slid right under me again. Her jaw, that digging jaw, clamped on my rear leg.

For the longest time, I felt nothing. Her grip, if anything, became firmer, and the pain began to pulse. I thought: She can't hold on for ever. Eventually she began to squirm beneath me, batting her wings in the dirt. Where I felt pressure, I tried to pull my body away. At one point I lifted so many legs that I almost fell over. And then, to my amazement, she toppled me. Me! I was four times her size. We rolled across the entrance to my burrow, and kept rolling, over and over. I caught myself hoping that no one was watching. Her blue body was streaked with dust, and her wings looked frayed, but those jaws still clamped tight.

And then…yeow! Right into my lower stomach. This time it was stunning, a sharp, deep scissor-cut. The worst pain I ever felt. Piercing. Deep. I shivered. But very soon—amazing—it was not so bad. Cool liquid seemed to flow up from my belly, out to all my extremities. I don't know how to explain it: there was warmth in the cool, if that makes sense. It relaxed me and took away the pain almost at once. My legs went soft, everything went soft, and there was a stillness. It was good, except I couldn't feel my heart. I listened. No, I definitely couldn't feel my heart. I knew I wasn't dead, though. You're not dead if you're listening for your heart.

You know what part of me was doing? Watching. Watching to see what was going to happen next. I saw my legs uncurl. Saw the tops of the trees, a patch of sky—I couldn't turn my head very much. And you know what was the weirdest thing? Another part of me was wondering how the whole thing would look if Horst Rhein was filming it, slowed to one sixty-fourth. Can you imagine? I wasn't afraid: I knew that if I was thinking these things I must still be alive. And I could tell that it was growing dark.

But it was midday. Why was it so dark?

She came closer, slowly. She looked like hell. Where were the pizzicato strings? I saw her licking a drop of blood from her stinger. Blood. Mine. She didn't ever look at me. Nathan, this I swear—the next pregnant digger wasp I come across, she's going to get the Tom Cruise treatment.

I was somewhat paralysed, I knew. But I thought that it would wear off.

I was moving again. Being moved, I should say. Sliding—being slid—over the ground. I could see her shadow at the fringe of my vision. Then I saw her with my leg in her mouth. She raised me up and put me in the hole. Upside down. I slid down slowly. Didn't hit bottom, though—there was still a bit of room below me. I could see the dark sky, a disc of it at least.

Then it blacked out. She came down on top of me. I could see her expression, which was no expression at all. She seemed completely detached, like she wasn't even there, wasn't part of what was going on. Down she came, looking, staring, but hardly even seeing me. And out of her belly came a goo, a greenish goo. It oozed over me. It was warm, and smelled like bad butter.

The next thing I knew, she was hovering again. Rolling her head, turning around in the hole. And what was this I could see coming out from between her legs: a jelly egg? It glittered in the dimming light. A single transparent egg fell on to the secretion and stuck fast to my stomach. Tarantulas watching this would be revolted.

She spun back up the passage, blocking the light for a moment.

Then she was gone. I could see sky again. I was pleased. I'll wait this out, I told myself. I'll be fine.

Then the dirt came, scooped down first in wispy puffs and then in a grainy stream. It fell into my mouth, my eyes. I couldn't spit or cough or hiss. There was almost no light, but I could still see my legs, and my strange wet stomach.

It's been quiet for hours. I say hours, but I have no idea how long she's been gone. It doesn't smell anymore, or maybe I've gotten used to it. I don't think I'm loco but there's definitely a sensation on my stomach. Some sort of movement. A quivering. Ooooooo: was that a sting? How could that be possible?

It's the egg. Scratching. Nibbling. Sucking my blood. *Interview with the Vampire*. Cruise again.

Nathan once told me that you can see your whole life spinning before you at the end. It doesn't. Nothing like that is happening. I know exactly where I am. In a hole, behind the parking lot of the El Capitan theatre in my beloved Lone Star State. Hook 'em Horns. They're showing *Kilimanjaro*.

There's a tearing at my stomach, a tearing. I can hear jaws. Maybe I'll *hear* my life spin past. At least, they sound like little jaws, but I can't be sure. I can't trust myself anymore.

Maybe. Maybe if I hadn't gotten so much Hollywood in my head. Maybe if I had been truer to my Tarantula self. That's what I seem to hear Nathan lecturing: Son, I warned you about *Pepsis*. Why didn't you listen? Why weren't you faithful to your nature? Why didn't you live Tarantula true?

And—*God, that little son-of-a-bitch is eating me alive!*—I shout back at Nathan: 'The Truth! You can't handle the Truth!' But I know he can't hear me, and wouldn't know what I meant if he could.

It feels best that I go to sleep for a while. Just a nap...to get some of my strength back. Unless I wake up a skeleton. I'm only kidding. You're not dead if you can crack a joke. □

Royal Festival Hall
Hayward Gallery
on the South Bank

BRUCE NAUMAN

16 JULY – 6 SEPTEMBER

Work spanning the 30 year career of one of the most important artists of the post-war avant-garde.

ADDRESSING THE CENTURY: 100 YEARS OF ART & FASHION

8 October – 11 January From Matisse to Miyake, this exhibition brings alive the creative relationship between art and fashion through the century.

Literature Highlights
Autumn 1998 *on the South Bank*

23rd September

**Terry Pratchett,
AS Byatt,
Alasdair Gray**
with **Jenny Uglow**
Discworlds Apart
Three world-class writers discuss their shared preoccupation with imaginary worlds.

3 – 17 October

The F-Word
Feminism: sex, lives and writing
A discursive series looking back, forward and side-ways at women's writing featuring writers such as
**Kate Figes,
Jacqueline Rose,
Linda Grant,
Beatrix Campbell**

30th October – 7th November

Poetry International
Writers taking part include
**Czeslaw Milosz,
Roger McGough,
Derek Walcott,
Anne Carson,
Olga Sedokova,
Tom Paulin,
Marge Piercy**

BOX OFFICE 0171 960 4242

For your FREE Literature and Hayward Bulletins with full details of all the above and more please call
0171 921 0734. OR SURF www.sbc.org.uk

Funded by
THE ARTS COUNCIL OF ENGLAND

sbc

GRANTA

BIG MILK
Jackie Kay

The baby wasn't really a baby any more except in the mind of the mother, my lover. She was two years old this wet summer and already she could talk buckets. She even had language for milk. Big Milk and Tiny Milk. One day I saw her pat my lover's breasts, in a slightly patronizing fashion, and say, 'Silly, gentle milk.' Another day we passed a goat with big bells round its neck in a small village near the Fens. The light was strange, mysterious. The goat looked like a dream in the dark light. The baby said, 'Look, Big Milk, look, there's a goat!' The baby only ever asked Big Milk to look at things. Tiny Milk never got a look in.

I never noticed that my lover's breasts were lopsided until the baby started naming them separately. The baby was no mug. The left breast was enormous. The right one small and slightly cowed in the presence of a great twin. Big Milk. I keep saying the words to myself. What I'd give for Big Milk now. One long suck. I was never that bothered about breasts before she had the baby. I wasn't interested in my own breasts or my lover's. I'd have the odd fondle, but that was it. Now, I could devour them. I could spend hours and hours worshipping and sucking and pinching. But I'm not allowed. My lover tells me her breasts are milk machines only for the baby. 'No,' she says firmly, 'they are out of bounds.' I should understand. 'You are worse than a man,' she tells me. A man would understand, she says. 'A man would defer.' I'm not convinced. A man would be more jealous than I am. Two years. Two years is a long time to go without a single stroke. I look over her shoulder at the baby pulling the long red nipple of Big Milk back and forth.

At night I lie in bed next to the pair of them sleeping like family. The mother's arms flailed out like a drowned bird. The baby suckling like a tiny pig. The baby isn't even aware that she drinks warm milk all night long. She is in the blissful world of oblivion. Limbs all soft and gone. I test the baby's hand, full of my own raging insomnia. The small fat hand lands back down on the duvet with a plump. She doesn't even stir. I try my lover's hand. She can tell things in her sleep. She knows the difference between me and the baby. In her sleep, she pulls away, irritated. I lie next to the sleeping mother and baby and feel totally irreligious. They are a painting. I could rip the canvas. I get up and open the curtains slightly. Nobody stirs. I take a peek at

VALERIE WINCKLER/RAPHO/NETWORK

Jackie Kay

the moon. It looks big and vain, as if it's saying there is only one of
me buster, there's plenty of you suckers out there staring at me. It is
a canny moon tonight, secretive. I pee the loudest pee I can manage.
I pour a glass of water. Then I return to bed next to the sleeping
mother and daughter. The baby is still suckling away ferociously, her
small lips going like the clappers. It is beyond belief. How many pints
is that she's downed in the one night? No wonder the lover is drained.
The baby is taking everything. Nutrients. Vitamins. The lot. She buys
herself bottles and bottles of vitamins but she doesn't realize that it
is all pointless; the baby has got her. The baby has moved in to
occupy her, awake or asleep, night or day. My lover is a saint, pale,
exhausted. She is drained dry. The hair is dry. Her hair used to gleam.
   I'm not bothered about her hair. I am not bothered about not
going out any more, anywhere. The pictures, pubs, restaurants, the
houses of friends. I don't care that I don't have friends any more.
Friends without babies are carrying on their ridiculous, meaningless
lives, pretending their silly meetings, their silly movies, their crazy
avant-garde theatre matters. Tottering about the place totally without
roots. Getting a haircut at Vidal Sassoon to cheer themselves up. Or
spending a whole summer slimming. Or living for the two therapy
hours per week. That's what they are up to. A few of them still bang
away at ideas that matter to them. But even they sound tired when
they talk about politics. And they always say something shocking to
surprise me, or themselves. I don't know which. I don't see any of
them any more.
   I see the baby mostly. I see her more than I see my lover. I stare
into her small face and see her astonishing beauty the way my lover
sees it. The big eyes that are a strange green colour. The lavish
eyelashes. The tiny perfect nose. The cartoon eyebrows. The perfect
babysoft skin. The lush little lips. She's a picture. No doubt about
it. My lover used to tell me that I had beautiful eyes. I'd vainly picture
my own eyes when she paid me such compliments. I'd see the deep
rich chocolate brown melt before me. The long black lashes. But my
eyes are not the subject these days. Or the object, come to think of
it. My eyes are just for myself. I watch mother and daughter sleeping
peaceably in the dark. Dreaming of each other, probably. There are
many nights I spend like this, watching. I haven't made up my mind

102

yet what to do with all my watching. I am sure it will come to some use. The baby dribbles and the lover dribbles. The light outside has begun. I've come round again. The birds have started up their horrendous opera. I'm in the best seat, next to the window with the theatrical tree. The baby has power. It is the plain stark truth of the matter. I can see it as I watch the two of them. Tiny puffs of power blow out of the baby's mouth. She transforms the adults around her to suit herself. Many of the adults I know are now becoming babified. They like the same food. They watch the same programmes. They even go to bed at the same time as the baby; and if they have a good relationship they might manage whispering in the dark. Very little fucking. Very little. I'm trying to console myself here. It's another day.

In the morning the baby always says 'Hello' to me before my lover gets a word in. To be fair, the baby has the nicest 'Hello' in the whole of the world. She says it like she is showering you with bluebells. You actually feel cared for when the baby talks to you. I can see the seduction. I know why my lover is seduced. That and having her very own likeness staring back at her with those strange green eyes. I can never imagine having such a likeness. I tell myself it must be quite creepy going about the place with a tiny double. A wee doppelgänger. It's bound to unsettle you a bit, when you are washing your hair, to look into the mirror and for one moment see a tiny toddler staring back at you. It can't be pleasant.

The feeding itself isn't pleasant either. Not when the baby has teeth. I've heard my lover howl in pain on more than one occasion when the baby has sunk her sharp little milk teeth into Big Milk. A woman is not free till her breasts are her own again. Of this I am certain. I am more certain of this than a woman's right to vote or to choose. As long as her breasts are tied to her wean she might as well be in chains. She can't get out. Not for long. She rushes home with her breasts heavy and hurting. Once we went out for a two-hour-and-twenty-minute anniversary meal. When we got home my lover teemed up the stairs and hung over the bathroom sink. The milk spilled and spilled. She could have shot me with it there was so much. Big gun milk. It was shocking. She swung round and caught me staring, appalled. She looked proud of the quantities. Said she could have filled a lot of bottles, fed a lot of hungry babies with that.

Jackie Kay

I tried to imagine the state of my life with my lover feeding hundreds of tiny babies. I pictured it for a ghastly moment: our new super king-size bed (that we got so that all three of us could sleep comfortably and are still paying for in instalments) invaded by babies from all over the world. My lover lying in her white cotton nightie. The buttons open. Big Milk and Tiny Milk both being utilized for a change. Tiny Milk in her element—so full of self-importance that for a second Tiny Milk has bloated into the next cup size. The next time she mentioned having enough milk to feed an army, I told her she had quite enough on her hands. And she laughed sympathetically and said my name quite lovingly. I was appeased for a moment until the baby piped up with a new word. 'Did you hear that?' she said, breathless. 'That's the first time she's ever said that. Isn't that amazing?' 'It is,' I said, disgusted at myself, her and the baby all in one fell swoop. 'It is totally amazing—especially for her age,' I added slyly. 'For her age, it is pure genius.' She plucked the baby up and landed a smacker on her smug baby cheek. The baby patted Big Milk again and said, 'Funny, funny, Milk. Oh look Mummy, Milk shy.' I left the two of them to it on the landing outside the toilet.

Even when I go up to my attic I can still hear them down below. Giggling and laughing, singing and dancing together. 'If you go down to the woods today, you're in for a big surprise.' The rain chaps on my tiny attic windows. Big Milk is having a ball. I climb down the steep stairs to watch some more. Daytime watching is different from night-time. Tiny details light up. The baby's small hands are placed protectively on the soft full breasts. The mouth around the nipple. Sometimes she doesn't drink. She just lies half asleep, contemplating milk or dreaming milk. I am never sure. It makes me wonder how I survived. I was never breastfed myself. My mother spoon-fed me for two weeks then left. I never saw her again. Perhaps I've been dreaming of her breasts all my life. Maybe that's what rankles with the baby taking Big Milk for granted. When her mouth expectantly opens there is no question that the nipple won't go in. No question. Every soft open request is answered. I try and imagine myself as a tiny baby, soft black curls on my head, big brown eyes. Skin a different colour from my mother's. I imagine myself lying across my mother's white breast, my small brown face suffocating in the pure joy of warm, sweet milk. The smell of it, recognizing the tender smell of it. I imagine my life if she had kept me. I would have been a hairdresser if I hadn't been adopted. I'm quite sure. I would have washed the dandruff off many an old woman's head. I would have administered perms to give them the illusion of their hair forty years before. I would have specialized in tints and dyes, in conditioners that give full body to the hair. I would probably have never thought about milk. The lack of it. Or the need of it.

I lie in the dark with the rain playing soft jazz on the window pane of our bedroom. I say our bedroom, but it is not our bedroom any more. Now teddy bears and nappies and ointment and wooden toys and baby clothes can be found strewn all over the floor. I lie in the dark and remember what it was like when I had my lover all to myself. When she slept in my arms and not the baby's. When she woke up in the night to pull me closer. When she muttered things into my sleeping back. I lie awake and remember all the different places my lover and I had sex. All the different ways, when we had our own private language. The baby has monopolized language. Nothing I say can ever sound so interesting, so original. The baby has converted me into a bland, boring, possessive lover who doesn't know her arse from her elbow. There are bits of my body that I can only remember in the dark. They are not touched. The dawn is stark and obvious. I make my decision. I can't help it. It is the only possible thing I can do under the circumstances.

I love my lover and I love her baby. I love their likeness. Their cheeks and eyes. The way their hair moves from their crown to scatter over their whole head in exactly the same place. Their identical ears. I love both of them. I love the baby because she is kind. She would never hurt anybody. She is gentle, silly. But love is not enough for me this time. I get up, get dressed and go outside with my car keys in my hand. I close my front door quietly behind me. My breath in my mouth. I take the M61 towards Preston. I drive past four junction numbers in the bleached morning. There are few cars on the road. I stop at a service station and drink a black coffee with two sugars. I smoke two cigarettes that taste disgusting because it is too early. I don't smoke in the day usually. I smoke at night. Day and night have rolled into one. The baby's seat in the back is empty. The passenger seat has a map on it. There is no lover to pass me an apple. There is just me and the car and the big sky, flushed with the morning. I put on a tape and play some music. I am far north now. Going further. I am nearly at the Scottish border. I feel a strange exhilaration. I know my lover and her baby are still sleeping, totally unaware of my absence. As I drive on past the wet fields of morning, I feel certain that there is not a single person in the world who truly cares about me. Except perhaps my mother. I have been told where she lives up north. Right at the top of the country in a tiny village, in a rose cottage. She lives in the kind of village where people still notice a new car. If I arrive in the middle of the day, the villagers will all come out and stare at me and my car. They will walk right round my car in an admiring circle. Someone might offer to park it for me.

I will arrive in the daytime. When I knock at the door of Rose Cottage, my mother will answer. She will know instantly from the colour of my skin that I am her lost daughter. Her abandoned daughter. I have no idea what she will say. It doesn't matter. It doesn't matter if she slams the door in my face, just as long as I can get one long look at her breasts. Just as long as I can imagine what my life would have been like if I had sucked on those breasts for two solid years. If she slams the door and tells me she doesn't want to know me, it will pierce me, it will hurt. But I will not create a scene in a Highland town. I will go to the village shop and buy something to eat. Then I will ask where the nearest hair salon is. I will drive there directly where a sign in the window will read, ASSISTANT WANTED. I will take up my old life as a hairdresser. When I say my old life, I mean the life I could have, perhaps even should have, led. When I take up my old life, old words will come out of my mouth. Words that local people will understand. Some of them might ask me how I came to know them. When they do, I will be ready with the answer. I will say I learned them with my mother's milk.

I am off the M6 now and on the A74. I read somewhere that the A74 is the most dangerous road in the country. Something new in me this morning welcomes the danger. Something in me wants to die before I meet my mother. When I think about it, I realize that I have always wanted to die. That all my life, I have dreamed longingly of death. Perhaps it was because she left. Perhaps losing a mother abruptly like that is too much for an unsuspecting baby to bear. I know now this minute, zooming up the A74 at 110 miles per hour, that I have wanted to die from the second she left me. I wonder what she did with the milk in her breasts, how long it took before it dried up, whether or not she had to wear breast pads to hide the leaking milk. I wonder if her secret has burned inside her Catholic heart for years.

I can only give her the one chance. I will knock and I will ask for her to let me in. But if she doesn't want me, I won't give her another chance. I won't give anyone another chance. It has been one long dance with death. I have my headlights on even though there is plenty of daylight. I have them on full beam to warn other cars that I am a fast bastard and they had better get out of my way. The blue light in my dashboard is lit up. It and the music keep strange company. Is there anyone out there behind or before me on the A74 who has ever felt like this? I realize that I am possibly quite mad. I realize that the baby has done it to me. It is not the baby's fault or her mother's. They can't help being ordinary. Being flesh and blood. The world is full of people who are separated from their families. They could all be on the A74 right now, speeding forwards to trace the old bloodline. It is like a song line. What is my mother's favourite song? 'Ae Fond Kiss'? 'Ae fond kiss and then we sever.' There is much to discover. I picture the faces of all the other manic adopted people, their anonymous hands clutched to the steering wheel in search of themselves. Their eyes are all intense. I have never met an adopted person who does not have intense eyes. But they offer no comfort. This is all mine.

I arrive in the village at three o'clock, exhausted. My mouth is dry, furry. It is a very long time since I have slept. I spot a vacancies sign outside a place called the Tayvallich Inn. It has four rooms, three taken. The woman shows me the room and I tell her I'll take it. It is not a particularly pleasant room, but that doesn't matter. There is no view. All I can see from the window is other parts of the inn. I close the curtains. The room has little light anyway. I decide to go and visit my mother tomorrow after sleep. When I get into the small room with the hard bed and the nylon sheets, I weep for the unfairness of it all. A picture of the baby at home in our Egyptian cotton sheets suckling away and smiling in her sleep flashes before me. My lover's open nightie. It occurs to me that I haven't actually minded all my life. My mother shipping me out never bothered me. I was happy with the mother who raised me, who fed me milk from the dairy and Scots porridge oats and plumped my pillows at night. I was never bothered at all until the baby arrived. Until the baby came I never gave any of it a moment's thought. I realize now in room four of Tayvallich Inn under the pink nylon sheets that the baby has engineered this whole trip. The baby wanted me to go away. She wanted her mother all to herself in our big bed. Of late, she's even started saying 'Go Away!' It is perfectly obvious to me now. The one thing the baby doesn't lack is cunning. I turn the light on and stare at the silly brown and cream kettle, the tiny wicker basket containing two sachets of Nescafé, two tea bags, two bags of sugar and two plastic thimbles of milk. I open one thimble and then another with my thumbnail. They are the size of large nipples. I suck the milk out of the plastic thimbles. The false milk coats my tongue. I am not satisfied. Not at all. I crouch down to look into the mirror above the dressing table. I am very pale, very peelie-wally. Big dark circles under my eyes. I do not look my best for my mother. But why should that matter? A mother should love her child unconditionally. My hair needs combing. But I have brought nothing with me. I did not pack a change of clothes. None of it matters.

I pass the nosy Inn woman in the hall. She asks me if I need anything. I say, 'Yes, actually I need a mother.' The woman laughs nervously, unpleasantly, and asks me if I'll be having the full Scottish breakfast in the morning. I tell her I can't think that far ahead. She hesitates for a moment and I hesitate too. Before she scurries off to tell her husband, I notice her eyes are the colour of strong tea. I open the door that now says NO VACANCIES and head for Rose Cottage. I can't wait for tomorrow, I must go today. I must find her today. My heart is in my mouth. I could do it with my eyes shut. I feel my feet instinctively head in the right direction. It is teatime. My mother will be having her tea. Perhaps she will be watching the news. My feet barely touch the ground. The air is tart and fresh in my face. Perhaps some of my colour will return to my cheeks before my mother opens

her front door. Will she tilt her head to the side gently when she looks at me? Following my nose miraculously works. There in front of me is a small stone cottage. Outside the roses are in bloom. There is a wonderful yellow rose bush. I bend to sniff one of the flowers. I always knew she would like yellow roses. I stare at the front door. It is painted plain white. Standing quietly next to the front door are two bottles of milk. I open the silver lid of one of them and drink, knocking it back on the doorstep. It is sour. It is lumpy. I test the other one. It is sour as well. I look into my mother's house through the letter box. It is dark. I can't see a single thing.   □

109

IMAGINED WORLDS

FREEMAN DYSON

"*Imagined Worlds* makes illuminating criticisms of what [Dyson] calls 'ideologically driven' technologies, which, because they symbolize national pride, are obliged to succeed...Ideologically driven technologies, Dyson argues, discourage the rigorous experimentation without which no technology can properly evolve."

—Timothy Ferris,
NEW YORK REVIEW
OF BOOKS

"This is an extraordinary book, written in the wisdom of old age but with the hopeful courage of a man whose commitment to science, if not necessarily to its products, has kept him young."
—NEW YORKER

"*Imagined Worlds*...deserves to be read for its elegance and sagacity."
—Michael Thompson-Noel,
FINANCIAL TIMES

Jerusalem-Harvard Lectures
$14.00 paper • £8.50 paper

THE KENNEDY TAPES

Inside the White House during the Cuban Missile Crisis

EDITED BY ERNEST R. MAY AND PHILIP D. ZELIKOW

"To read [*The Kennedy Tapes*] is to be in the White House in those fateful days of October, 1962... This immediacy is new, and it is endlessly fascinating...*The Kennedy Tapes* is a must-read, not only for the student of history or international affairs, but for citizens of any country who hold out the hope that the Earth will never face such a crisis again."
—James Baker,
THE OBSERVER

"Riveting...*The Kennedy Tapes*... [is] a suspenseful, self-contained narrative of a single intense episode."
—Hendrik Hertzberg,
NEW YORKER

Belknap Press • 20 halftones •
$16.95 paper • £10.50 paper

THE ANATOMY OF DISGUST

WILLIAM IAN MILLER

"[A] most useful book...one that takes its readers, however reluctantly, down alleys of life worth traversing. One wouldn't have thought that the subject of disgust could exfoliate so elaborately, or throw off so many provocative insights, as it does in these pages."
—Joseph Epstein,
NEW YORKER

"While *The Anatomy of Disgust* does disgust, it also enthralls, enlightens, dazzles, and entertains...What this beautifully written book reminds us so brilliantly is how much the humanities—and in some ways only the humanities—can tell us about the empirical world, the world of physical sensation, social behavior, and political conflict."
—Andrew Stark,
TIMES LITERARY SUPPLEMENT

$15.95 paper • £9.95 paper

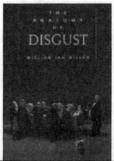

HARVARD UNIVERSITY PRESS

US: 800 448 2242 • UK: 0171 306 0603 • www.hup.harvard.edu

GRANTA

MY FROZEN FATHER
Deborah Levy

STRAND EN SEE
NET BLANKES

BEACH AND SEA
WHITES ONLY

← →

ORDE ELIASON/LINK

Jan Smuts Airport, South Africa, 1991. Three grown-up children visit the country they were born in for the first time in twenty-three years. As they walk through customs busting with love for their dad whom they have not seen for a year, they glimpse him waiting at the barrier. He is wearing a suit and holds a new brown leather briefcase under his arm.

The children wave frantically. Their father appears not to see them. They shout out to him but he does not appear to have heard them. And then they know why. He has seen a comrade, a friend of the family who must have been on the same plane, and he is holding out his arms to welcome her.

The old woman shuffles towards their father. She seems to take for ever. They stand behind her while he hugs and kisses her. They watch him animated and affectionate, as he exchanges addresses and news with her. They stand glumly waiting for their father to acknowledge them. And in that wait, the unspeakable happens. They feel their cheeks burning with anger. Its force is so overwhelming they feel dizzy and cold and shameful. When he finally turns towards them he is not met by the loving, adoring children they so badly want to be, but by a hostile silent trio who are battling with a rage they do not yet understand. Their father makes a joke. He says, 'Tell me about your lives in thirty seconds.'

When and where does Exile begin?

They sit in the airport bar with their father waiting for the connection to Durban where he now lives. He asks them if they'd like something to drink? They can see a juice machine on the counter. Guava juice. The thick pink sweet juice of their childhood. Dad buys them each a juice in white plastic cups. Black airport staff sweep trash from under their feet. Dad looks strained because they are strained.

They don't know what to talk about and they don't know what to do with the force of what they are feeling. In fact they dare not catch each other's eye. There is an uncomfortable, sullen silence. They want to joke and laugh but don't know how to. Who is this man anyway? What sort of things do you talk to him about?

'Um, so, um what's it like to be back? What's it like to live here?'

Their father begins to talk. He systematically lists the changes for the better since Nelson Mandela's release. He describes the mood in the country, the inevitable transition to democracy and the complexity of the future. This is the future their father has devoted his life to.

His children's minds are elsewhere. They cannot listen because they don't seem able to recover from being ignored when they waved and shouted at the barrier. In fact they are trying hard to do an emergency operation on their insides, but they don't seem to have the right instruments. While he talks and they arrange their faces into some version of dutiful children privileged to hear the cutting-edge news, first-hand, of a country in transition, they hear the rasp of the broom sweeping rubbish under their feet. They glance at the deadpan face of the black man pushing his broom and hear their father's voice as if it is a soundtrack to a film. Something is being announced in Afrikaans. The guava juice is finished. It sticks to their lips, this thick sweet syrup. Cigarettes have been ground out in ashtrays. At last, their flight connection to Durban. They busy themselves adjusting suitcases, doing up buttons and zips, activities that mean they do not have to speak. From the plane window they glimpse the skyscrapers of subtropical Durban, which will soon be renamed KwaZulu/Natal. Their father turns to his eldest daughter, Deborah, and says,

'You were last here when you were three years old.'

Durban, 1962

Deborah is three years old, paddling in the polluted warm ocean on Durban's main beach. These are the days when beaches and toilets and park benches are for Whites Only. The massacre outside Sharpeville police station, when security forces opened fire on demonstrators protesting against pass laws, has happened two years before. Sixty-nine people were killed and hundreds wounded. Soon after, membership of the African Nationalist Party and the Communist Party is made illegal. Both Deborah's parents are members of these organizations.

Durban. Sun, sea, apartheid and sharks. These are notoriously shark-infested waters. Early each morning lifeguards patrol the beach checking the shark nets. While paddling in the sea, three-year-old Deborah hears a voice speaking through a tannoy. She notices that everyone is running out of the ocean and starts to run with the crowd. She can't see her mother and father anywhere. A voice is crackling through the tannoy trying to calm the crowd who are shouting and beckoning to bodies they can still see in the water.

A shark has somehow swum through the nets and been spotted in the shallows. A *Jaws*-style attack is about to begin. A lifeguard finds the three-year-old, and she explains that she is lost. He kneels down on the sand and picks the little girl up, explaining that he's going to take her to the lifeguard's hut and make an announcement. But first of all he needs to know her name. For some reason she lies. Instead of saying Deborah, she says Beatrice.

'C'mon then, Beatrice, your Mom and Dad will come and get you in no time at all.' He carries her across the sand to the lifeguard's hut. It seems to Deborah, who is now Beatrice, that there are miles and miles of sand; she is excited and scared.

In the long walk to the hut she wonders whether she should tell him her real name? No, it's too late now. He's called her Beatrice three times already. She can't undo this recent transgression, and anyway she's not supposed to talk to strangers so changing her name might give her some protection.

Meanwhile Deborah's mother stares out to sea, weeping. She thinks she can see pools of blood congealing in the water. There is no doubt about it. Her three-year-old daughter has been eaten by a shark. She hears another announcement echo over the vast expanse of beach.

'A little girl, about two or three years old, is lost and cannot find her parents. Her name is Beatrice. Could her parents pick her up from the lifeguard's hut?'

Deborah's father is walking the beach in a panic. How can he go back to his wife and say their daughter is nowhere to be found? He too hears the announcement about Beatrice. Perhaps he should go to the lifeguard's hut anyway and report that his daughter is missing? He starts to run.

Their daughter is sitting in the shade, under an assumed name, drinking the lovely can of cold orangeade the lifeguard has given her. She has no doubt that her parents are going to find her. In fact it's a test. If they can find her despite the obstacles she's put in their way, it must really mean they want her!

Deborah Levy

Johannesburg, 1964

Deborah is with her father in their suburban garden making a snowman. She is now five years old. This is a freak winter and she has never seen snow before. Father and daughter start making the body, a great round ball of filthy Johannesburg snow, patting it down with their hands. Then they start on the snowman's head. It's getting dark and they quickly find a stick to trace a big smile from one end of the snow head to the other.

Then they go inside their little bungalow with its green veranda and peach tree, now heavy with white ice. Deborah thinks of her snowman standing under the stars. Tomorrow she plans to make him even taller and fatter; she will give him a nose and even a scarf like they have on the front of Christmas cards.

That night, while she lies in bed, the special branch of the security police knock down the door of their home. Her parents are not too sure which, if not both of them, is going to be taken away. They want Deborah's father and tell him to pack a suitcase. For some reason the police are digging up the garden, watched by the snowman with whom Deborah is in secret communion. She speaks to him the way people speak to God, she speaks to him in her head, and he answers her. She is saying, 'Why are they digging up the garden?' and he replies, 'They think something is buried there.'

What is a snowman? A snowman is a friendly stranger, here today, gone tomorrow. A round jovial paternal presence, built by children to watch over the house. He is weighty, full of substance, but he is also temporary and spectral. He is a father who is going to come unstuck, soften and liquefy. He starts off as an image clear in the mind, frozen in time, and then becomes a muddled memory. The snowman is her father who is going to disappear.

The police find nothing but earth and snails, cat shit and stones, but they do take away her father. He has already packed his suitcase. He has been arrested under the Suppression of Communism Act. This is 1964 and there have been many other political arrests. These burly men in khaki uniforms have their big hands on her father's shoulders, one on either side. Dad kisses his family goodbye and they watch him get into the back of a small shiny red car. Dad who first got interested in politics because when he was twelve years old he had to stuff newspaper into the holes in his shoes. At school he wore his Lithuanian mother's spectacles because she could not afford to buy him his own. He wanted to understand why people were poor, and like many of his generation, Marx explained his life to him. And now he is being marched off at a pace to somewhere terrible, marched off by men who torture other men and who sometimes have swastikas tattooed on their wrists. The car pulls away with her father inside it. They all wave until their wrists ache but their father doesn't wave back. This is the first and only goodbye in the small girl's life. 'Goodbye' is never again going to mean that people come back after they've said it.

Maria is a large, fierce Zulu woman who has a secret stash of chewy oblong sweets wrapped in waxy paper. These are called Pinkies, and are hidden in her apron pocket. The police have also searched her room because she is nanny to the children in this household, and she is furious, sad. A tear slips down her cheek as she strokes the little girl's hair, not stroking gently, gripping the five-year-old's head with both her hands, swearing. Maria has seen all this before. It's part of her life. She absolutely knows the score and she suspects the girl is not going to see her father for a long time. Meanwhile Deborah's mother is making phone calls to lawyers and friends, her one-year-old son, Sam, sleeping on her shoulder.

Maria takes the girl into the kitchen. It's five in the morning and despite the snow of yesterday, the sun is beginning to push through the sky. Maria is saying something but Deborah is elsewhere. She can hear her mother talking on the telephone in hushed, urgent tones. Maria holds up a pineapple for her to see, and when the girl doesn't react, she starts sawing at it with a carving knife. She sprinkles a slice of the fruit with cinnamon powder and sugar and hands it to her.

'Deb,' she says quietly, in a matter-of-fact voice. 'You're going to have to be very brave.'

Is South Africa a beautiful country? The veldt, the sunshine, the sunsets, the rivers and ocean? No, it is not. There is no escaping an interior geography that smells of tears and pinched lips and being brave.

Her father will spend a year on trial and be sentenced to three years' imprisonment in Pretoria Central. Deborah is five years old now and will not see him until she is nine. During that time the interrogators will make him stand for 114 hours. When he faints they will throw cold water on his face and then stand him up again. The home is filled with the absence of her father. His photograph stands on a cabinet next to the phone. Absence is a very present emotion in the house. Every room is full of Dad's absence. Apartheid means 'apartness' after all. A separation. Is he dead and Mom isn't telling them? The hallway, the bathroom, the bedrooms, the cupboard with brooms and buckets, the lounge with its two tall doors—push them open—where is Dad? The kitchen that leads to the green veranda overlooking the back garden where the grass is high and peaches lie rotting under the tree. Where is he?

Durban, 1962

Deborah has not yet seen snow. Nor has she built a snowman. She is three years old, lost on Durban beach, and has changed her name to Beatrice. Sharks have escaped from the nets, she is sitting in the lifeguard's hut and no one has come to collect her. The kindly bronzed lifeguard picks up the tannoy and belts out the same announcement he's been making for the last hour.

'We have a little girl here. Her name is Beatrice, she's got blonde curls and a red swimming costume.'

Someone knocks on the door of the hut. The lifeguard puts down the tannoy and saunters to the door. Deborah's father is hot and breathless.

'I've lost my daughter,' he says.

'Is her name Beatrice?'

'No.'

'What does she look like?'

'She's got blonde curly hair and she's wearing a red swimming costume.'

The lifeguard, puzzled, opens the door. Her father glimpses his daughter sitting on the bench swigging fizzy orange.

'Hello Dad.'

Her father (who has many pseudonyms himself in The Movement) does not appreciate his daughter's early attempt at negotiating an enigmatic identity. He picks her up in his arms and whacks her. Then he hugs her. And whacks her again. They walk hand in hand, barefoot across the burning sand listening to the tinkle of the ice-cream seller's bell as he cries, 'ESKIMO PIE, ESKIMO PIE.'

A childhood treat, Eskimo pie is vanilla ice cream coated in chocolate and not a reference to food eaten in Alaska, Greenland and Eastern Siberia. But in terms of internal weather, a psychological climate, the ice of the Arctic has a metaphorical place in this story. Dad was a political prisoner for four years. He came out frozen. He went into Pretoria Central as one man and came out another. He went in as A and came out as X. The colour of his face was ice blue from lack of air and colour and family. Four years after he built the snowman with his five-year-old daughter, he arrived back at the house and looked for it in the garden. He expected it to be there. His own thaw had yet to take place. He had yet to 'become warm enough to lose numbness', to become 'less cold or stiff in manner'. He went in as a man and came out as a snowman.

In flight, 1991

Deborah sits in silence with her father on the connecting flight from Johannesburg to Durban. The father who held out his arms to welcome a comrade but who did not welcome her. In Durban there will be no such thing as a Whites Only beach. The ANC, PAC and the Communist Party are legalized. Nelson Mandela has been released. The convention for a new democratic South Africa has begun negotiations on the formation of a multiracial transitional government. It is a time of celebration and hope.

Yet now on the aeroplane the atmosphere is more like a funeral. It seems to Deborah, and to her brother and sister sitting next to their father in silence, as if there is no language they share. How different it might have been if their father had greeted them with his arms wide open—Hello! Hello! Hello!—and embraced his nervous brats with their English accents and muddled relationship with the country they were born in and left for ever when Deborah was nine years old.

Deborah Levy

Dad, stern and distressed, rips open a packet of in-flight peanuts. The nuts spill on to the lap of his new suit. He asks, 'What the hell is wrong with you?'

Deborah does not know what to say. Or where to begin. She could say, 'Why didn't you wave when you saw me?' This sounds incredibly childish. She could say, 'Because you never write or phone and I always pretend it's OK. Because unlike me you have done something useful with your life.' Instead, she says nothing.

As the plane begins its descent she stares out of the window at the Indian Ocean. She thinks that Dad may not be the snowman after all. He lives in the sun, in the new South Africa. It is Deborah who is frozen vapour. □

GRANTA

THE SCENE OF THE CRIME

PHOTOGRAPHS BY SIMON NORFOLK
INTRODUCED BY MICHAEL IGNATIEFF

Translators' headphones, the International Criminal Tribunal for Rwanda

Your genocide, my self-defence

The photographs by Simon Norfolk [*opposite and from page 129*] are a selection from his essay on genocide in the twentieth century and how, and if, we choose to remember it. Genocide: a new word for an old crime. Compounded of the Greek word for tribe and the Latin suffix for murder, it was coined in 1943 by a Polish jurist, Raphael Lemkin, to describe any systematic attempt to exterminate a people or its culture and way of life. It is a 'crime against humanity', one of a select body of offences which even though directed at particular tribes are crimes against all.

Genocide is a violation of certain universal intuitions about when it is appropriate for human beings to die: when they are ready, when their time is up, when they take up arms, when they are guilty, and so on. That they should die simply because of the colour of their skin or the contours of their face violates a basic presumption of human innocence. No one should be killed simply for being who they are. If there are moral universals in the world, one would have thought that this would be one.

It is not. To understand this point simply imagine what would happen if an exhibition of Simon Norfolk's photographs were mounted in the main lobby of the United Nations building in New York. The Turkish delegation would protest against the inclusion of the Armenian photographs; the Americans would be outraged at the inclusion of Vietnam; the British would object bitterly to the inclusion of Dresden; and Russians might well be indignant at the inclusion of the Ukrainian famine. Perhaps only the Germans would keep quiet. The genocide committed in their name remains the only one beyond argument.

The truths we hold to be self-evident are the truths that divide us. This year marks the fiftieth anniversary of the Genocide Convention, passed by the United Nations in December 1948 and ratified by the parliaments of all but a handful of member states. But it remains a nullity, never once applied or enforced. None of the perpetrators of the genocides committed since 1948—not even Cambodia—has been punished. The larger the crime, it seems, the greater the chances of impunity. There has been talk since 1948 of a permanent international tribunal to try such crimes, but none has

Michael Ignatieff

been created because most nations won't accept their citizens being tried by a foreign court, even one mandated by the United Nations. In the absence of such a court, genocide has never acquired the clear meaning which only successful prosecutions ever give to crime. Deprived of a sustaining jurisprudence, the word has fallen into a dubious moral limbo. Perpetrators excuse themselves of the charge of genocide by claiming that they were merely defending themselves against the genocidal intentions of their enemies, thus getting their retaliation in first. Victimized peoples inflate the injustices they have suffered into genocide in order to seek absolution and sympathy. To claim to have been the victim of a genocide can be an essential moral step in claiming reparations, self-determination and statehood. In the process, the coinage has been debased. What remains is not a moral universal which binds us all together, but a loose slogan which drives us apart.

By including Dresden in his collection of photographs, Simon Norfolk raises the question of these suspect moral equivalences. Genocide is a crime whose identity turns on intention. What intention was at work in RAF Bomber Command in February 1945? To harm and punish German civilians, certainly. To exterminate them as a people? Certainly not. Moreover, victims whose state is engaged in war belong in a different category to victims who have not taken up arms. The people of Dresden were citizens of a state waging an exterminatory war and the bombing was an act of war. Once the conflict was over, the bombing ceased. It was as just a war as ever was fought, but its justice does not justify war crimes. And a war crime Dresden most certainly was: indiscriminate slaughter of a civilian population for no military or tactical objective, or none that can be subsequently defended. That no one was punished for Dresden is an inequity of victor's justice. But injustice is not undone by misdescribing the crime.

Likewise, the indiscriminate bombing of civilians and the defoliation of jungles in Vietnam were war crimes. Anyone who doubts this should inspect the consequences, unsparingly catalogued in the photographs of deformed children and their fiercely accusing stares. But genocide is not a simple synonym for horror. It is a category of horror, distinct unto itself. Instead of defining a discriminate

124

category of evil, the word genocide has become an invitation to abandon all discrimination. It might seem better to abandon the word altogether, were it not that the crime it describes continues to exist.

Genocide as utopia

The impulse to commit genocide is ancient. The list of tribes which have been exterminated may be as long as the list of animal and plant species which we have rendered extinct. This exterminatory impulse is much misunderstood. It is actually a kind of longing for utopia, a blood sacrifice in the worship of an idea of paradise. What could be more like paradise on earth than to live in a community without enemies? To create a world with no more need for borders, for watch-posts, a world freed from fear in the night and war by day? A world safe from the deadly contaminations and temptations of the other tribe? What could be more beautiful than to live in a community with people who resemble each other in every particular? We all long for harmony, for an end to the seemingly interminable discord of human relations. What could be more seductive than to kill in order to put an end to all killing? This utopia is so alluring that it is a wonder the human race has been able to survive it at all. Certainly genocide enlists lower motives than the longing for utopia. The men with the machetes may have no utopia in mind higher than at last possessing their neighbour's farm or property. But genocide is such a radical cleansing, such a violation of the normal order of things, that it must enlist the highest of motives, the biggest of dreams. Most genocides begin with orders from above, with rabid invocations of the people's need to cleanse themselves of pollution. Beyond the hate, however, the authorities promise a calm after the cleansing storm and a world freed of enemies and fear. This utopia both glorifies venal motive and silences residual scruple.

At the end of this century, we can see from Bosnia and Rwanda that such impulses have not ended with the defeat of fascism and the collapse of communism. They remain permanent human temptations; the way to a utopia so appealing that for millennia the violence used to achieve it was not perceived as a crime. What could be more sensible than to rid the forest of the tribe whose existence menaces your own? Until very recent times, it was not self-evident that other tribes belonged to the same species. While human life may have existed on the planet for a million years, it is possible that only in the last thousand have men believed that we belong to a single tribe. The crime of genocide could not exist as a moral category until this consciousness was established. This was the work of the monotheistic religions, who bound the tribes together by preaching that all men were subject to the same master. It was not until the European Enlightenment that this religious intuition was secularized, when it became a commonplace to think of human beings possessing a common nature and a common set of moral obligations. And only in our century, in the last fifty years, has it become possible to declare a set of universal human rights. So the history of genocide teaches us something about the history of the century in general: ours has been the first to perfect mass murder and the first to understand the exact sense in which this is a crime. Our future depends on whether our consciousness of it as a crime is equal to the strength of it as a temptation.

The scene of the crime

In the mission school in Nyarubuye, Rwanda, the bodies of the children have decomposed. The ragged clothes which shroud their skeletons are falling apart. The bones are white, picked clean.

Near the ruins of the crematoria at Auschwitz, Mogen David stars in wood were once placed to mark the spot where human ash drifted down upon the ground. But the ash has now returned to the earth and the wooden stars themselves are turning to dust.

The malignity in these places is dissolving. Bones crumble; human ash returns to soil; teeth, sandals, hair, bullets, axes disperse into atoms and molecules. The evidence of evil, like the evidence of good, obeys the universal laws of entropy. Heat cools, matter disintegrates, memories fade.

These photographs document the downward drift of forgetting: how flowers push up through graves, how birds fill the sky over Dresden, a sky that once was thick with bombers; how snow is covering over the mass graves of the Ukraine, and the fields of Anatolia where Armenians were marched to their deaths; and how the sands of the Namibian desert have covered the final traces of the Herero people.

Were we ignorant of what happened in such places, the sunlit snow of eastern Anatolia and the patterned sand of the Namibian desert might seem sublime. But since we know what nature has witnessed, nature loses its innocence. The desolation in these photographs is beautiful, but their beauty is suspect. They play on the basic amorality of the aesthetic. But they are not guilty—so it seems to me—of the charge that they beautify what is obscene. They are documenting vanished crimes and in doing so they put their own beauty into question. A sand dune no longer looks innocent when we know that it covers the traces of a death march.

What these photographs tell us is that even infamy is subject to entropic decay. Even large and terrible crimes are eventually forgotten; even horror turns into dust and sand. This is hard to bear. We do not want to live in a world where crime escapes punishment, where evil escapes being called by its proper name, where infamy is swallowed up by sand and wind. Entropy is a moral scandal. For if everything is forgotten, if all headstones decay, what is the point of grieving?

Evil counts on the certainty that grass will cover the limepits, that the ground will swallow up the bullet-casings, that human voices will eventually fall silent and memory fail. A German history of the destruction of the Herero in 1904 speaks of the 'sublime silence of infinity' stifling the cries of the dying. Demonic cynicism often lays claim to the sublime. For if everything ends in the silence of infinity, why should evil matter?

Entropy makes remembering an obligation. In remembering we make our stand against the indifference of nature. But these pictures make clear what memory is up against and why remembering takes faith. Nature will not help. The best markers are those entered in the human mind and transmitted from generation to generation, though even these are no match for nature. Photographs decay; books disintegrate; stories falsify and beautify and finally betray those they wish to save. For as these pictures show, nothing, not even infamous crime, is immortal.

In the Russian Orthodox memorial service for the dead, the believers sing the *Viechnaya Pamyat*: 'Eternal Memory, Eternal Memory grant him O Lord.' The memory in question here is God's. It is perfect: every hair on our head is counted, and every one of our

Michael Ignatieff

sins too. If we are forgotten by men, we will still be remembered by God. This is the consolation of the faithful. But where is the consolation of the faithless? The only consolation seems to lie in being reconciled to erasure by the winds.

It is not easy to be at peace with what these pictures tell us: that everything slowly vanishes, including our best efforts to remember. All human culture is an attempt to inscribe significance on life and to make human meaning and human connections endure. In our century, the crimes we have committed against each other have been so large, so persistent, so insane that they make us wonder whether this struggle has any point. For we have become a force of entropy ourselves; we have unleashed our own nihilism, our own drive to nothingness.

Genocide is the perfection of this drive towards oblivion. The dead are hurled into mass graves; corpses are piled on top of each other in a defilement which eliminates all singularity, dignity and meaning from dying. The difficulty of mastering genocide lies in the impossibility of restoring to each victim the singular attention which is due all humans in the hour of their deaths. We cannot now rescue each one of the victims from the anonymity of mass graves. Only God's memory could and then only if we could believe.

Belief is difficult because we have good reason to lack belief in ourselves. We were the ones who mechanized death, who created instruments—crematoria, shooting pits, death marches—which violated our own injunction that each human death should be given significance. And so a great work of reparation has been going on throughout the century, an unending, futile, yet essential attempt to undo the harm we have done to ourselves. We erect museums; statues; exhibitions; we collect the pictures of those who have died to restore an identity to their facelessness. These photographs express this universal need to redeem the dead through memory. Each photograph here is like those pebbles placed on the top of gravestones in Jewish cemeteries, the symbol of a link which not even death can destroy. But these photographs also tell us that nature will wash away both pebbles and headstones alike. All we can do is to place them there, over and over, from generation to generation, for as long as we can.   □

Classroom, Nyarabuye Parish School, Rwanda

RWANDA, 1994

An estimated 7,000 Rwandans died each day over three months in 1994 when the long-running hostility between the Hutu and Tutsi peoples turned murderous. Much of the killing was inspired by the Hutu government. On 15 April, the government militia killed 2,600 refugees who had sought shelter in the church and school at Nyarabuye.

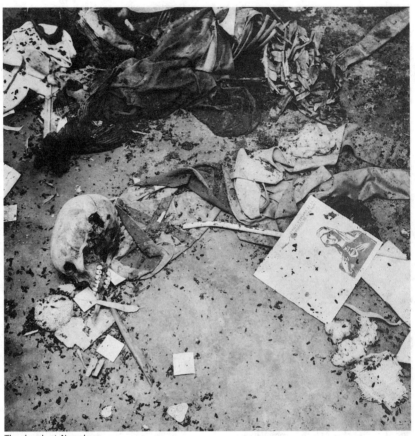

The church at Nyarabuye

Battleground, Kigali

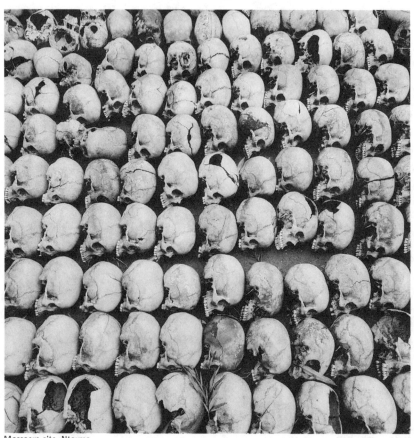
Massacre site, Ntarma

'Reactionaries'

CAMBODIA, 1975-9

After Phnom Penh fell to the Khmer Rouge, led by Pol Pot, more than a
million Cambodians were executed or died of starvation in labour camps. The
portraits above of some of the dead are exhibited at a former interrogation
and torture centre in Phnom Penh.

The torture centre, Phnom Penh

Bed at the torture centre

Map of Cambodia

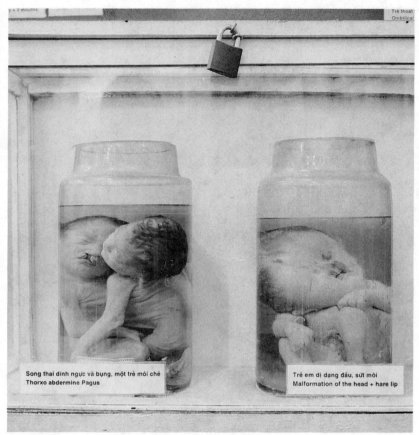

y + 3 mouths

Trẻ thoát
Ombilical

Song thai dính ngực và bụng, một trẻ mối chế
Thorxo abdermine Pagus

Trẻ em dị dạng đầu, sứt môi
Malformation of the head + hare lip

Agent Orange

VIETNAM, 1964-75

About four million Vietnamese were killed during the Vietnam war, many of
them by American bombing. The results of chemical defoliants are preserved
at the Museum of the American War Atrocity in Ho Chi Minh City.

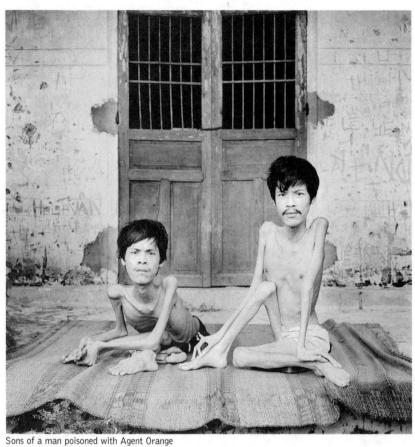
Sons of a man poisoned with Agent Orange

Tourist trinkets, Ho Chi Minh City

Crematoria

AUSCHWITZ-BIRKENAU, 1942-5

The museum at Auschwitz contains the remains of about 1.25 million people, most of them Jews who were liquidated as part of Hitler's 'final solution'. The site forms the largest cemetery in the world.

Part of 7,000 kilograms of women's hair

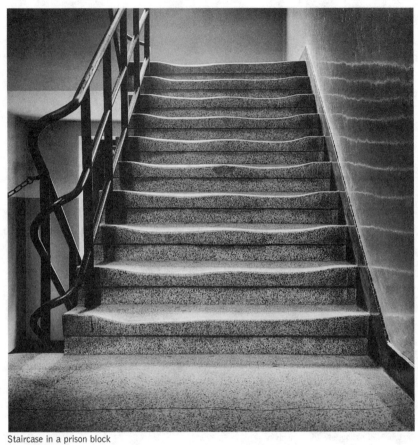
Staircase in a prison block

Memorial

DRESDEN, 1945

On the night of 13 February, around 100,000 Germans were killed in a single indiscriminate Allied bombing raid, many by burning or choking to death in the firestorm. In the bombing of Coventry, in 1940, 582 people died.

Augustus the Strong, Dresden's founder

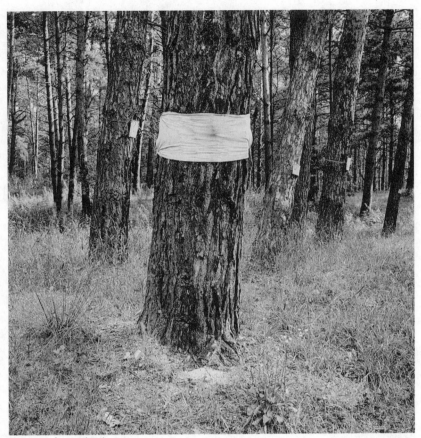

The scene of mass shootings

UKRAINE, 1932-33

The Stalin-inspired famine that starved anything between six and eleven
million Ukrainians became known as *shtuchnyl holod*—the man-made famine.

Haystacks, Ukraine

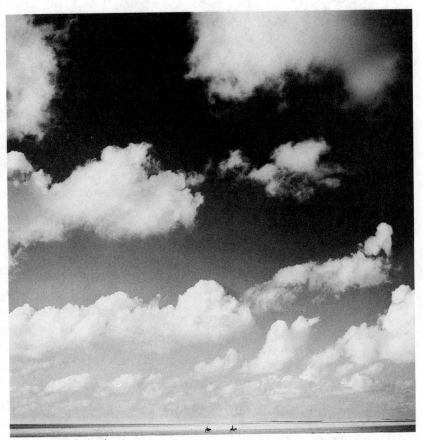

The flight to the Syrian desert

ARMENIA, 1915

During the First World War, the Turkish government deported 1.75 million Armenians to Syria. Up to one million people died on the journey, through starvation and dehydration or in round-ups. When the killings began on 20 April, they were coordinated by telegraph.

Telegraph, the Kachkar Mountains

NAMIBIA, 1904

Germany's colonial army drove the indigenous Herero people of south-west Africa away from their water and into the Omaheke desert. Eighty per cent of the Herero nation died. In his memoirs, General von Trotha wrote: 'It goes without saying that war in Africa cannot be waged according to the Geneva Convention. A nation does not perish so quickly.'

GRANTA

RUST
T. Coraghessan Boyle

LANA WONG/THE SPECIAL PHOTOGRAPHERS LIBRARY

That was the sky up above, hot, with a fried egg of a sun stuck in the middle of it, and this was the ground down here, hard, with a layer of parched grass and a smell of dirt and leaf mould, and no matter how much he shouted there didn't seem to be much else in between. What he could use was a glass of water. He'd been here, what—an hour, maybe?—and the sun hadn't moved. Or not that he could see, anyway. His lips were dry and he could feel all that ultraviolet radiation cooking the skin off his face, a piece of meat on the grill, turkey skin, crisp and oozing, peeling away in strips. But he wasn't hungry—he was never hungry anymore. It was just an image, that was all. He could use a chair, though, and somebody to help him up and put him in it. And some shade. Some iced tea, maybe, beads of moisture sliding down the outside of the glass.

'Eunice!' he called out in a voice that withered in his throat. 'Eunice, goddamnit, Eunice!' And then, because he was old and he was angry and he didn't give a damn anymore, he cried out for help. 'Help!' he croaked. 'Help!'

But nobody was listening. The sky hung there like a tattered curtain, shreds of cloud draped over the high green crown of the pepper tree he'd planted forty years ago, the day his son was born, and he could hear the superamplified rumble of the TV from behind the shut and locked windows and the roar of the air-conditioner, and where was the damn dog anyway? That was it. He remembered now. The dog. He'd come out to look for the dog—she'd been gone too long, too long about her business, and Eunice had turned her parched old lampshade of a head away from the TV screen and said, 'Where's the dog?' He didn't know where the dog was, though he knew where his first bourbon and water of the day was—right there on the TV tray in front of him—and it was eleven a.m. and plenty late enough for it. 'How the hell would I know,' he'd said, 'you were the one let her out,' and she'd come right back at him with something smart, like, 'Well you'd better just get yourself out there in the yard and see, hadn't you?'

He hadn't actually been out in the yard in a long while—years, it seemed—and when he went out the back door and down the steps he found himself gaping at the bushes all in flower, the trumpet vine smothering the back of the house, and he remembered a time when

T. C. Boyle

he cared about all that, about nature and flowers, steer manure and potting soil. Now the yard was as alien to him as the Gobi Desert. He didn't give a damn for flowers or trees or the stucco peeling off the side of the house and all the trim destroyed with the blast of the sun or anything else. 'Booters!' he'd called, angry suddenly, angry at he didn't know what. 'Booters! Here, girl!'

And that was when he fell.

Maybe the lawn dipped out from under him, maybe he stepped in a gopher hole or tripped over a sprinkler head—that must have been it—but the long and short of it was that he was here, on the grass, stretched out like a corpse under the pepper tree, and he couldn't for the life of him seem to get up.

*I've never wanted anybody more in my life, from the minute I came home from Rutgers and laid eyes on you, and I don't care if you are my father's wife, I don't care about anything anymore...*Eunice sipped at her drink—vodka and soda, bland as all get-out, but juice gave her the runs—and nodded in complete surrender as the former underwear model-turned-actress fell into the arms of the clip-jawed actor with the ridge of glistening hair that stood up from his crown like a meat loaf just turned out of the pan. The screen faded for a moment before opening on a cheery ad for rectal suppositories, and she found herself drifting into a reverie about the first time Walt had ever taken her in his arms.

They were young then. Or younger. A whole lot younger. She was forty-three and childless, working the checkout desk at the library while her husband ran a slowly failing quick-printing business, and Walt, five years her junior and with the puffed-up chest and inflated arms of the inveterate bodybuilder, taught phys. ed. at the local high school. She liked to stop in at the Miramar Hotel after work, just to see who was there and unwind a bit after a day of typing out three-by-fives for the card catalogue and collecting fifteen- and twenty-cent fines from born-nasty rich men's wives with beauty parlour hair and too much time on their hands. One day she came in out of the flaming nimbus of the fog and there was Walt, sitting at the bar like some monument to manhood, his tie askew and the sleeves of his white dress shirt rolled up to reveal the squared-off blocks of his forearms. She sat at one of the tables, ordered a drink—it was vodka and grapefruit in those days, tall—and lit a cigarette. When she looked up, he was standing over her. 'Don't you know smoking's bad for your health?'

She took her time, crossed her legs under the table and squirmed her bottom around till she was comfortable. She'd seen Ava Gardner in the movies. And Lauren Bacall too. 'Tell me that,' she said, slow and languid, drawing it out with the smoke, 'when I'm an old lady.'

Well, he laughed and sat down and they got to talking and before long he was meeting her there every afternoon at five while her husband moaned and fretted over last-minute rush jobs and his wife drank herself into oblivion in her own kitchen. And when that moment came—their first embrace—she reached out for his arms as if she were drowning.

But now the screen flickered and *The Furious Hours* gave way to *Riddle Street* and she eased back in her chair, the vodka and soda at her lips like recirculated blood flowing back into her, and watched as the heroine—one of the towering sluts of daytime television—carved up another man.

The funny thing was that nothing hurt, or not particularly or any more than usual, what with the arthritis in both knees and the unreconstructed hernia that felt as if some animal were living under his skin and clawing to get out—no, he hadn't broken anything, he was pretty sure of that. But there was something wrong with him. Desperately wrong. Or why else would he be lying here on his back listening to the grass grow while the clouds became ghosts in winding-sheets and fled away to nothing and the sun burned the skin right off his face?

Maybe he was dying, maybe that was it. The thought didn't alarm him, not especially, not yet, but it was there, a hard little bolus of possibility lodged in his brain. He moved the fingers of his right hand, one by one, just to see if the signals still carried that far, and then he tried the other side, the left, and realized after a long moment that there was nothing there, nothing he could feel anyway. Something whispered in his ear—a single word, *stroke*—and that was when he began to be afraid. He heard a car go by on the street out front of the house, the soughing of the tyres, the clank of the undercarriage, the smooth fuel-injected suck of the engine. 'Help!' he cried. 'Somebody help!'

And then he was looking up into the lace of the pepper tree and remembering a moment on a bus forty-five years ago, some anonymous stop in Kansas or Nebraska, and he on his way to California for the first time and every good thing awaiting him. An old man got on, dazed and scrawny and with a long whittled pole of a neck and a tattered straw hat set way back on his head, and he just stood there in the middle of the aisle as if he didn't know where he was. Walt was twenty-nine, he'd been in the service and college too, and he wasn't acquainted with any old people or any dead people either—not since the war, anyway. He lifted weights two hours every morning, rain or shine, hot or cold, sick or well, and the iron suffused him with its power like some magic potion.

He looked up at the old man and the old man looked right through him. That was when the driver, oblivious, put the bus in gear and the old man collapsed in his shiny worn suit like a puppet with the strings cut. No one seemed to know what to do, the mother with her mewling baby, the teenager with the oversized shoes, the two doughy old hens with the rolled-in-butter smiles fixed on their faces, but Walt came up out of his seat automatically and pulled the old man to his feet, and it was as if the old guy wasn't even there, nothing more than a suit stuffed with wadding—he could have propped up ten old men, a hundred, because he was a product of iron and the iron flowed through his veins and swelled his muscles till there was nothing he couldn't do.

Eunice refreshed her drink twice during *Riddle Street*, and then she sat through the next programme with her eyes closed, not asleep—she couldn't sleep anymore, sleep was a dream, a fantasy, the dimmest recollection out of an untroubled past—but in a state suspended somewhere between consciousness and its opposite. The sound of a voice, a strange voice, speaking right to her, brought her out of it—*It was amazing, just as if she knew me and my whole life and she told me I was going to come into some money soon, and I did and the very next day I met the man of my dreams*—and the first thing she focused on was her husband's empty chair. Now where had he got himself off to? Maybe he'd gone to lie down, maybe that was it. Or maybe he was in the kitchen, his big arms that always seemed to be bleeding pinioning the wings of the newspaper, a pencil in his big blunt fingers, his drink like liquid gold in the light through the window and the crossword all scratched over with his black glistening scrawl. Those were skin cancers on his arms, she knew that, tiny dots of fresh wet blood stippling the places where his muscles used to be, but he wouldn't do anything about it. He didn't care. It was like his hernia. 'I'm going to be dead soon anyway,' he said, and that got her down, it did, that he should talk like that. 'How can you talk like that?' she'd say, and he'd throw it right back at her. 'Why not? What have I got to live for?' And she'd blink at him, trying desperately to focus, because if she couldn't focus she couldn't give him a look, all pouty and frowning, like Marlene Dietrich in *Destry Rides Again*. 'For me, baby,' she'd say. 'For me.'

The idea of the kitchen sent her there, a little shaky on her feet after sitting so long, and her ankles weren't helping, not at all—it felt as if somebody'd sneaked in and wrapped truck tyres around them while she was watching her programmes. The kitchen was glowing, the back windows glazed with sun, and all the clutter of their last few half-eaten meals invested with a purity and beauty that took her breath away and made her feel like crying, the caramel of the maple syrup bottle and the blue of the Windex and red of the ketchup as vibrant and natural there as flowers in a field. It was a pretty kitchen, the prettiest kitchen in the world. Or it had been once. They'd remodelled in '66—or was it '69? Double aluminium sink, self-cleaning oven, cabinets in solid oak and no cheap lamination, thank you very much. She'd loved that kitchen. It was a kitchen that made her feel loved in return, a place she could retreat to after all the personal nastiness and gossip at the library and wait for her man to come home from coaching football or basketball or whatever it was, depending on the season.

The thought came to her then—or not a thought, actually, but a feeling because feelings were what moved her now, not thoughts— that she ought to maybe fix a can of tomato soup for lunch, and wouldn't it be nice, for a change, to fix some for Walt too? Though she knew what his reaction would be. 'I can't eat that,' he'd say, 'not with my stomach. What do you think, I'm still thirty-eight?'

Well, yes, she did, as a matter of fact. And when he was thirty-eight and he took her away from Stan Sadowsky and blackened both of his eyes for him when he tried to get rough about it, he'd eat anything she put down on the table in front of him, shrimp cocktail in horseradish sauce right out of the jar, pickled cherry peppers, her special Tex-Mex tamales with melted cheese and Tabasco. He loved her then too. Loved her like she'd never been loved before. His fingers—his fingers were magic, the fingers of a masseur, a man who knew what a deep rub was, who knew muscle and ligament and the finer points of erectile tissue and who could manipulate her till she was limp as a rag doll and tingling all over.

Sure, sure he could. But where in the Lord's name was he?

The sun had moved. No doubt about it. He'd been asleep, unconscious, delirious, dehydrated, sun-poisoned—pick an adjective—and now he was awake again and staring up at that yellow blot in the sky that went to deep blue and then black if you stared at it too long. He needed water. He needed bourbon. Aspirin. Ibuprofen. Two of those little white codeine tablets the doctor gave him for the pain in his knees. More than anything, though, he needed to get up off this damn lawn before the grass grew through the back of his head. Furious suddenly, raging, he gave it everything he had and managed to lift his right shoulder and the dead weight of his head from the ground—and hold it there, hold it there for a full five seconds, as if he were bench-pressing his own body—before he sank back down again. It wasn't going to work, he could see that now, nothing was going to work, ever again, and he felt himself filling up with despair, a slow dark trickle of it leaking into the black pool that was already inside him.

With the despair came Jimmy. That was the way it always was. When he felt blue, when he felt that life was a disease and not worth the effort of drawing the next contaminated breath, Jimmy was there. Seven years, six months and fourteen days old, sticks for legs, his head too big for his body and his hair like something you'd scour pans with. Jimmy. His son. The boy who grew up teething on a catcher's mitt and was already the fastest kid in the second grade. Walt had been at school the day he was killed, spotting for the gymnastics club as they went through their paces on the parallel bars. Somebody said there was smoke up the street—the paint store was on fire, the whole block going up, maybe even the bank—and the vaulted cathedral of the gym went silent. Then they smelled the smoke, musty and sharp at the same time, and then they heard the sirens. By the time Walt got out to the street, his gymnasts leading the way in a blur of flying heels, the fire engine was skewed across the sidewalk in the oddest way, three blocks at least from the fire, and he remembered thinking they must have been drunk or blind, one or the other. When he got there, to where the fire company was, smoke crowding the sky in the distance and the taste of it, acid and bitter, on his tongue, he asked the first person he saw—Ed Bakey, the assistant principal—what was the matter. 'One of the kids,' Ed said, and he was shaking so badly he could hardly get the words out, 'one of the kids got hit by the truck.'

He drifted off again, mercifully, and when he came to this time the sun was playing peek-a-boo with the crown of the pepper tree, and the field of shade, healing redemptive shade, spread almost to his feet. What time was it, anyway? Three, at least. Maybe four. And where the hell was Eunice? Inside, that's where she was, where time was meaningless, a series of half-hour slices carved out of the programme guide, day melding into night, breakfast into dinner, the bright electrons dancing eternally across the screen. He dug his elbows into the lawn then, both of them, and yes, he could feel his left side all of a sudden and that was something, and he flexed every muscle in his body, pecs, delts, biceps, the long striated cords of his back and the lump of nothing that was his left leg, but he couldn't sit up, couldn't so much as put an inch between him and the flattened grass. That frustrated him. Made him angry. And he cried out again, the driest faintest bleat of rage and bewilderment from the desert throat of a man who'd never asked anybody for anything.

She called him for lunch, went to the foot of the stairs and called out his name twice, but it was next to impossible to wake him once he went off, soundest sleeper in the world—you'd need a marching band just to get him to blink his eyes—so she heated the tomato soup, cleared a place at the table and ate by herself. The soup was good, really hit the spot, but they put too much salt in it, they all did, didn't matter which brand you bought. It made her thirsty, all that salt, and she got up to make herself a fresh vodka and soda— there was no sense in traipsing round the house looking for the other glass, which, as she knew from experience, could be anywhere. She couldn't count the hours she'd spent shuffling through the bathroom, kitchen and living room on her feet that felt as if they'd been crimped in a vice, looking for one melted-down watery drink or another. So she took a fresh glass, and she poured, and she drank. Walt was up in the bedroom, that's where he was, napping, and no other possibility crossed her mind, because there was none.

There was the usual ebb and flow of afternoon programming, the stupid fat people lined up on a stage bickering about their stupid fat lives and too stupid to know the whole country was laughing at them, the game shows and teenage dance shows and the Mexican shows stocked with people as fat and stupid as the Americans only bickering in Spanish instead of English. Then it was evening. Then it was dusk. She was watching a Mickey Rooney/Judy Garland picture on the classic movie channel when a dog began barking on the screen and she was fooled, just for a second, into thinking it was Booters. That was when she noticed that Booters was gone. And Walt: whatever could he be doing all this time?

She went up the stairs, though each step seemed to rise up insidiously to snatch at her just as she lifted her foot, and saw that the bedroom was empty and that neither dog nor man was in the upstairs bathroom enjoying the monotonous drip-drip-drip of the faucet that never seemed to want to shut itself off. Twice more she went round the house, utterly bewildered, and she even looked in the pantry and the broom closet and the cabinet under the sink. It was nearly dark, the ice cubes of her latest vodka and soda tinkling like chimes in her hand, when she thought to look out back.

'Walt?' she called, thrusting her head out the door. 'Booters?'

The frail bleating echo of her own voice came back to her, and then, slipping in underneath it, the faintest whisper of a sound, no louder than the hum of a mosquito's wings or the muffled cry of a bird strangled in the dark. 'Help!' she heard, or thought she heard, a sound so weak and constrained it barely registered.

'Walt?' she tried again.

And then: 'Eunice, goddamnit, over here!'

She was so startled she dropped her drink, the glass exploding on the flagstones at her feet and anointing her ankles with vodka. The light was fading, and she didn't see very well anymore, not without her glasses, anyway, and she was puzzled, truly puzzled, to hear her husband's voice coming out of nowhere. 'Walt?' she murmured, moving across the darkened lawn as through a minefield, and when she tripped, and fell, it wasn't over a sprinkler head or gopher's mound or a sudden rise in the lawn, it was over the long attenuated shadow of her husband's still and recumbent form.

Eunice cried out when she went down, a sharp rising exhalation of surprise, followed by an acquiescent grunt and the almost inevitable elision of some essential bone or joint giving way. He'd heard that sound before, too many times to count, on the football field, the baseball diamond, the basketball court, and he knew right away it was trouble. Or more trouble, if that was possible. 'Eunice,' he croaked, and his face was cooked right down to the bone, 'are you hurt?'

She was right there, right there beside him, one of her legs thrust awkwardly over his, her face all but planted in the turf. She was trying to move, to turn over, to right herself—all that he could feel, though he couldn't for the life of him swivel his head to see—but she wasn't having much success. When finally, after a protracted effort, she managed to drag her living leg across his dead one, she took what seemed like an hour to gulp at the air before her lips, tongue and mouth could form a response. 'Walt,' she gasped, or moaned actually, that's what it was, moaning, 'my...I think...oh, oh it hurts...'

He heard a car race up the street, the swift progress of life, places to go, people to meet. Somewhere a voice called out and a door slammed.

'My hip, I think it's my hip—'

It was all he could do to keep from cursing, but he didn't have the strength to curse and there was no use in it, not now. He gritted his teeth. 'Listen, I can't move,' he said. 'And I've been laying here all day waiting for somebody to notice, but do you think anybody'd even poke their damn head out the door to see if their husband was dead yet and fried up in the sun like a damn pork rind?'

She didn't answer. The shadows thickened round them. The lawn went from grey to black, the colour drained out of the treetops and the sky grew bigger by the minute, as if invisible forces were inflating it with the stuff of the universe. He was looking up at the emerging stars—he had no choice, short of closing his eyes. It had been a long time since he'd looked at the stars, indifferent to any space that didn't have a roof over it, and he was strangely moved to see that they were all still there. Or most of them, anyway, but who was counting? He could hear Eunice sobbing in the dark just to the left of him, and for a long while she didn't say anything, just sniffed and snuffled, gagging on every third or fourth breath. Finally her voice came at him out of the void: 'You always blame me for everything.'

Well, there was truth in that, he supposed, but no sense in getting into it now. 'I don't know what's wrong with me, Eunice,' he said, trying to keep his voice level though his heart was hammering and he foresaw every disaster. 'I can't get up. I can't even move. Do you understand what I'm saying?'

There was no response. A mosquito lighted on his lower eyelid, soft as a snowflake, and he didn't have the power to brush it away. 'Listen,' he said, speaking to the sky and all the spilled paint of the stars, 'how bad are you? Can you—you think you can crawl?'

'It hurts,' she gasped, 'Walt, it hurts,' and then she was sobbing again, a broken dry nagging rasp that cut into him like the teeth of a saw.

He softened his voice. 'It's OK, Eunice. Everything's going to be OK, you'll see.'

It was then, just as the words passed his lips, that the familiar music of Booters' jingling tags rang out ecstatically from the far corner of the yard, followed by a joyful woof and the delirious patter of approaching paws. 'Booters!' they cried out simultaneously, 'good girl, Booters. Come here, come here, girl!'

Eunice was expecting a miracle, nothing less—she was an optimist, always was, always would be—and the minute she heard the dog she thought of all the times Lassie had come to the rescue, Rin Tin Tin, Old Yeller, Buck, Toto and she didn't know who else. She was lying face down on the lawn and her cheek had begun to itch where it was pressed into the grass and the grass made its snaking intaglio in the flesh, but she didn't dare move because of the pain in her hip and lower back that made her feel as if she were being torn in two. She was scared, of course she was, for herself and for Walt, but when Booters stood over her and began to lick the side of her face she felt a surge of hope. 'That's a girl,' she said. 'Now speak, Booters, speak!'

Booters didn't speak. She settled her too-big paws down in the grass beside Eunice's head and whined in a soft puppyish way. She wasn't much more than a puppy, after all, a big lumpish stupid dog of indeterminate breed that couldn't seem to resist soiling the carpet in the hallway no matter how many times she was punished for it. The last dog they'd had, Booters the First, the original Booters, now that was a dog. She was a Border collie, her eyes bright with alertness and suspicion, and so smart you could have taught her the multiplication tables if you had a mind to. It was a sad day when they had to have her put down, fifteen years old and so stiff it was like she was walking on stilts, and Walt felt it as much as she did herself, but all he said was, 'You measure your life in dogs, and if you're lucky you'll get five or six of them,' and then he threw the dirt in the hole.

For the next hour, while the mosquitoes had a field day with her face and the back of her neck and her unprotected legs, Eunice kept trying. 'Speak, girl!' she said. 'Go get help. Get help! Speak!' At first, Walt did his part too, growling out one command after another, but all Booters did was whine through her slushy jowls and shift position to be near whichever one of them was exhorting her the most passionately. And when the automatic sprinklers came on with a hiss of air and the first sputtering release of subterranean pressure, the dog sprang up and trotted over to the porch, smart enough at least to come in out of the rain.

He was dozing when the sprinklers came on. He'd long since given up on the dog—what did Eunice expect her to do, flag down an ambulance?—and he was dreaming about nothing more complicated than his bed, his bed and a glass of water, half a glass, anything to soothe his throat, when the deluge began. It was a mixed blessing. He'd never been so thirsty in his life, baked and bleached under the sun till he felt mummified, and he opened his mouth reflexively. Unfortunately, none of the sprinklers had been adjusted to pinpoint the gaping maw of a supine old man stretched out in the middle of the lawn, and while the odd drop did manage to strike his lips and even his tongue, it did nothing to relieve his thirst and he was soon soaked through to the skin and shivering. And yet still the water kept coming like some sort of oriental water torture until finally the pipes heaved a sigh and the flow cut off as abruptly as it had begun.

He felt bad for Eunice, felt powerless and weak, felt dead, but he fought down the despair and tried to sit up again. Or his brain tried. The rest of him, aside from the sting of his sun-scorched face and the persistent ache of his knees and the shivers that shook him like a rag, seemed to belong to somebody else, some stranger he couldn't communicate with. After awhile, he gave it up and called out softly to his wife. There was no response. Then he was asleep and the night came down to lie on him with all its crushing weight.

Toward morning he woke and saw that Eunice had managed to crawl a few feet away—if he rolled his eyes all the way to the left he could just make her out, a huddled lump in the shining grass. He held his breath, fearing the worst, but then he heard her breathing— or snoring, actually—a soft glottal in-suck of air followed by an even softer puff of exhalation. The birds started in then, recommencing their daily argument, and he saw that the sky had begun to grow light, a phenomenon he hadn't witnessed in ages, not since he was in college and stayed up through the night bullshitting about women and metaphysics and gulping beer from the can.

He could shake it off then. Push himself up out of the damp grass, plough through ten flapjacks and half a dozen sausage links and then go straight to class and after that to the gym to work out. He built himself up then, every day, with every repetition and every set, and there was the proof of it staring back at him in the weight-room mirror. But there was no building now, no collecting jazz albums and European novels, no worrying about brushing between meals or compound interest or life insurance or anything else. Now there was only this, the waiting, and whether you waited out here on the lawn like breakfast for the crows or in there on the recliner, it was all the same. Nothing mattered anymore but this. This was what it all came down to—the grass, the sky, the trumpet vine and the pepper tree, the wife with her bones shot full of air and her hip out of joint, the dog on the porch, the sun, the stars.

Stan Sadowsky had tried to block the door on him the day he came to take Eunice away, but he held his ground because he'd made up his mind and when he made up his mind he was immovable. 'She doesn't want to be with you anymore, Stan,' he said. 'She's not going to be with you.'

'Yeah?' Stan's neck was corded with rage and his eyes leaped right out of his head. Walt didn't hate him. He didn't feel anything for him, one way or the other. But there behind him, in the soft light of the hall, was Eunice, her eyes scared and her jaw set, wearing a print dress that showed off everything she had. 'Yeah?' Stan repeated, barking it like a dog. 'And what the fuck do you know about it?'

'I know this,' Walt said, and he hit him so hard he went right through the screen door and sprawled out flat on his back in the hallway. And when he got up, Walt hit him again.

But now, now there was the sun to contend with, already burning through the trees. He smelled the rich wet chlorophyll of the grass and the morning air off the sea, immemorial smells, ancient as his life, and when he heard the soft annunciatory thump of the paper in the front drive he called out suddenly but his voice was so weak he could scarcely hear it himself. Eunice was silent. Still and silent. And that worried him, because he couldn't hear her snoring anymore, and when he found his voice again he whispered, 'Eunice, honey, give me your hand. Can you give me your hand?'

He could have sworn he saw her lift her shoulder and swivel toward him, her face alive and glowing with the early light, but he must have been fooling himself. Because when he summoned everything he had left in him and somehow managed to reach out his hand, there was nothing there. □

"A sardonic divertissement that concerns itself with fundamental problems of man's existence—a tale that is sad-eyed, witty, and often very funny."

—Charles J. Rolo, *New York Times Book Review*

A Dog's Head

JEAN DUTOURD

Translated by **Robin Chancellor**
With a new foreword by **Wendy Doniger**

Paper $12.00 / £9.50

"A Dog's Head is an excellent joke in the worst possible taste, and its author, M. Jean Dutourd, is a satirist of the first rank."—Anthony West, *New Yorker*

"A Dog's Head is a book of unusual craftsmanship and sensibility. Its theme is based on the fundamental problems of every man's life, and the sparks of its wit are struck by the impact of fantasy and realism."
—*Times Literary Supplement*

"A tiny masterpiece in the French classical tradition."—P. L. Travers, *New York Herald Tribune*

Available at your bookseller.

THE UNIVERSITY OF CHICAGO PRESS

Visit us at *www.press.uchicago.edu* to read an excerpt from *A Dog's Head*

9999
John Barth

The word *odometer* dates from 1791, but mileage indicators didn't appear as standard equipment on automobile instrument panels until after the First World War. George Parker's memory, therefore, of his parents bidding him and his older sister, in the rear seat of the family sedan—the big black Buick, it must have been, the family's first post-war conveyance, and most likely during one of their ritual Sunday-afternoon drives down-county—to 'Watch, now: she's all nines and 'bout to come up zeros,' can be dated no earlier than 1919, George's eighth year and sister Janice's eighteenth, nor later than 1922, the year newly-wed Jan moved with her husband from Maryland's Eastern Shore to upstate New York. And Jan is very much a feature of this memory; more of a mother to him through that melancholy period than his disconsolate mother was (still grieving for her war-lost first-born), it could even have been she who called her kid brother's attention to that gauge on the verge of registering its first thousand or ten thousand miles. In any case, in his eighty-fifth year George well recalls a long-ago subtropical Delmarva afternoon (automotive air-conditioning was yet another world war away), his Sunday pants sticky on the grey plush seat, the endless marshes rolling by, and that row of nines turning up not quite simultaneously from right to left to what his father called 'goose eggs'.

For our George—who just two hours ago (at a few minutes past nine p.m. on Sunday 7 September 1997, to be more if not quite most exact) was prepared to end his life, but has not done so, yet—each of those limit-years has its private significance. Certain sentimental reasons, to be given eventually, incline him to prefer 1919, in particular the third Friday of that year's ninth month: tidewater Maryland could well have been still sweltering then, and the new Buick might feasibly have been turning up its first thousand. But 1922 (though not its summer) was likewise a milestone year, so to speak, in what passes for this fellow's life story.

A consideration now occurs to him: Wouldn't the digits 9999, for reasons also presently to be explained, have 'freaked out' his mother altogether, as Americans say nowadays? Perhaps she had already taken to the bed whereof she became ever more a fixture, tended first by Janice and their tight-visaged father, subsequently (after Jan's escape to Syracuse) by a succession of 'coloured' maids,

ALEX MACLEAN/PHOTONICA

as Americans said back then. In which case it would have been Jan herself in that front passenger seat, 'playing Mom' (it was no game), and not impossibly young George who, bored with counting muskrat-houses to pass the sweatsy time, leaned over the front seatback, noticed the uprolling odometer, and said 'Hey, look,' etc. It doesn't much matter, to this story or generally; George just likes to get things straight. 1919 was the second and final year of the great influenza pandemic, which killed perhaps twenty-five million people worldwide (more than the Great War), including some half-million Americans—among them young Hubert Parker, who was serving in France with the American Expeditionary Force and was felled in '18 not by the Hun but by the deadly myxovirus. Baseball players in that season's World Series wore cotton mouth-and-nose masks, as did many of their spectators; 'open-faced sneezing' in public was in some venues declared a crime, as were handshakes in others. George's odometer memory includes no face masks, but then neither does his recollection of the family's home life generally in that glum period.

In a misanthropic mood, Leonardo da Vinci called the mass of humankind 'mere fillers-up of privies'. True enough of this story's mostly passive protagonist, George supposes; likewise even of his (late, still inordinately beloved, *indispensable*) spouse, their four parents and eight grandparents and sixteen great-grandparents et cetera ad infinitum, as far as George knows; likewise of their middle-aged son (his wife felled by a heart attack before his mother succumbed to a like misfortune) and their sole, much-doted-upon grandchild. Prevailingly, at least, they have all as far as George knows led responsible, morally decent if perhaps less than exemplary lives: no known spouse- or child-abusers among them; no notable greedheads, programmatic liars, cheaters, stealers, or exploiters of their fellow citizens. One drunk bachelor uncle on George's mother's side, but he injured none except himself. George and Pamela Parker, we can assert with fair confidence, in their lifetimes have done (*did*...!) no or little intentional harm to anybody, and some real if not unusual good. Pam by her own assessment was a reliable though unremarkable junior-high mathematics teacher, George by his a competent though seldom more than competent public-school administrator, the pair of them at best B-plus at worst B-minus parents and citizens, perpetuating the cycle of harmless fillers-up of privies, all soon enough forgotten after their demise. If anything at all has distinguished this pair from most of their fellow filler-uppers...

There on his night stand is Cabernet Sauvignon to dull his senses for the deed. There are the sleeping pills, of more than sufficient quantity and milligrammage; the completed note of explanation To Whom It May Concern (principally his retirement-community neighbours and his granddaughter) and the sealed letter to his Personal Representative (George Parker, Jr.). There is the plastic bag recommended by the Hemlock Society to ensure quietus, but which our man fears might prompt an involuntary suffocative panic and blow the procedure; he may well opt not to deploy it when the hour arrives.

And what, pray, might be that Estimated Time of Departure?

If anything, we were saying, has distinguished this now-halved pair of Parkers from the general run of harmless, decent folk, it is (*was...!*) their reciprocally abiding love—which psychologists maintain ought most healthily to extend outward from self and family to friends, community and humankind, but which in George and Pam's case remained for better or worse largely intramural—and a shared fascination with certain *numbers*, especially of the calendric variety: certain patterns of date notation. If one could tell their story in terms of such patterns—and one could, one can, one will—that is because, as shall be seen, after a series of more or less remarkable coincidences had called the thing to their attention, they saw fit to begin to arrange certain of their life events to suit it, telling themselves that to do so was no more than their little joke, a romantic game, an innocent tidiness, a kickable habit.

But let's let those dates tell their story. The late Hubert Parker, George's flu-felled eldest sib, happened to be born on the ninth day of September, 1899: in American month/day/year notation, 9/9/99; in the more logical 'European' day/month/year notation, also 9/9/99, or 9.9.99 (we now understand the possibly painful association of that on-the-verge odometer reading back in the family sedan). Very well, you say: No doubt sundry notables and who knows how many mere privy-fillers shared that close-of-the-century birth-date, as will a much larger number its presently upcoming centenary. But did they have a next-born sib who first saw light on New Year's Day, 1901 (1/1/01 American, ditto European, and a tidy alternating-binary 01/01/01 by either), birthday of the aforementioned Janice Parker? The coincidence was a neighbourhoodwide How-'bout-that and a bond between brother and sister, even before its remarkable compounding by George Parker's birth in 1911 on what, beginning with his seventh birthday, would mournfully be dubbed Armistice Day and later, on his forty-third, be grimly, open-endedly renamed Veterans' Day.

By either system, 11/11/11: the century's only six-figure 'isodigital', as a matter of fact. (It will be Pam, the seventh-grade-math-teacher-to-be, who early on in their connection offers George that Greeky adjective, together with the datum that his birthday's 'precurrence' in the twelfth century—11/11/1111—was the only *eight*-figure Isodigital in their millennium. Work it out, reader, if such things fascinate you as they did them; you may note as well that no date in either the preceding or the succeeding millennium of the Christian era will exceed seven isodigits.) Not surprisingly, even without those parenthetical enhancements George's birth-date was the occasion of considerable family and neighbourhood comment. He recalls his parents joking, before Hubie's death ended most levity in their household, that they had planned it that way, and that they were expecting young Hube to supply their first grandchild on either Groundhog Day (2/2) or George Washington's birthday (2/22) in 1922.

When those dates arrived, Hubert Parker was dead; sister Jan (nicknamed for her birth-month) was a registered nurse whose chief patient was her mother and whose impending marriage would soon leave the family 'on its own'; and young George was a somewhat introverted fifth-grader in East Dorset Elementary, his fascination with such calendrics understandably established. It was on one or the other of those two February holidays that he reported to Miss Stoker's class the remarkable coincidence of his and his siblings' birth-date patterns, called their attention to the phenomenon of 'all-the-same-digit' dates, projected for them the eleven-year cycle of such dates within any century (2/2/22, 3/3/33, etc.), and pointed out to them what the reader has already been told: that the constraints of a twelve-month year with roughly thirty-day months make 11/11/11 the only six-figure 'same-digiter' in any century. Miss Stoker was impressed. Nine months later, on that year's Armistice Day, when like every elementary-school teacher in America his (then sixth-grade) teacher, Miss Scheffenacher, observed to the class that the Great War had ended on the *eleventh hour* of the eleventh day of the eleventh month just four years past, they sang a mournful-merry Happy (eleventh) Birthday to our protagonist. After everyone had stood with heads bowed as the town's fire sirens sounded that eleventh hour, the boy responded with the observation that even those few of his classmates who hadn't turned eleven yet were nevertheless in their eleventh year; additionally, that while the date of his war-lost brother's death in France had not been a Same-Digiter, it had been the next best thing (for which George hadn't yet found a name): 8/18/18—when, moreover, luckless Hubie had been eighteen years old.

His comrades regarded him as more or less special, whether charmed or spooked. Miss Scheffenacher (having provided the term 'alternating-digiter', which George shortened to Alternator) opined that he would go to college and become somebody some day, and then set the class to listing all the Samers and Alternators in the century, using the American style of date notation. Not even she had previously remarked the curious patterns that emerged from their blackboard tabulations: that among the Samers, for example, there were none in the century's first decade, four in its second (all in 1911, culminating in George's birthday), two in its third (the aforenoted February holidays of their present year), and only one in each of the decades following. She thought George should definitely go on to college, and would have declared as much to his parents had the mother not been an invalid and the father a non-attender of parent-teacher meetings and most other things.

Except for the Miss Stokers and the Miss Scheffenachers, however, who 'went off' to the nearby State Normal School to become teachers, not many young people in small-town tidewater Maryland in those days were inclined or able to pursue their formal education past the county school system; most were proud to have achieved their high-school diplomas instead of dropping out at age sixteen, by choice or otherwise, to begin their full-time working lives. But with his family's blessing George did, in fact, complete his first year in that little teachers' college and begin his second before the combined setbacks of his mother's death and the Great Depression obliged him to leave school—on 1/31/31, he noted grimly—and work as bookkeeper and assistant manager of his father's foundering car-sales business.

There he might have remained and our story be stymied had not his ever-more-dispirited father committed suicide on the first or second day of May 1933. Shot himself in the starboard temple with a small-bore pistol, he did, late in the evening of 5/1; lingered unconscious in the county hospital for some hours; expired before the dawn of 5/2, his son at his bedside, his harried daughter en route by train and bus from Syracuse. Although the date was numerically insignificant (so George thought), he happened two months earlier to have sighed, in his bookkeeper's office, at the approach, arrival and passage of 3/3/33, the first Samer since Miss Scheffenacher's fifth-grade February. The fellow had attained age twenty-one, still single and living in his parents' house, now his. The tidy arithmetic of double-entry bookkeeping he found agreeable, but he had neither taste nor knack for selling motor vehicles, which few of his townsfolk could afford anyhow in those hard times. On a determined impulse he sold the automotive franchise that summer, rented out the house, and with the meagre proceeds re-enrolled to complete his interrupted degree in secondary education.

Three years after his receipt thereof, our calendric love-chronicle proper begins. Twenty-six-year-old George, having mustered additional accreditation, is teaching math and 'science' to the children of farmers and down-county watermen in a small high school near his Alma Mater; he looks forward already to 'moving up' from the classroom (which has less appeal for him than does the subject matter) to school administration, for which he feels some vocation. He has dated two or three women from among the limited local supply, but no serious romance has ensued. Is he too choosy, he has begun to wonder? Are they? Is he destined never to know the experience of love? In early March 1938, he surprises his somewhat diffident self by inviting his principal's new young part-time secretary, barely out of high school herself and working her way through the teachers' college, to accompany him to a ham-and-oyster supper at the local Methodist church, the social hub of the community. Despite the eight-year difference in their ages and some good-humoured 'razzing' by the townsfolk, the pair quite enjoy themselves; indeed, George feels more lively and at ease with pert young Pamela Neall than he has ever before felt with a female companion. On her parents' screened front porch later that evening, he finds himself telling her of his calendrical claim to fame: his and his siblings' birth-dates, his brother's death-date, the Alternator 1/31/31 that marked his leaving college, and the Samer 3/3/33 that prompted his return. Miss Neall's interest is more than merely polite. Her ready smile widens in the lamplight as he runs through the series. All but bouncing with excitement beside him on the porch glider, she challenges him to guess her own birth-date, and when he cannot, offers him the clue (she's a quick one, this hard-working aspirant to math-teacherhood) that just as he was born on the century's only six-digit Samer, she was born on its only *seven*-digit Alternator.

George feels...well, beside himself with exhilaration. 'Nine Nineteen Nineteen-Nineteen!'

Moved by the same delight, they kiss.

Did the course of true love ever run smooth? Now and then, no doubt, but not inevitably. The couple were entirely pleased with their 'first date' (George's joke, which won him another kiss; but it was Pamela who remarked before he did that the date of that date was another Alternator, 3/8/38) and no less so with their second and third. Pam's mother and father opposed any sequel, however, on grounds of their daughter's youth and the age differential. Common enough in that time and place for girls of eighteen to marry, but they had hoped she would finish college first. A firm-willed but unrebellious only child who quite returned her parents' love, Pam insisted that the four of them reason it out together, listening with respectful courtesy to all sides' arguments. Hers and George's (they're a team already): that their connection was not yet Serious and would not necessarily become so, just a mutual pleasure in each other's company and some shared interests; that should it after all develop into something more (they exchanged a smile), she was determined not to be diverted from the completion of her degree and at least a few years' experience of teaching—a determination that George applauded and seconded. Her parents': that they had no objections to George as a person, only as a premature potential suitor of a girl who one short year ago could have been his high-school student; that however their daughter might vow now her determination to finish her education (for which she was largely dependent on their support), love 'and its consequences' could very well override that resolve, to her later regret. Better to avoid that risk, all things considered—and no hard feelings, George. In the end the four agreed on a compromise: a one-year moratorium on further 'dates' while Pam completed her freshman year at the normal school, spent the summer camp-counselling up in Pennsylvania as planned, and returned for her sophomore year. During that period the pair would not refrain from dating others, and if next spring—at ages nineteen and twenty-seven, respectively—she and George inclined to 'see' each other further, her parents would withdraw their objections to such dates.

Each repetition of that word evoked the young couple's smiles, as did such now-voltaged numbers as *nineteen*; without knowing it, Pam's well-meaning parents had undermined their own case and increased the pair's interest in each other. When the girl agreed to have no further dates with Mister Parker before the date 3/9/39, George understood that the campaign which he had not till then particularly set out to wage was already half won. As good as their word, for the promised year they refrained from dating each other, though not from exchanging further calendrics and other matters of mutual interest in their frequent letters and telephone conversations; and they dutifully if perfunctorily dated others—Pamela especially—with more or less pleasure but no diminution of either's feelings for her/his predestined soulmate.

Quite the contrary, for so they came ever more to regard each other with each passing month. Had George noticed, Pam asked him in one letter from Camp Po-Ko-No, that if his sister Jan had managed to be born on the first of October instead of the first of January, then her birth-date (10/1/01) would be the only 'patterned' date, whether Samer or Alternator, in the century's first decade? And would he please *please* believe her that although the senior counsellor with whom she had dutifully 'gone out' once or twice had proposed the fancy word *isodigitals* to describe what they called Samers, she had found the fellow otherwise a bore? He would indeed, George promised, if she would ask him the Greek word for Alternators and not date him a third time, as *he* was not re-dating his history colleague Arlene Makowski. Meanwhile, had Pam noticed that the date of her latest letter, 8/3/38, was a Palindrome, a numerical analogue to 'Madam, I'm Adam'? And that her remarkable birth-date, 9/19/1919, could be regarded as a Palindromic Alternator, as for that matter could sister Jan's? And that he loved her and missed her and was counting the days till 3/9/39?

One weekend shortly thereafter he drove all the way up into the Pennsylvania mountains in order to see and talk with her for just one surreptitious lunch hour, the most they felt they could allow themselves without their meetings becoming a 'date'. They strolled through the little village near Pam's camp, holding hands excitedly, stopping to kiss beside a shaded stream that ran through the tiny town park with its monuments to the Union dead and the casualties of the Great War.

'*Sequentials*,' he offered, 'like Straights in a poker hand. The first in this century was One Two Thirty-Four, and there won't be another till One Twenty-Three Forty-Five.'

She hugged him, pressed her face into his shirt-front, and reckoned blissfully. 'But then the next one comes later that same year: December Third!'

He touched her breast; she did not move his hand away.

'We give up,' her good-natured parents declared that fall. Their daughter was back at the normal school, their future son-in-law back in his high-school classroom, and the pair were still not actually 'dating', but telephoning each other daily and seeing each other casually as often as manageable on the weekends. 'You're obviously meant for each other.'

But it pleased the couple, perversely, to let their reciprocal desire ripen through that winter without further intimacies until the agreed-upon date, meanwhile reinforcing their bond with the exchange of Reverse Sequentials (3/2/10, 4/3/21, etc.) and the touching observation—Pamela's, when George happened to recount to her in more detail the story of his father's suicide—that the date of that sad event was not as 'meaningless' as he had supposed, for while it might be tempting to regard 3/3/33 (George's 'career change' day) as marking the end of the century's first third, the actual 'thirty-three per cent date' of 1933—i.e. its 122nd day—would be 2 May, when Mr Parker died. Indeed, since 365 divided by three gives not 122 but 121.666...n, it was eerily appropriate that the poor man shot himself on the evening of 1 May and died the following morning.

Much moved, 'The fraction is so *blunt*,' George almost whispered: 'One-third, and that's that. But *Point three three* et cetera goes on for ever.'

'Like our love,' Pam declared or vowed, thinking *infinite isodigitality*—and herself this time placed his hand, her own atop it, where it longed to go.

On the appointed date, 9 March '39, they declared their affiancement. In deference to Pam's parents' wishes, however, they postponed their marriage nearly a full two years: not quite to her baccalaureate in May 1941, but to the first day of the month prior, trading off their friends' April Fools' Day teasing for the satisfaction of the American-style Alternator plus European-style Palindrome. Moreover, just as George felt his 'true' eleventh and twenty-second birthdays to have been not the November Elevenths of those years but 2/22/22 and 3/3/33 respectively, so the newly-wed Mr and Mrs Parker resolved to celebrate their wedding anniversaries not on the actual dates thereof but on the nearest Alternator thereafter: 4/2/42, 4/3/43, etc.

And so they did, though not always together, for by the arrival of that first 'true' anniversary the nation was at war. Not to be conscripted as cannon fodder, thirty-year-old George enlisted in the Navy and after basic training found himself assigned to a series of logistical posts, first as a data organizer, later as an instructor, finally as an administrator. Pam's profession and the couple's decision to put off starting a family 'for the duration' made her fairly portable; although they missed their first True Anniversary (George couldn't get leave from his Bainbridge boot camp) and their fourth (story to come), they celebrated 4/3/43 at his base in San Diego and 'the big one', 4/4/44—their third True Anniversary, George's thirty-third True Birthday, and their first Congruence of Samers and Alternators, a sort of calendrical syzygy—at his base in Hilo, Hawaii, where Pam happily taught seventh-grade math to the 'Navy brats'. Whether owing to the tropical ambience, the poignancy of wartime, the specialness of the date, or the mere maturation of their love, she experienced that night her first serial orgasm; it seemed to her to extend like the decimal equivalent of one-third, to the edge of the cosmos and beyond.

4/5/45 saw them separated again, this time by a special assignment that George was dispatched to in the South Pacific. Forbidden to mention to her even the name of his island destination, much less the nature of his duty there (it will turn out to be to do with logistical support for the bombing of Hiroshima and Nagasaki four months later), all George could tell her was that while the first of that year's two Straights (1/23/45) saw the war still raging in both the European and the Pacific Theater of Operations, he wouldn't be surprised if the show was over by the second. And did his dear Pammy remember first flagging that notable date during their non-date in that little park near Camp Poke-Her-No-No?

How swiftly a good life runs. By their first 'irregular' or 'corrective' anniversary (4/1/50: the zero in any decade-changing year will spoil their romantic little game but remind them of their wedding's actual date) they were resettled in Pam's home town, George as assistant superintendent of the county school system, Pam as a teacher in that same system on more or less open-ended leave to deliver—on an otherwise 'meaningless' date in May—their first and, it will turn out, only child, George Junior. He grew; she returned to teaching; sister Jan's husband deserted her in Syracuse for a younger woman; all hands aged. Some calendar-markers along their way, other than their always-slightly-later True Anniversaries: 7/6/54, a Reverse Sequential on which George Junior's baby sister miscarried and the Parkers called it a day in the reproduction department; 5/5/55, their Second Syzygy (fourteenth True Anniversary and George's forty-fourth True Birthday), when thirty-five-year-old Pam enjoyed by her own account the second best orgasm of her life; 23 November 1958, when George came home from the supervisor's office (he had been promoted the year before) to find his wife smiling mysteriously, his third-grade son bouncing with excitement as Pam had once done on her parents' front-porch glider, and on the cocktail table before their living-room fireplace, champagne cooling in a bucket beside a plate of...dates. The occasion? 'One one two three five eight,' she told him happily when he failed to guess: 'the only six-number Fibonacci in the century.' 'Get it, Dad?' George Junior wanted to know: 'One and one makes two, one and two makes three, two and three makes five, and three and five makes eight!' 'You can pop my cork later,' Pam murmured into his ear when he opened the bottle, and they happily fed each other the hors d'oeuvre.

By their Third Syzygy—George's fifty-fifth True Birthday, their Silver True Anniversary (a full two months later now than their Actual), and the twenty-second of the D-Day landings of Allied invasion forces in Normandy—George Junior was a high-school sophomore less interested in the Fibonacci series or any other academic subject than in getting his driver's licence, his girlfriend's attention, and the Beatles' latest album; Pam was recovering from a hysterectomy; George Senior had taken up golf and looked forward already to retirement in Florida, like Pam's parents. No orgasms that night, but contented toasts to 'the Number of the Beast and then some' and the True end of their century's second third (its Actual .6666...n point, they would have enjoyed pointing out to young George if he ever stayed both home and still long enough to listen, was not 6/6/66 but the year's 243rd day, the last of August).

Life. Time. The Parkers subscribed to both, enjoying the former much more than not while the latter ran in any case. 7/7/77 ought to have been their luckiest day: the expense of their son's lacklustre college education (Business Administration at the state university) was behind them, as was the suspense of his being drafted for service in Vietnam. Now twenty-seven, the young man was employed as an uncertified accountant at, of all history-repeating businesses, a large Chevrolet-Buick dealership—across Chesapeake Bay in Baltimore, where he lived with his wife and baby daughter. George himself was retired more or less contentedly and in good health though somewhat pot-bellied, eager to move south (Pam's parents, alas, had died) but resigned to waiting four more years for his wife's retirement and Social Security eligibility at sixty-two. They doted on their grandchild, wished that Baltimore weren't so long a drive and that their daughter-in-law weren't so bossy, their son so submissive. In the event, nothing special happened in their house that July Thursday except that George Senior managed a usable morning erection despite his hypertrophic prostate; aided by a dollop of personal lubricant to counteract Pam's increasing vaginal dryness, they made pleasurable love. Lying post-coitally in each other's arms three dozen years into their marriage, they agreed that every day since 3/8/38 had been a lucky day for them.

8/8/88 already! George's seventy-seventh True Birthday, the couple's forty-fourth True Anniversary, Pam's sixty-ninth year! They've settled in a modest golf-oriented retirement community in south-west Florida and would normally be Back North this time of year, escaping the worst of the heat and hurricane season and visiting their granddaughter (now twelve) and her maritally unhappy dad. But George Senior is in hospital, pre-opping for the removal of a cancerous kidney (he'll recover), and so they're toughing out their Fifth Syzygy on location. Pam limps in at Happy Hour (arthritic hip) with a smuggled split of Piper-Heidsieck and a zip-lock plastic bag of dates; they kiss, nibble, sip, sigh, hold hands, and reminisce about that Big One back in Hilo back in '44, when she went Infinitely Isodigital.

'I wonder what ever happened to that handsome Senior Counsellor at Po-Ko-No,' she teases him, and crosses her heart; 'the one that never laid a digit on me.'

'Maybe he ran off with my alternative Alternator,' George counters: 'Arlene Whatsername. Did I ever tell you she was born on One Six Sixteen?'

In their latter age, Pam busies herself volunteering at the county library and playing bridge with other women in their retirement-community clubhouse. George, as his body weakens, has in his son's words 'gone philosophical': he reads more than he ever did since college days—non-fiction these days, mostly, of a speculative character, and *Scientific American* rather than *Time* and *Life*—and reflects upon what he reads, and articulates as best he can some of those reflections to his mate. His considered opinion (he endeavours to tell her now, lest he happen not to survive the impending surgery) is that like the actual alignment of planets, these calendrical 'syzygies' and other date-patterns that he and she have taken such playful pleasure in remarking are as inherently insignificant as they are indeed remarkable and attractive to superstition. Human consciousness, George Parker has come to understand—indeed, animal consciousness in general—has evolved a penchant for noting patterns, symmetries, order; in the case of *Homo sapiens*, at least, this originally utilitarian penchant (no doubt a great aid to survival) tends to acquire a non-utilitarian, 'gee whiz' value as well. Certain patterns, symmetries and coincidences become fascinating in themselves, aesthetically satisfying. Even non-superstitious folks like himself and Pam, if they have a bit of the obsessive-compulsive in their make-up, may take satisfaction in noting correspondences between such patterns and their significant life-events, and be tempted to jigger such correspondences themselves into a pattern—which may then become causative, influencing the course of their lives in the same way that superstition would maintain, but for opposite, non-mystical reasons.

'You know what?' said Pam (for so swiftly does time run, this pre-op tête-à-tête is already past tense): 'George Junior is right.'

Operation successful, but along with his left kidney the patient lost much of his appetite for both golf and food. Pam underwent a hip replacement, also reasonably successful. George Junior's wife's heart without warning infarcted; she died cursing God and her milktoast husband. The latter within the year remarried (a divorcee five years his senior, with two teenagers of her own) and moved the 'blended family' to Santa Fe, New Mexico, where he took a job in his new bride's father's accounting firm. Granddaughter Kimberly pleaded with her paternal grandparents to rescue her from her stepfamily; aside from their increasing frailty, however, they thought it best for the girl to accommodate to her new situation. In just a few short years, they reminded her, she would be off to college with their financial assistance and virtually on her own.

'Are we aware,' Pam asked George on April Fools' Day 1990—their 'corrective' forty-ninth anniversary—'that our Golden True Anniversary will also be my very first True Birthday?' For so indeed 9/1/91 would be, within the parameters of their game: a Syzygy of a different stripe! They would celebrate it, they decided, by taking fifteen-year-old Kimberly to Paris, the first trip abroad for any of them if one discounts a Caribbean cruise the February past. The girl was thrilled, her grandparents if anything more so; the three made plans and shared their anticipatory excitement by telephone and e-mail, crossing their fingers that the Gulf War wouldn't spoil their adventure. More charmed by the date-game than her father had ever been, Kim proudly announced her 'discovery' that the Golden Alternator 9/1/91 would in France become a Golden Palindrome: 1.9.91.

'That girl will amount to something,' George proudly predicted. Amended Pam, 'She already does.' In mid-August, however, shortly before Kim joined them in Florida for their departure from Miami to Paris, Pam suffered the first of what would be a pair of coronaries. It left the right side of her body partially paralysed, impaired her speech, cancelled all happy plans, and constrained the 'celebration' of her True seventy-second birthday and their Golden True Anniversary to a grim reversal of 8/8/88: Pam this time the pale and wheelchaired patient; George the faux-cheery singer of Happy Birthday, their granddaughter harmonizing by long-distance telephone.

Through that fall and winter she regained some range of motion, but never substantially recovered and had little interest in continuing so helpless a life solely on the grounds of their surpassing love. Together they discussed, not for the first time, suicide. Neither had religious or, under the circumstances, moral objections; their impasse, which Pam declared unfair to her, was that George made clear his resolve to follow suit if she took her life, and she couldn't abide the idea of, in effect, killing him.

'Couldn't you have lied,' she complained, 'for my benefit?'

Her husband kissed her hand. 'No.'

On the last day of February, her second and fatal stroke resolved the issue for them before it could harden into resentment. The widower postponed his own termination to see the last rites through, for which his son and granddaughter, but not the rest of that family, flew out from Santa Fe (sister Jan was ten years dead of breast cancer; her grown children had never been close to their Aunt Pam and Uncle George). Kimberly, tears running, hugged her grandpa goodbye at the airport afterward and pointed out that by European notation, it being a leap year, Nana Pam had died on a five-digit Palindromic Alternator: 29.2.92. George wept gratefully into her hair.

Through half a dozen hollow subsequent 'anniversaries', mere dumb habit has kept him alive after all, though ever more dispirited and asocial. George Junior's second marriage has disintegrated. Feeling herself well out of that household, Kim attends a branch of Florida State University, in part to be near her grandfather, and in fact their connection, though mainly electronic, remains the brightest thing in the old man's life. Plump and sunny, more popular with her girlfriends than with the boys, she discusses with him her infrequent dates and other problems and adventures; she visits him on school holidays, tisks maternally at his bachelor housekeeping, and cheerily sets to work amending it. And without fail she has noted and telephoned him on 9/2/92, 9/3/93, 9/4/94, 9/5/95, 9/6/96—not to wish him, grotesquely, a happy anniversary, but merely to let him know that she remembers.

It is the expectation of her sixth such call that has delayed George's calm agenda for this evening, his and Pam's fifty-sixth True Anniversary. The man is eighty-five, in pretty fair health but low on energy and no longer interested in the world or his protracted existence therein. His son and namesake, nearing fifty, currently manages a General Motors dealership back in the tidewater Maryland town where he was born and raised; the two exchange occasional cordial messages, but seldom visit each other. Granddaughter Kim, having spent the summer waitressing at a South Carolina beach resort and the Labor Day holiday with her bachelor father ('a worse housekeeper than you, Grandpa!'), should be returning to Orlando about now to begin her junior year in hotel management; as a special treat from her grandfather she'll spend part of this year as an exchange student in France. Usually she telephones in the early evening, just after the rates go down. Last September, though, come to think of it, she merely e-mailed him a hurried THINKING OF YOU, GRANDPA!!! KIM:-) XOXOXOX 9/6/96.

He has eaten, appetiteless, his microwaved dinner, cleaned up after, poured himself a second glass of red wine, made his preparations as aforenoted, and rechecked the computer (YOU HAVE NO NEW MAIL). Kim's recent messages have spoken of a new

9999

boyfriend, one of her co-workers at the resort, whom she'll 'miss like crazy' when they return to their separate colleges and has hoped to touch base with between her visit home and her rematriculation; perhaps in the unaccustomed excitement of romance she has lost track of the date. She knows that he goes to bed after the ten o'clock news; he'll give her till then, although his self-scheduled exit-time was 9.19. A touch muzzy-headed from the wine, as that hour approaches he changes into pyjamas (wondering why), wakes the computer one last time, then shuts it down for good—a touch worried, a touch irritated. Call George Junior? No need to worry him; he'll know nothing that Kim's grandfather doesn't. Call the college? She has no new phone number there yet. Her summer workplace, then. But this is silly; she simply though uncharacteristically forgot the date, or remembered but got somehow sidetracked.

Now it's half past nine, and he's annoyed: if he ends his life per programme, the girl may blame herself for not having telephoned. So he'll leave her a message, reassuring her of his love and her non-responsibility for his final life-decision. All the same, she'll feel guilty for not having spoken with him one last time. So what? Life goes on, and on and on.

It's just a senseless pattern, he reminds himself: he doesn't have to turn himself off on 9/7/97 or any other 'special' date. He can wait to be sure that Kim's OK, tease her for forgetting her old gramps, then do his business when he's sure she won't in any way blame herself—on 9/20, 10/2, whenever. *Not* doing himself in tonight simply for the sake of repudiating the Pattern, he recognizes, would be a backhanded way of acknowledging the thing's ongoing hold on him; but he has these other, perfectly reasonable reasons for delay...

Or is he merely temporizing, rationalizing the Pattern's grip? Mightn't his freedom be better demonstrated (to himself, as no one else will know or care) by going ahead now as planned, following the Pattern precisely in order to prove (to himself) that he's under no compulsion either to follow it or not?

Our George is sleepy: the uncustomary wine, the hour, the weight of these considerations. He could get a good night's sleep and kill himself *mañana*, with a clear head. He could do it next May, the sixty-fifth anniversary of his father's suicide. He could put it off till

185

John Barth

9/9/99, his and Pam's fifty-eighth Anniversary, his eighty-eighth True Birthday and his brother's one hundredth Actual. He could for that matter put it off till the next 11/11/11, the ultimate full cycle, and be the first centenarian ever to autodestruct.

Sitting up in his half-empty bed at ten past eleven, with his left foot he pushes off and lets fall to the hardwood floor his right bedroom slipper, the better to scratch a little itch on his starboard instep. 9/9/99, he wearily supposes, would after all be the aptest date for his final Date: the next day his life's odometer would roll up straight zeros, as the calendar's never does.

Or he could do the damned thing right now.   □

GRANTA

AFTER AMNESIA
Joyce Carol Oates

Joyce Carol Oates

We enter the world as purely physical beings; and leave it in the same way. In between, through our lifetimes, we labour pridefully to establish *identities*, *selves* distinct from our bodies. Not *what* we are but *who* we are. This is the crux of our humanity.

I had reason to believe myself established in my identity. I had been a professional woman for more than twenty years, and had been attached to Princeton University for some time; a woman who had earned, it might be argued, the privilege of being no longer a *woman* exclusively but a *person*. Of course, I didn't think of such things. It would not have occurred to me to think of such things. I had assimilated these assumptions over two-thirds of my lifetime the way food is broken down and assimilated into the body's bones, flesh and blood.

This episode, this humiliating experience, occurred in March 1984. I told no one about it afterwards, failing to find an adequate language in which to transpose it into an entertaining anecdote; and not wanting to embarrass others, in any case. For perhaps eleven years I did not think of it. I had not so much forgotten it as dismissed it—a cluster of blurred, vaguely malevolent images, and smells; a dreamlike event to which confused emotions were attached, perhaps not even my own.

The occasion was a guided tour through a New Jersey prison facility. The Millstone County Detention Center, I'll call it, named for a river that flows nearby in an anonymous urban area not unlike the outskirts of Newark, New Jersey. Less than an hour's drive from Princeton, where I live; but so wholly unlike Princeton as to seem a separate state. (It's part of my amnesia that I'm unable to recall who arranged for me to visit the facility. I'm sure I didn't make a personal request. More likely, a friend of a friend, or a professional acquaintance, had arranged for the invitation. I've said yes to most invitations of a seemingly 'broadening' and 'enriching' nature out of a dread of saying no to the one crucial invitation that might make a difference in my life.)

From the outside, the Millstone County Detention Center did not appear conspicuously different from the old weather-worn factories, warehouses and trainyards in the vicinity, which I had only glimpsed from time to time, in passing, from an interstate highway.

The walls were high, ten or twelve feet of grey discoloured concrete that appeared to be exuding an oily damp, topped with 'razor wire' in sinuous coils. When I parked my car in the visitors' parking lot, which was almost empty, I smelled a sharp odour in the air as of coins held in a sweating palm, that might have been blown from a chemical factory near the river, but was concentrated in the area around the detention centre.

As soon as I entered the building through a metal detector checkpoint, past uniformed guards from the Millstone County Sheriff's Office, I thought *This is a mistake: turn back*. But of course I did not turn back. Pride and curiosity in equal measure would never have allowed me to turn back. The tour group was small, only five or six of us. A professor from Rutgers-Newark Law School, a visiting criminologist, lawyers from the New Jersey State Department of Public Advocacy. My identity that day was not 'writer' but 'professor of humanities, Princeton University'. I'm unable to remember the names, even the faces, of these other visitors, except that they were all men, and, like me, Caucasian. The fact of race would not seem significant outside the context of a state prison in which so many inmates are black; 'Caucasians' rarely feel any binding principle otherwise. Majority populations take themselves for granted as the norm; not accident, still less historical privilege, but 'nature' would seem to define us.

Our tour guide was an officer from the New Jersey State Correctional Facility, wearing a bright coppery badge that identified him as a sergeant and an instructor of firearms. An affable, smiling, stocky-muscled man of vigorous middle age with a flushed face and a habit of winking, or seeming to wink, as he spoke; eyes like transparent blue glass, alert, intelligent, yet cast for the most part over our heads. You could not tell if he took pride in his role, guiding civilian visitors through the facility, or if he merely tolerated it, and us. His uniform was pale blue and around his waist he wore a smartly gleaming leather holster conspicuously missing a pistol.

Here was the first ominous note. Though the sergeant explained the situation with a smile. Outside the security checkpoints, county sheriff's guards were armed; inside, guards in beige-brown uniforms carried no weapons, or even holsters. One of us enquired about the policy and the sergeant said, matter-of-factly, 'If guards carry guns there's the possibility the inmates will take the guns from them.' He paused; his manner mildly teasing, as if a joke hovered in the air close about us and he was the only one to discern it. Seeing the expressions on our faces, he went on, 'Millstone is a maximum security facility and once the alarm goes off, if it goes off, you couldn't get out in a tank. Every door, every gate, every elevator is bolted electronically. And there's no windows—you'll notice there's no windows to the outside.'

One of the men in our group asked what would happen if someone was taken hostage. The sergeant smiled, peering over our heads, and with the air of one who has uttered certain words many times and has yet to be disappointed in his listeners' reactions, said, 'Policy is, if they take you, they take you. If they take me, they take me. No negotiations with inmates at Millstone. No hostages.'

The tour began, no turning back. Checkpoints, beady blinking camera-eyes overhead, ponderous metallic doors like those in spaceships in sci-fi movies of the 1950s. Without my handbag, which had to be checked at the front desk, my hands were loose and empty. Entering the maximum security unit we had to be frisked, but because I was female none of the male guards could touch me; the sergeant telephoned the women's unit on the seventh floor to summon down a matron. She was a black woman in the same beige-brown uniform who briskly patted my body up and down and passed me on with a murmured 'OK', not a glance of acknowledgement. It struck us as odd that the sergeant too was frisked by a guard. He said, with his affable smile, a just-perceptible hint of a wink, 'A county officer might smuggle in contraband, like anybody else. Like some lawyers have been known to do, eh?'

We were marched along a windowless corridor. Instructed *You will not speak with any inmate, you will not make eye contact with any inmate, you will follow me closely at all times and direct any questions exclusively to me.* The odour of coins in a sweating hand grew more intense, a greasy odour beneath, a faint stench as of overripe oranges. We were told a brief history of Millstone, 'old' facility and 'new'. Statistics, dates. The sergeant informed us in a clipped voice that there were four categories of inmates in the facility:

those who'd been arrested and couldn't make bail; those presently on trial; those who'd been convicted and were awaiting sentencing; and overflow from other state facilities. The women's unit was segregated, of course. Don't feel sorry for any inmate. Most of them, they've worked damn hard to get in here. All kinds of crimes: theft, arson, drugs and drug-dealing, armed robbery, rape, manslaughter, murder. Drunk and disorderly, wife-beating, child-beating, child molesters. No 'white-collar' crimes—the perpetrators can make bail. A serious sex offender, like that guy raped the little girl a few weeks ago, they're segregated from the general population.

Before one of the hefty metal doors the sergeant called, 'Key up!' A black guard appeared with a key to let us into the kitchen unit which was an older unit, the sergeant said, with a door still manually operated, by key rather than TV monitor and code. The door swung open, we were led inside and abruptly found ourselves in the presence of inmates. A number of men, dark-skinned, working in the kitchen, a cavernous fluorescent-lit space. There was a hum of ventilators and fans but the air was thick with smells of grease, yeasty baked rolls, scorched tomato sauce, cleanser, ammonia, disinfectant. Smells of hair oil, perspiration. The kitchen workers wore baggy uniforms, coveralls, of the green hue of stagnant water. As we civilians entered in suits, ties, blazers and polished shoes their eyes shifted to us and away in a single swerve of a motion as if seeing and not-seeing were simultaneous. In his rapid, affable, overly loud voice the sergeant continued to speak as if the inmates could not hear him, and indeed they appeared oblivious of us as if on the other side of a plate glass barrier. It was embarrassing, awkward, unnatural and yet clearly routine. White visitors, 'professionals'; black inmates, 'criminals'. Yet how close we were, only a few yards separating us. A lanky black man of about thirty with his springy-woolly hair caught tight in a hairnet was scouring the interior of a badly crusted giant baking tin; another was unpacking a cardboard box of what appeared to be gallon-sized cans of Montco peaches; another, heavyset, with a raddled black face and wearing an upright dazzling-white chef's hat like a figure in a cartoon, worked at a giant stove. *You will not make eye contact with any inmate* and so I did not, fixing my attention on the canned food which was stacked on counters and shelves. These were comically oversized cans of familiar brand names, Hunt's Tomato Sauce, Heinz's Pork & Beans, Campbell's Chicken Noodle Soup, Montco Sliced Peaches, like a pop-artefact by Andy Warhol. I could see, though I tried not to look at him, the inmate in the hairnet watching me out of the corner of his eye as, with a fist-sized clump of steel wool, he scoured, scoured, scoured the baking tin in furious circles.

'At Millstone, inmates feed in their cell blocks,' the sergeant was saying. 'A big dining hall isn't looked to be practical here.'

Uneasy in our professional clothes and Caucasian skin the five or six of us were led through the kitchen unit as if on a march across a special ramp laid down in a swamp—you wouldn't wish to step off that ramp, not for an instant.

Next we were taken through the laundry unit which was another cavernous, windowless, fluorescent-glaring space, warm as a slow oven and smelling of damp laundry, disinfectant and oily male sweat. A half-dozen inmates were working, dark-skinned, silent, all with sizeable stomachs. Except for their sullen faces and their resolutely downcast eyes, these men too gave not the slightest sign of being conscious of their observers. They might have been performers in a long-running play at which we, visiting tourists, were just another audience. The sergeant talked, the inmates went about their work. Folding sheets, towels and uniforms; hauling more laundry out of enormous dryers. Their faces oozed sweat. They moved mechanically, yet with no perceptible beat or rhythm. There could be no pleasure in such work, nor even the angry satisfaction of displeasure. Within minutes the laundry unit became unbearably warm. We visitors were uncomfortable in our winter clothes, our 'professional' uniforms. I wore dark wool, a blazer and a long skirt, and my clothes weighed heavily on me. It was becoming increasingly difficult to concentrate on the sergeant's relentless voice. How mixed up with the glaring fluorescent light, that voice of seemingly casual authority. I too had begun to sweat inside my clothes. Like the other visitors I dared not look too closely at inmates who so stonily, with such dignity, refused to look at us. I was thinking *We didn't put you here! We aren't the ones.*

We ascended in an elevator and were led briskly along a corridor and through an electronically monitored checkpoint (the sergeant punched in a code to open the door) and invited then to contemplate through a wire-enforced plate glass window the 'volleyball court'—a flat asphalt roof with a lank net strung up, and no players. An icy rain had begun to fall. A half-mile beyond the facility's concrete wall was the expressway, and beyond that the river, only barely visible, of the colour this morning of stainless steel cutlery. Recreation for most inmates was two hours a day when practical, the sergeant was saying, but now that the gym was used for beds there was a problem, the prison population being mainly young men, blacks and some Hispanics, eighteen to twenty-five years of age on the average, street kids, lots of energy they got to work off. Lots of anger.

We stared at the deserted volleyball court for a while. We were then led back through the checkpoint and to the elevator. One of the men in our group asked about violence in the facility, and the sergeant said affably, 'Violence? Here? Nah,' but this was a joke evidently, for he went on to say, still more affably, 'Sure, there's always a problem in any prison facility. Inmates extorting other inmates, like they do on the street. A detention centre is basically the street with walls around it. It's a population can't make bail. It's a population where everybody knows everybody else. You're connected, or you're not. There's guys hitting up other guys for money, ganging up on them in the showers. Five minutes in, a guy's weak, without connections, everybody knows it. It's in the showers they're vulnerable. Beatings, rapes. Nobody ever informs on anybody. Unless he's finished anyway. They make a 'woman' of him, he's dead meat from then on.' The sergeant paused and then added, 'Sometimes a certain class of white guy, not segregated, he'll have a serious problem. Other white guys, you'll be seeing them, can handle it OK.'

We were not to be taken through the segregated unit on the fourth floor but were allowed to peer into it through another wire-enforced plate glass window in a guard station, as the sergeant explained the circumstances of 'segregation'. It seemed to be an important term to him, a category of distinction. We saw little except a long brightly lit corridor with cells opening off it, at the far end of which two guards stood talking together. The cells had canvas padding, the sergeant said, and the guards here knew First Aid. Inmates who lost control in their cell blocks, attacked their attorneys for instance, or attacked guards—they were brought here, and closely monitored. The protective-custody unit was next door, only a few inmates in it at the present time including the white guy who raped and killed a little girl.

In one of the cells we could see, dimly, a figure lying on a cot. This was a 'suicide watch cell' where inmates were watched twenty-four hours a day. No suicides at Millstone, not if they could be prevented. The facility had a high rating in this respect. Still, sometimes an inmate will surprise everybody, the sergeant said, shaking his head. Sometimes they can kill themselves in the damnedest ways if they're desperate. We watched the motionless figure in the cell.

One of the lawyers in our group persisted in asking about violence in the facility, rape for instance. The sergeant said with a shrug that sure it happened, men going after men, healthy young guys of that age, late adolescence but with the emotional age of children, what would you expect? We were in an elevator in which a guard accompanied a stony-faced black man in handcuffs, both of them ignoring our presence. A woman in such company, I assumed the attitude of an honorary man. A professional woman, in a sense, *is* an honorary man. So I, too, had questions to ask of the sergeant: what did he think of the newly revived death penalty in New Jersey? Wasn't it the case that there was a disproportionate number of black men sentenced to death throughout the United States, compared to the general prison population? The sergeant said, shrugging, 'That's how the system works out.'

Adding, as if reluctantly, 'There's advantages and disadvantages to the death penalty. The advantage is, you put away a dangerous criminal for a long time, all these guys on Death Row, and society is protected. The disadvantage is, for law enforcement officers, you encounter a more dangerous type of criminal. What's he got to lose, he's thinking. And probably he's right.' The sergeant's voice was still resolutely affable. 'Some of these guys, their lives aren't worth much to them. Like it's a match they lit and they can blow out any time.

That's the type of inmate you're basically dealing with in Millstone.'

We were not to be taken through the women's unit on the seventh floor but on our brief tour through the infirmary unit we encountered a number of female inmates waiting to see the doctor, supervised by a matron. The matron was black, and it seemed that all of the women were black, and of varying ages though mainly young, several looking no more than sixteen. They wore baggy coveralls or dresses of the same washed-out sickly green as the male inmates. Like the men, they did not look at us after the initial sullen glance. One young woman was bloated with pregnancy; another, her hair braided in dozens of delicate cornrows, had a bruised-looking face and furious eyes. *What you lookin' at, you!* The sergeant was saying matter-of-factly that the female population at Millstone was between eight and ten per cent of the male, but it was going up, like it was going up nationally. The crimes were mainly drug-related, prostitution, bad cheques. Mostly the crimes were tied in with male perpetrators. Though sometimes you'd be surprised, women were turning up for armed robbery, assault, murder. All across the country.

Women didn't mind incarceration the way men did, the sergeant said. The worst thing was being deprived of their children if they had children but, overall, they were protected in the facility—'Protected from the men.'

Was this meant to be funny, or ironic? A few of us laughed uncertainly.

The air about us was becoming thick, more difficult to breathe, as though too many breaths had already been expelled into it. Now we were in the interior of the facility, where the prison population was housed. We stared through another wire-enforced window in a guard station on the fifth floor, into a scene of disconcerting intimacy, a gym made over into a 'temporary dorm' for newly arrested prisoners. The 'temporary dorm', the sergeant said, had been in use for over a year. Mattresses were spread out in almost uniform rows on the hardwood floor of the windowless fluorescent-lit space—'The lights are never turned off,' the sergeant said. What a shock: dozens of men in dull-green baggy clothes amid rumpled sheets, towels, clothes, shoes, toiletries. Nearly all were black or swarthy-skinned but there was one man with the look of a skinned rabbit, bloodless-pale amid his fellows, with a dome of thinning white hair. Most of the men were of ordinary height and girth but there were several who were as tall and solid as horses. Unaware of being observed, or indifferent, the inmates seemed to be pantomiming 'real' people. Some lay on mattresses asleep in the glaring light or comatose and others sat sorting through their possessions as if they'd been doing so for a long time; still others stood motionless as if arrested in thought, or walked about aimlessly like somnambulists, or stood talking together in small groups. Near the guard station was a long table at which inmates sat conferring with men in civilian clothes—their attorneys. Over all was an air of passivity, withheld power. No sound penetrated the plate glass window through which we looked, adding to the atmosphere of strangeness. There was a heraldic simplicity about the inmates as if they were figures in a twelfth-century fresco, charged with a symbolic meaning of which they themselves were ignorant, and wholly without self-consciousness. The sergeant was saying, 'Your average inmate in the system, if he's in for a prison term, would be waiting, about now, for lunch. Mainly they're waiting for the next meal. These men are waiting to be moved somewhere else. If they get lucky, they could be back on the street tomorrow. If not, not. Whatever it is, they're waiting. Lots of them got scores to settle so they think about that. What they don't like, what pisses them off, is a glitch in their routine.'

The pointlessness of it. The futility. I would not ask about remorse, conscience—I did not want the sergeant to laugh at me. It might be argued that the human condition was not tragic after all, nor even spiritual. A matter of waiting, eating, settling scores. Not that the inmates in the 'temporary dorm' were estranged from common humanity but that this, in its starkest, least sentimental essence, *was* humanity. If we could observe ourselves through wire-enforced plate glass windows twenty-four hours a day.

If the tour had ended at this point, my impressions would have been disturbing, even depressing, but not annihilating, in no way personal. The dominant sensation was physical: extreme fatigue, eye ache. I was not thinking any longer of injustice—or justice—or of the tragic inequities of black and white America—but only of the anticipation of my own release. Within the hour!—freedom.

But, unfortunately, the tour did not end at that point. We were observing a cell block on the fifth floor, one of numerous thirty-man cell blocks in the facility, the 'heart' of the modern prison system, the sergeant explained, replacing the old-style tiers of cells that you'd see in the movies. The thirty-man block was structured with cells arranged around an open space like a common room, containing tables and chairs; the fourth wall of this rectangular space was an elevated guard station in which a window, wire-enforced as usual, was inset. No privacy for these men except at the very rear of their cells, and these cells measuring six feet by eight. The effect was like that of a zoo enclosure or an aquarium. Here as elsewhere the dominant majority of the population was dark-skinned and young. There was more movement here, more restiveness, than in the gym. *Don't make eye contact with any inmate* an inner voice admonished even as I drifted close to the window. Perhaps I was trying to ease away from the sergeant's droning voice. Perhaps by this time I was not thinking very coherently. I might have come to assume that, in my Caucasian skin, protected by plate glass, I was invisible. Certainly I'd grown dazed. And in this state I was careless, and met the startled gazes of two young inmates standing near the window, about ten feet below. They were husky black men in their mid-twenties. They were frowning at me, staring at me, as if they'd never seen anything quite like me before in their lives. Their faces showed consternation, resentment, fury. It was a reflexive act on my part: I was confused, and smiled.

The most natural of female reactions: the first impulse, frightened of the male, you smile. Not with the eyes which show fear but with the mouth, promising compliance.

Now came an immediate, extraordinary reaction—as if I'd flung open a window to call attention to myself, as if I'd waved a flaming torch.

A ripple of excited interest passed among the inmates. Suddenly everyone was looking at me. *A woman! There's a woman!* In the instant of knowing my blunder, already it was too late. I'd been sighted, discovered and exposed, there could be no discreet withdrawal. My skin flushed, my heart beat rapidly with a rush of adrenalin. I would have liked to cringe from view and did in fact look to see if I could position myself behind the sergeant's stocky frame, as a child might, but, perversely, I'm sure it was coincidentally, the sergeant had seated himself on the edge of a desk; the first time since the tour had begun that he'd taken a seat.

Excited calls and cries spread through the cell block, muffled behind the soundproof glass. Even older inmates slouched dispiritedly at the margins of the enclosure were roused to life. Others leaned out of their cells to stare. In idle-seeming but purposeful eddies, younger men began to drift boldly forward to within a few feet of the window. They bared their teeth, grinned and rolled their eyes. Their mouths shaped words I could not hear. I stood paralysed, stricken with embarrassment and mounting panic. Males, in a pack. The female terror of becoming an object of male sexual desire, prey. Multiple rape, rape to the death, a frenzy of propagation. The life-force gone wild, blocked-up seed yearning only to be spilled. Why didn't the sergeant, or the guards in the station, notice? Didn't my tour companions notice? Yet the sergeant continued to speak. Citing statistics, the names of New Jersey politicians. How could he keep us here, talking with such calm, maddening persistence, as agitation built up in the cell block?

Certain of the younger, more emboldened inmates were flashing outright grins and their hands moved suggestively. *White bitch! White cunt!* They appeared about to break into a rowdy dance, like mocking children. Yet I could not look away, as if I'd been hypnotized. Perhaps I was still smiling, in my terror, a ghastly fixed smile like a death's head. It was as if I stood naked before strangers, utterly exposed and in such exposure annihilated. A woman in her mid-forties—too old! But that was not the point. Sexual desirability was not the point, nor even attractiveness. Mere sexual identity was all that mattered. *A woman: cunt.* What these eager men would do to me, if they could get hold of me: that was the promise of their eyes, their mouths. How I would beg, plead, scream. How I would sacrifice in an instant all that remained of my dignity, if only I could be spared. *But this isn't me! I am so much more than what you see.*

The episode could not have lasted more than a few minutes, and yet those few minutes were excruciating. As I was the lone woman in the inmates' mocking and enraged eyes, so I was the lone woman in the guard station. Was it possible the sergeant and the other officers were unaware of the inmates' excitement? Yet no one intervened, nor even glanced at me. No one offered to lead me out, to spare me the humiliation I was obviously enduring. Maybe I deserved it? Maybe the ravening inmates deserved it? For the one, a lesson of knowing, *This is just to show you what you would experience except for us, your protectors.* For the others, *This is your punishment, what we've deprived you of, behind bars—the female body.*

So at certain junctures of experience we who are women are made to realize, as no man would ever be made to realize in quite the same way, that our identities as individuals are provisional. A professional woman, particularly one who associates herself with an institution, or has a public reputation substantial enough to characterize her, believes that, by having distinguished herself from others of her category (that is, her sex), she might have achieved a distinctive identity; through this identity, she might be in the possession of some measure of power. (For what is 'identity' but our power to control others' definitions of us?) In this, she is mistaken. A woman's 'identity' is one granted her by men; it is a neutral identity, an honorific. The fiction is *We grant you your putative identity apart from being merely female; but we retain the privilege of revoking it at any time.* In this fiction, the 'professional woman' is a desexualized female. But a desexualized female is an impossibility. Never in any plausible scenario could a professional man be unwillingly divested of his identity in such a way, becoming, in others' eyes, a sheerly sexual being; a genitalia-bearing body. To be reduced to a body is to be contemptible, because anonymous, mass-produced.

Of course I was not thinking of such speculative matters that morning in March 1984; nor would I think of them in the intervening years. Shame is the emotion that most effectively blocks memory. Amnesia is the great solace, the most available form of self-protection. For one to whom anger, let alone rage, is not an option, what recourse but forgetfulness?

Only years later would I begin to remember. My memory triggered by another woman saying, with an air of bemusement: Why do we instinctively smile when men stare at us? insult us? threaten us sexually? Only then, after eleven years. How like actual mist the amnesia seemed as it lifted and dissolved.

The tour was over, or nearly. Two hours and five minutes had passed, leaving us as drained as eight or twelve hours might have done. The sergeant smiled at us, looking at us directly for the first time. 'Tired, eh?' We were on the ground floor, towards the rear of the facility, in the control centre, where officers sat smoking and drinking coffee and staring at TV monitors in a double row on a concrete wall. Now that the adrenalin rush had subsided, my head throbbed with pain. I must have looked sickly. Every drop of pride and integrity had been drained from me; it was my great accomplishment simply to have finished the tour. Not to have broken down in my companions' eyes.

As we left the facility, the sergeant called, teasing, after us, 'Be sure to come back again soon, eh?'

Now that I had my handbag and my coat, I felt more possessed of myself. I departed the oppressive building quickly, ahead of my male companions, without a backward glance. If someone called goodbye to me, I did not hear. Free! A fine icy rain was being blown slantwise by the wind, smelling of the river. But how wonderful the icy rain, the chemical odour! I smiled in relief and gratitude as I unlocked my car, giddy as if my life had been spared; better yet, as if I'd slipped away unapprehended from the scene of a shameful crime.　　　　□

GRANTA

FIFTEEN LASHES
Anwar Iqbal

Anwar Iqbal

I was an apprentice newspaper reporter when General Zia ul-Haq came to power in Pakistan in the military coup of 1977. That was more than twenty years ago; but there are scenes from his reign that I shall always remember. The general was keen on Islamic law and Islamic punishment, but, though stonings and amputations of the hands were often talked of, the general came down in favour of flogging, a form of punishment which in Pakistan owes as much to an inherited British colonial tradition as to the penal code of Islam. Floggings were always a part of prison life in Pakistan. The general's innovation was to make them public, *pour encourager les autres.*

Soon after he took over, the general arranged a big public flogging-show and I, as a reporter, was sent to watch. The victims were lined up in white pyjamas, loose white shirts and white caps. They looked like circus animals waiting for the crack of the trainer's whip. All were men, most of them middle-aged. They looked pale, and they shook with fear. Some even wet their trousers when the flogging began, but it had little effect on their captors or the doctor whose job it was to examine each victim and declare him fit to be flogged. The stage was built in a big open space between the old city of Rawalpindi and the new capital Islamabad; the two places adjoin each other. Normally, children played football, cricket and hockey there. It was an open platform, about fifteen feet high, and could be viewed from every corner of the huge ground. A wooden frame was fixed in the middle of the platform where every victim was to be tied, his hands and feet separately as on a cross. His face would be turned towards the stage where the policemen, the magistrate, and other important people were sitting; the press had special seats so that they could watch the flogging closely and report every detail. His hips, which would receive the whip, were to face the audience. A microphone was fixed on the frame, near where the victim's mouth was to be, so that everybody could hear him scream. Centre stage stood a tall and well-built man wearing only a loincloth. He was rubbing oil all over his body. Then he did some push-ups to show his muscles. When he finished, he picked up a big stick, soaked in oil, from a corner where about half a dozen such sticks were kept for him to choose from. He picked one and tried it in the air. The whip made a horrible hissing noise every time he cut the air with it. The whipper, who was a convict himself, had been brought specially from the prison to perform the job, which earned him privileges inside. He received superior food and spent most of his time exercising. He was in great demand and toured Pakistan from city to city to flog whenever the government thought it needed to scare people. He looked very intimidating. He was now ready to flog. All his muscles tightened and bulged like the feathers of a rooster ready to fight. As those on the stage prepared for the flogging, thousands of people had already gathered to watch it. The ground was full to capacity. So were the neighbouring roads and side streets. There were people on the rooftops of nearby buildings. Some even clung to the trees and electricity poles around the ground. The poor watched with a cautious nonchalance; they have learned not to appear too interested in such things because they tend to supply the victims whenever their rulers need to demonstrate their strength. The rich behaved differently. They had come by car and on their motorbikes and were cruising around, waiting for the spectacle to begin. The young among them were dressed in tight jeans and bright shirts and some of them had brought their girlfriends with them. Some might have committed the same sin for which the fifteen victims were to be flogged: drinking alcohol and having sex with women other than their wives. But they did not seem bothered. They were safe in doing whatever they did because they belonged to the so-called 'VIP' class where no law, religious or secular, applies. They also had better, safer places in which to drink or screw and did not have to frequent cheap hotels which the police would raid whenever their bosses felt the need to impress the public with activity. All the victims were arrested from a hotel in a lower-middle-class neighbourhood of the old city. The raiding party, so it was said, had found more than fifty people drinking alcohol and having sex. All of them were convicted in a trial completed in three days. Most of them were over fifty and so found unfit for flogging. The women involved in this crime were also convicted but were spared the whip. Those men found fit were brought for flogging.

Now the flogging was to start. The man with the stick indicated that he was ready. An official came on to the stage, detached the microphone from the wooden frame and announced the name of the first man who was to be whipped. He then read out the allegations against him and signalled the guards to bring him on to the platform. Two constables brought the convict on to the stage. He looked utterly helpless. He was not trembling. He did not even look afraid. He looked more like an animal about to be slaughtered and unable to understand what was happening to him. He could not follow verbal commands. So to make him move, one of the constables had to give him a little push. He moved, and then kept walking so that he would have fallen off the opposite end of the stage if the other constable had not stopped him. It was as if his mind had stopped functioning. There seemed to be no coordination between his thoughts and his actions. Each of his hands and feet appeared to be moving separately. The constables led him to the frame. Then the doctor came, examined him, listened to his heart with a stethoscope, and declared him fit for flogging. The man listened to the pronouncement with indifference, as if it did not concern him. He even nodded his head twice, as if endorsing the doctor's decision. By now the crowd was completely silent. Even the hawkers, selling ice cream and fresh fruits to the crowd, were quiet. The constables lifted the man up on to the frame, and tied his hands and feet to the scaffolding: his face was turned towards the stage and his buttocks exposed to the crowd. They tied another piece of cloth above his hips to mark the target. Then they moved aside. Now all eyes were fixed on the whip-man who was fiercely slashing the air with his whip. The crowd was so quiet that the microphone picked up the slashing of the whip and carried it everywhere. The man on the scaffolding also heard the sound. So far he had been very quiet but the slashing sound changed him. He started trembling and then cried, very loudly. The loudspeakers carried his voice to the crowd and beyond, but nobody spoke a word. Now a magistrate, also sitting on the stage, asked the whip-man to begin. He tested the whip for the last time, slowly hitting his left palm, and then came running, stopped a foot or two from the scaffolding and hit the victim with full force. The whip touched his skin, went into his flesh and came out again. The man shrieked in agony. Those sitting on the stage could see blood oozing from the wound. *One*, said the official counting the whips. The man was sobbing now which could be heard on the loudspeakers. The whipper went back to his mark and came running again when the magistrate signalled him to resume. The whip hit the flesh, the man shouted for help, the flogger withdrew, came back again, hit him and withdrew. Once this sequence was broken when the doctor came to examine the victim. After his examination, he invited the whip-man to continue. The constable untied the man after the fifteenth lash and he fell on to the stage. They removed him on a stretcher and brought the next man.

This was my first public flogging. Several months later I went to a *maidan*, a public space, in Rawalpindi where a blind woman was to be flogged for sexual misbehaviour. An audience of hundreds of men surrounded the stage where she was to be whipped. They displayed neither sorrow nor passion. They chatted about politics and sport as they waited for the flogging to begin. Then a police officer came and asked them to go home because a higher court had suspended the flogging. Soon the *maidan* rang with voices of disapproval. The men wanted to watch the *tamasha*, the hullabaloo. They were there to watch the woman's helplessness and to enjoy it. But the policemen were ready with their batons, so they had to disperse. And the truth was that I shared their disappointment. Although I had been writing against public flogging ever since it began, I wanted to watch it. I might go back to my typewriter and condemn it, but I did not want to miss the spectacle.

This was an unpleasant discovery to make about myself. A sorrowful, angry disgust—with myself and the country I lived in—thus became a feature of my life. □

The Prime of Miss Jean Brodie

in a newly revised version by Jay Presson Allen
adapted from the novel by Muriel Spark

"Fresh, distinctive and
highly entertaining...
the night belongs to
Fiona Shaw, a funny
and poignant Miss
Brodie from an actress
undoubtedly in her prime"
Daily Telegraph

"**Phyllida Lloyd's**
ingeniously staged,
pulsating production"
Evening Standard

"An invigorating
new adaptation"
Time Out - Critics' Choice

"TRULY
REMARKABLE"
Independent

Sponsored by
**The Royal Bank
of Scotland**

In repertoire in the Lyttelton

Royal National Theatre
Box Office 0171-452 3000
www.nt-online.org

Reg'd Charity

GRANTA

THE COINCIDENCE
OF THE ARTS
Martin Amis

Martin Amis

'This is a farce, man. Have you read my novel yet?'

'No.'

'Well why's that now?'

'I've been terribly—'

Across the road a fire truck levered itself backwards into its bay with a great stifled sneeze. Round about, a thousand conversations missed a beat, gulped, and then hungrily resumed.

'The thing is I've been terribly busy.'

'Aren't those the exact same words you used last time I asked you?'

'Yes.'

'Then how many more times do I got to hear them?'

The two men stood facing each other on the corner: that mess of streets, of tracks and rinks, where Seventh Avenue collapses into the Village... He who posed the questions was thirty-five years old, six foot seven, and built like a linebacker in full armour. His name was Pharsin Courier, and he was deeply black. He who tendered the answers was about the same age; but he was five foot eight, and very meagre. Standing there, confronted by his interrogator, he seemed to be lacking a whole dimension. His name was Sir Rodney Peel, and he was deeply white.

They were shouting at each other, but not yet in exasperation or anger. The city was getting louder every day: even the sirens had to throw a tantrum, just to make themselves heard.

'Find time for my novel,' said Pharsin. He continued to urge such a course on Rodney for a further twenty minutes, saying, in conclusion, 'I gave you that typescript in good faith, and I need your critique. You and I, we're both artists. And don't you think that counts for something?'

In this city?

The sign said: OMNI'S ART MATERIAL—FOR THE ARTIST IN EVERYONE. But everyone was *already* an artist. The coffee-shop waiters and waitresses were, of course, actors and actresses; and the people they served were all librettists and scenarists, harpists, pointillists, ceramicists, caricaturists, contrapuntalists. The little boys were bladers and jugglers, the little girls all ballerinas (bent over the

208

tables in freckly discussions with their mothers or mentors). Even the babies starred in ads and had agents. And it didn't stop there. Outside, sculptors wheelbarrowed chunks of rock over painted pavements past busking flautists, and a troupe of clowns performed mime, watched by kibitzers doing ad lib and impro. And on and on and up and up. Jesters teetered by on ten-foot stilts. Divas practised their scales from tenement windows. The construction workers were all constructivists. The AC installers were all installationists.

And, for once, Sir Rodney Peel happened to be telling the truth: he *was* terribly busy. After many soggy years of artistic and sexual failure, in London, SW3, Rodney was now savouring their opposites, in New York. You could still see this failure in the darkened skin around his eyes (stained, scarred, blinded); you could still nose it in his pyjamas, unlaundered for fifteen years (when he got out of bed in the morning he left them leaning against the wall). But America had reinvented him. He had a title, a ponytail, a flowery accent, and a pliant paintbrush. He was an unattached heterosexual in Manhattan: something had to give. And Rodney now knew the panic of answered prayers. Like a bit-part player in a dream, he looked on as his prices kept doubling: all you needed was an aristocratic wag of the head, and a straight face. Under the floorboards of his studio, in brown envelopes, lurked ninety-five thousand dollars: cash. And every afternoon he was climbing into an aromatic bed, speechless, with his ears whistling like seashells.

Rodney still felt that he had a chance of becoming a serious painter. Not a good chance—but a chance. Even he could tell that his artistic universe, after ten months in New York, had undergone drastic contraction. The journey into his own nervous system, the groping after spatial relationships, the trawl for his own talent—all this, for the time being, he had set aside. And now he specialized. He did wives. Wives of wealthy professionals and executives: wives of the lions of Madison Avenue, wives of the heroes of Wall Street. His brush flattered and rejuvenated them, naturally; but this wasn't especially arduous or even dishonest, because the wives were never first wives: they were second wives, third wives, subsequent wives. They gazed up at him righteously, at slender Sir Rodney in his smudged smock. 'Perfect,' he would murmur. 'No. Yes. That's quite lovely...' One thing sometimes led to another thing; but never to the real thing. Meekly, his love life imitated his art. This wife, that wife. Rodney flattered, flirted, fumbled, failed. Then change came. Now, when he worked, his paint coagulated along traditional lines, and conventional curves. In between the sheets, though, Rodney felt the terrible agitation of the innovator.

'There's been a breakthrough,' he told Rock Robville, his agent or middleman, 'on the uh, "carnal knowledge" front.'
'Oh? Do tell.'
'Quite extraordinary actually. Never known anything quite...'
'The fragrant Mrs Peterson, mayhap?'
'Good God no.'
'The bodacious Mrs Havilland, then, I'll wager.'
Twenty-eight, sleek, rosy, and darkly balding, Rock, too, was English, and of Rodney's class. The Robvilles were not as old and grand as the Peels; but they were much richer. Rock was now accumulating another fortune as an entrepreneur of things British: holiday castles in Scotland, Cumbrian fishing rights, crests, titles, nannies, suits of armour. Oh, and butlers. Rock did much trafficking in butlers.
'No. She's not a wife,' said Rodney. 'I don't want to say too much about it in case it breaks the spell. Early days and all that.'
'Have you two actually "slimed"?'
Rodney looked at him, frowning, as if in effortful recall. Then his face cleared and he answered in the negative. Rock seemed to enjoy scattering these phrases of the moment—these progeriac novelties—in Rodney's path. There was another one he used: 'playing Hide the Salami'. Hide the Salami sounded more fun than the game Rodney usually played with women. That game was called *Find* the Salami.
'We uh, "retire" together. But we haven't yet done the deed.'
'The act of darkness,' said Rock, causing Rodney to contemplate him strangely. 'How sweet. And how retro. You're getting to know each other first.'
'Well that's just it. She doesn't... We don't...'
Rock and Rod were leaning backwards on a mahogany bar, drinking Pink Ladies, in some conservatorial gin-palace off Lower

Park Avenue. Inspecting his friend's anxious leer, Rock felt a protective pang and said suddenly,

'Have you done anything about your money yet? Talk to Mr Jaguar about it. Soon. Americans are very fierce about tax. You could get locked up.'

They fell silent. Both of them were thinking about the four or five seconds Rodney would last in an American jail. Now Rodney stirred and said,

'I'm in a mood to celebrate. It's all very exciting. Let me get you another one of those.'

'Ah. You're a white man,' said Rock absent-mindedly. 'And do let me know,' he added, 'when you've slimed.'

Rodney was one of those Englishmen who had to get out of England. He had to get out of England and grow his hair. Helpless against his mother, his grandmother, helpless against each dawdling, prating, beaming milady they somehow conscripted him to squire. When he tried to break out they always easily reclaimed him, drawing him back to what was theirs. They owned him... Rodney had a fat upper lip which, during those soggy years, often wore a deep lateral crease of resignation—of vapid resignation. In the Chinese restaurants of Chelsea you might have glimpsed him, being lunched and lectured by a heavy-smoking aunt, his arms folded in the tightness of his jacket, his upper lip philosophically seamed.

'Y̲ou get to my novel yet?'
'What?'
'Have you read my novel yet?'
'Ah. Pharsin.' Rodney collected himself. 'The thing is, I've been trying to make time for it in the afternoons. But the thing is...' He gazed unhappily down Greenwich Avenue. Sunday morning, and everyone was staggering around with their personal burden of prolixity, of fantastic garrulity, of uncontainable communicativeness: the Sunday *Times*. 'The thing is...'

The thing was that Rodney worked every morning and drunkenly socialized every evening, and in the afternoons—the only time of day he might conceivably pick up a book, or at any rate a magazine or a catalogue—he went to bed. With humming ears. And perpendicular in his zeal.

'Come on, man. This is getting insane.'

Rodney remembered a good tip about lying: stay as close to the truth as you dare. 'I've been trying to make time for it in the afternoons. But in the afternoons... My lady friend, do you see. I uh, "entertain" her in the afternoons.'

Pharsin assumed a judicious air.

'For instance,' Rodney enthused, 'on Friday afternoon I was just settling down to it. And in she came. I had your novel on my lap.'

This was of course untrue. Pharsin's ruffled, slewing typescript had never made it on to Rodney's lap. It was still under the piano, or in whatever corner or closet he had booted it into, months ago.

'She come every day?'

'Except weekends.'

'So what's your solution, Rod?'

'I'm going to clear some evenings. Settle down to it.'

'You say Friday afternoon you had my novel on your lap?'

'Just settling down to it.'

'OK. What's the title?'

Pharsin stood there, skyscrapering over him. Each of his teeth was about the size of Rodney's head. When he leaned over to spit in the gutter, you'd think someone had voided a bucket from the third floor.

'Give it up! What's the fucking title?'

'Um,' said Rodney.

Pharsin he had first encountered in the south-west corner of Washington Square Park, that inverted parliament of chess, where the junkies were all Experts, the winos were all Grand Masters, and the pizza-bespattered babblers and bums were all ex-World Champions. Rodney, who for a year had played second board for the University of Suffolk, approached the marble table over which Pharsin showily presided. In half an hour he lost a hundred dollars.

Never in his dealings with the thirty-two pieces and the sixty-four squares had Rodney been so hilariously outclassed. He was a mere centurion, stupidly waiting, in his metal miniskirt, his short-sword at his side; whereas Pharsin was the career gladiator, hideously experienced with the weighted net and the bronze trident. After half a dozen moves Rodney could already feel the grip of the cords, the bite of the tines. In the third game Pharsin successfully dispensed with the services of his queen: things looked good until Black drove the first of his rooks into the groin of White's defence.

They got talking as they loped together, serenaded by saxophones and sirens, past the bobbing dope-dealers of the north-west corner and out on to Eighth Street.

'Do you uh, "make a living" at it?'

'Used to,' said Pharsin through the backbeat of nineteen different boomboxes and radios turned out on to the road. 'Chess hustling is down with the economy. Forcing me to diversify.'

Rodney asked him what kind of thing.

'It's like this: chess is an art. You can do one art, you can do them all.'

Rodney said how interesting, and toddled on after him. It seemed to Rodney that he could walk through Pharsin's legs and out the other side. No, not enough room: muscles stood like heavies leaning against the tunnel walls. Pharsin's head, perched up there on that body, could only look to be the shape and size of a car neckrest. Rodney experienced respect for Pharsin's head. Whatever chess was (an art, a game, a fight), chess was certainly a mountain. Rodney strolled its foothills. Whereas the forward-leaning cliff face that closed out the sky had Pharsin halfway up it.

'You see this?'

Halting, Pharsin from inside his hoodie produced a fistful of scrolled paper: an essay, a polemic, entitled 'The Co-Incidence of the Arts, Part I: The Indivisibility of Poetry, Photography, and Dance.' Rodney ran his eye down the opening sentence. It was the kind of sentence that spent a lot of time in reverse gear before crunching itself into first.

'Are you sure you mean "coincidence"? Not uh, "correspondence"?'

'No. Co-incidence. The arts happen in the same part of the brain. That's how come I hyphenate. Co-incidence.'

Rodney had a lot of time for coincidence. Everything he now had he owed to coincidence. It happened on a country lane half a mile from his grandmother's house: a head-on collision between two

Martin Amis

Range Rovers, both of them crammed with patrilinear Peels. All else
followed from this: title, nerve, Rock, America, sex, and the five
thousand twenty-dollar bills underneath his studio floor. And talent
too, he thought: maybe.

'You English?'

'Oh, very much so.'

'My wife is English also. The oppressiveness of the class system
cause her to leave your shores.'

'I sympathize. It can be very wearing. Is she in the arts too, your
wife?'

'Yeah. She does—'

But Pharsin's monosyllable was quite cancelled by city stridor—
someone detonating a low-yield nuclear weapon or dropping a
dumpster from a helicopter. 'And yourself?' said Rodney.

'Sculptor. Mathematician. Choreographer. Percussionist. Essayist.
Plus the art you and I engaged in some while ago.'

'Oh, I remember,' said Rodney humbly. 'I'm a painter. With
other interests.' And he said what he usually said to Americans,
because it was virtually true, geographically (and what would *they*
know?): 'I studied literature at Cambridge.'

Pharsin gave a jolt and said, 'This intrigues me. Because I've
recently come to think of myself as primarily a novelist. Now, my
friend. There's something I'm going to ask you to do for me.'

He listened, and said yes. Why not? Rodney reckoned that
Pharsin, after all, would be incredibly easy to avoid.

Pharsin said, 'I'll be in an excellent position to monitor your
progress with it.'

Rodney waited.

'You don't recognize me. I work the door of your building.
Weekends.'

'Oh of course you do.' In fact, Rodney had yet to begin the task
of differentiating the three or four black faces that scowled and
glinted through the gloom of his lobby. 'The coincidence,' he mused,
'of the arts. Tell me, are you all a little family down there?'

'Why would we be? I don't associate with those animals. Now.
I'll bring you my novel early tomorrow. Casting all false modesty
aside, I don't believe you'll have a problem falling under its spell.'

'Um,' said Rodney.

'Three months you been sitting on it, and you don't even know the fucking *title*?'

'Um,' he repeated. Like the novel itself, the title, Rodney recalled, was very long. Pharsin's typescript ran to more than 1,100 pages: single-spaced. Pharsin said it comprised exactly one million words—a claim (Rodney felt) that few would ever call him on. 'It's very *long*.' He looked up into Pharsin's blood-spoked eyes and said, '"The..."'

'*The* what?'

'"The Words of..." Wait. "The Noise of the..."'

'Sound.'

'"The Noise of the Sound..."'

'Bullshit! *The Sound of the Words, the Sound of the Words,* man. *The Sound of the Words, the Sound of the Words.*'

'Exactly. *The Sound of the Words, the Sound of the Words.*'

'Commit the fucking energy, man. I say this because I'm convinced that your effort will be rewarded. The structure you'll particularly relish. And also the theme.'

After another forty column-inches of reproach, dissimulated threat, moral suasion and literary criticism, Pharsin wrapped things up, adding, as an audible afterthought,

'Thirteen weeks. And he doesn't even know its *name*?'

'Forgive me. I'm stupefied by, uh, "amorous excess".'

'That I can believe. You look totally fucked out. Man, take care: you're going to blow away on the wind. My marriage has survived thus far, but woman action and woman trouble I know all about. What's her name?'

Rodney murmured some feminine phoneme: Jan or Jen or June. But the truth was he didn't know *her* name either.

'We've slimed.'

'Good man. Tell all.'

This time Rod and Rock were to be found in some kind of *Irish* restaurant high up on Lexington Avenue. They occupied two places near the head of a table laid for eighteen. Their practice on such occasions was to meet an hour early, to chat and drink cocktails,

Martin Amis

before some Americans showed up and paid for it all. This night, in
Rock's comfortable company, Rodney belied his eight and a half
stone. Pared down to the absolute minimum (carrying just two or
three extra grams in that buxom upper lip), he nevertheless seemed
to share in his friend's bland rotundity; they both wore the
cummerbund of inner fatness conferred by their class. Black Velvet,
quaffed from pewter tankards, was their tipple of the hour.

'What's there to say?' said Rodney. 'Frankly, I'm speechless.
Words cannot...'

'Dear oh dear. Well describe her body at least.'

'Actually I'd rather not. I mean there's nothing to say, is there,
when things go so gloriously?'

'...It's Mrs Peterson, isn't it?' Rock paused unkindly. 'No. Far too
swarthy for you. You like the dairy-product type. Raised on curds and
whey. They have to look like English roses. Or you get culture shock.'

'How very wrong you are,' said Rodney in a strained voice. 'It
may interest you to know that my inamorata happens to
be..."bleck".'

'Bleck?'

'Bleck,' said Rodney with emphasis. It sounded more like *blick*
than *black*. A year or two ago they might have said *bluhck*. But
having largely shed their class signatures, the two men were now
recultivating them.

'Bleck?' repeated Rock. 'You mean a proper...? What are they
calling themselves these days. A proper American-African?'

'African-American.' As he continued, Rodney's voice grew
drowsy, and it was with a haggard sensuality—slow inhalations,
feeding some inner fire—that he relished his nightly cigarette. 'Well,
African. I sense Africa in her. I taste Africa in her. One of the French
bits, probably. Senegal, perhaps. Sierra Leone. Guinea-Bissau.'

Rock was looking at him.

'She moves like an empress. A Dahomey Amazon. Cleopatra
was very dark, you know.'

'So she's posh, too, is she? As well as bleck. Where does *she* say
she's from?'

Simultaneously ignoring this and rousing himself, Rodney said,
'It's what's so wonderful about America. There *aren't* any good bleck

girls in London. All they've got there are those squeaky Cockneys. Magnificent creatures, some of them, but—quite impossible. Simply not on the cards, over there. But over here, in the great uh, "melting pot".'

'The salad bowl.'

'I beg your pardon?' said Rodney, looking around for the salad bowl.

'They call it the salad bowl now. Not the melting pot.'

'Do they indeed.'

'In a way, you could say that English blecks are posher than their American cousins.'

'How so?'

'How *so*?'

Here were two men living in a silent movie: when they were alone together, the millennium seemed about a century away. Rock was now about to speak of the historical past; but his urbanity faltered, and he suddenly sounded sober.

'Oh come on. We know a little bit about this, don't we? The English contingent, they were shipped in after the war. To run the tubes and so on. And the buses. Contract labour. But not—but not like American blecks.'

'Same stock, though. One imagines.'

Rod and Rock: their family trees stood tall. Their family trees stood tall and proud. But what kind of trees were they—weeping willow, sallow, mahogany, ash? And something ailed or cankered them, shaping their branches all arthritic and aghast... The Peels had been among the beneficiaries when, on a single day in 1661, Charles II created thirteen baronetcies on the plantation island of Barbados. Rock's lot, the Robvilles, rather disappointingly (rather puzzlingly, from Rodney's point of view), didn't go back quite so far. But the Peels and the Robvilles alike had flourished at a time when every English adult with cash or credit owned a piece of it: a piece of slavery. The place where Rock's dad lived had been assembled by massive shipwright profits out of Liverpool, circa 1750. Intelligence of these provenances could never be openly acknowledged by either of the two men. Lifelong inhibition protected them: in their childhood it was like something terrible hiding under the bed. Still, Rock was a businessman. And he had never expected business to be pretty. He said,

'There's not much in it, I suppose. But the English contingent were freed longer ago.'

'Yes, well,' pondered Rodney, 'I suppose you can't get much less posh than being a slave. But that's to forget what they might have been originally.'

'Posh in Africa.'

'In a way. You know, Africa was quite advanced for a while. I mean, look at African art. Exquisite. Ancient, but immediate. Immediate. They had great civilizations there when England was just a sheep-dip. Ages ago.'

'What have you been reading? The *Amsterdam News*?'

'No. *Ebony*. But it's true! We're just upstarts and counterjumpers compared to them. Scum, Rock. Anyway I have a hunch my one came direct from Africa. The Sudan, quite possibly. Timbuktu was apparently an incredible city. Crammed with princes and poets and amazing houris. Jezebel was of—'

'Did you say amazing hoorays? Sorry? Oh never *mind*. What sort of accent does she have? Your one.'

'I don't know.'

'What's her name?'

'I don't know.'

Rock paused and said, 'Pray describe this relationship. How did you meet? Or don't you know that either?'

'We met in a bar. But it wasn't like that.'

They met in a bar but it wasn't like that. It was like this.

Rodney had just asked for a Bullshot. Consisting of vodka and consommé, a Bullshot is arguably a bullshit drink; but Rodney, his eyes lurking and cowering behind his dark glasses, badly needed his Bullshot. What he really felt like was a Bloodshot. He wore a pinched seersucker suit and a grimy cravat. He had spent the morning in a sepulchral brownstone on East Sixty-fifth Street, doing what he could with the long upper lip and ridiculously interproximate eyebrows of a Mrs Sheehan—wife to the chat-show king.

'Worcestershire sauce, if you please, and the juice of at least one lemon.'

'You know something? I could listen to your voice all day.'

It was not the first time Rodney had been paid this compliment. Sequestered in a deceptively mild cocaine hangover, he said, 'How sweet of you to say so.'

'No. Really.'

'So kind.'

This waitress at some point or other might have wanted to be an actress. She might have had the odd prompting towards the stage. But not recently. And anyway Rodney was looking past her, Rodney was flinching past her...

So. She was up on a stool at the counter—and up on the turret of her swivelling haunches, rising in her seat whenever they crossed or uncrossed, uncrossed or crossed. Rodney stared. There she sat, drinking milky tea from a braced glass, being bawled at by some ballgame on the perched TV, and exchanging vigorous but inaudible small talk with a hidden figure behind the bar. Unquestionably she was a person of colour, and that colour—or so it seemed to Rodney—was *american*. As in black, brown, american; then beige, white, pink... Beyond this room lay another room, where some kind of talent contest was being noisily disputed. Poetry readings. Monologues. Stand-up.

Rodney was staring at her with a pang of recognition, although he knew she was a stranger. He thought he had seen her before, in the neighbourhood. But never fully seen her. Because she was the woman on the street whom you never see fully, sent here to elude you, always turning away or veering off, or exactly maintaining parallax with mailbox or tree bole, or vanishing for ever behind the burning glass of a phonebooth or under the black shadow of a truck. Indignant poems have been written about these women—about these *desaparacidas*. Even the douce Bloom grew petulant about them. Men mind, because for once they are demanding so little, no contact, just a free gaze at the moving form. And this was Rodney's initial disposition. He didn't want to date her. He wanted to paint her.

'There you go, sir.'

'Thank you most awfully.'

'That voice!'

Even now, at the bar, she always seemed to be occluded or

eclipsed. In particular a pink lady, a Germanic middle-aged blonde with a whole reef of freckles and moles on her bared throat (how Rodney struggled, each day, with such imperfections in his sitters) kept masking her, kept hiding her and then revealing her. Suddenly the view cleared, and he absorbed the lavish power of her thighs— then her face, her glance, her unspecific smile. What she said to him was Talent. Not just *her* talent. His talent, too.

'Waitress! Waitress! Ah. Thank you. I wonder if you would very kindly lend me your pen there. For just a couple of minutes.'

'Certainly!'

'Thank you *so* much.'

He knew what to do. At his agent's prompting, Rodney had had some cards printed up, headed: SIR RODNEY PEEL (BARONET): PORTRAITIST. The flipside gave an example of the portraitist's art: looking like non-identical twins, the wife and daughter of a burglar-alarm tycoon were pooling their repose on a pair of French armchairs. Rodney started writing. He still wasn't entirely reconciled to that bracketed 'Baronet'. At first he had argued for the more discreet and conventional abbreviation, '(Bt)'. But he had eventually submitted to the arguments of his agent: according to Rock, Americans might think that Bt was short for Bought.

In the great wreaths and plumes of his embarrassing calligraphy Rodney said that he was an English painter, come to America; said how rare it was, even in this city, with its famed diversity, to encounter a face so *paintable* as her own; said he would, of course, remunerate her for her indulgence; said his rates were high. Rodney then used up a second card and most of a third with a fantastic array of apologies and protestations, of microscopic diffidencies—and then added a fourth, for her reply.

'Waitress? Excuse me! Excuse me!' Rodney's voice was having to contend with the espresso machine and the robust applause coming from the back room, as well as with the gasps and hiccups of human communion, all around: like a school yard. But Rodney's voice was bigger than he was. Trained by centuries of hollering across very large rooms.

'Ah. There you are.'

The waitress stood there as Rodney outlined her mission. And it seemed that her avowed preparedness to listen to Rodney's voice all day came under immediate strain. Her face toughened, and she knocked a fist into her hip as her shoulders gave a single shrug or shudder. But Rodney just tapped his calling cards into alignment and contentedly added,

'Now, not the orange-haired one, do you see, with all the freckles. Behind her. The dark one.' Rodney had a witty notion. His interlocutor was a cocktail waitress: why not speak her language? 'The Pink Lady: no. By no means. Rather, the Black Velvet. The Black Velvet.'

He tried to watch as the waitress delivered his note. Its recipient, again, seemed to glance and smile his way; but then a wall of new bards or jokesmiths, heading for the back room, interposed itself, and when the room cleared she was gone.

The shadow of the waitress dropped past him. He looked down at the tray she had placed on his table: the check, plus the fourth postcard, which said tersely and in neat small caps: 'You talk too much.'

Triple-lipped, Rodney paid and added fifteen per cent and took his leave.

It was as he crossed Tenth Street that he realized she was following him. Realized, too, in the light of day, that she was as black as night. And twice his size. His first impulse (one not quickly overcome) was to make a run for it. On Eleventh Street the darkened window of Ray's Pizza told Rodney that she was still behind him. He halted and turned, weakly squinting, and she halted, intelligently smiling, and he took a step towards her, and she took a step back, and he moved on, and she followed. Across Twelfth Street. Now with every step his legs were getting heavier and tenderer; it felt like the marrow-ache of adolescent growth. Despairingly he turned left on Thirteenth Street. She stopped following him. She overtook him. And as her pace slowed and slackened, and as he attended to the amazing machine of her thighs and buttocks, the parts accommodating themselves so equably in the close quarters of her skirt, all his fears (and all thoughts of his easel) gave way to a reptile vacuity. For the first time in his life Rodney was ready for anything. No questions asked.

When she reached his building she turned and waited. He

summoned breath to speak—but she smoothly raised a vertical forefinger to her lips. And he understood, and felt like a child. He talked too much. He talked too much... Mounting the steps, he pushed the inner glass door and held it open behind him; when he felt the transfer of its weight he withstood a rush of intimacy, as intimate as the press of boiling breasts on his spine. Dismissing the elevator as an impossibility, he began the long ascent, afraid to turn but minutely alert to her tread. His door. His keys all jammed and tangled in their ring, which he weepily picked at. Each lock turned a different way, the English way, the American way. He pushed, and felt the air rearrange itself as her shape moved past his back.

Many times, during that first half-hour, speech gulped up in Rodney's throat—and just as often her forefinger sought her lips (and there would be a frown of real warning). The finger side-on, always. But then they were standing near the piano, when she had completed her tour of his space; Rodney swallowed his most recent glottal stop, and her finger was once again raised; only now she turned it, rotating her whole hand through ninety degrees, showing him the bruised pink of the nail. After a beat or two Rodney took this as an invitation. He hovered nearer still and strained upwards. He kissed.

'Well what the fuck's the story, Rod? You read my novel yet or what?'

Jesus: the guy was like a neighbour's dog that just kept on hating you. You never gave him an instant's thought until there he was, balanced upright on the tautness of his leash, and barking in your face.

'Not yet,' Rodney conceded, as he stepped out of the elevator.

'Now this is basically some *rude shit* we're looking at here. Why the contempt, Rod? What's your answer?'

Rodney wrongly regarded himself as an expert at excuses. After all, he and excuses had been through a lot together. Gazing upwards, with tubed lips, he softly said,

'You're going to hate me for this.'

'I hate you already.'

Feeling a furry hum in either armpit, Rodney decided to change tack. The occasion called for something more than a negligent simper. 'But there was nothing I could do,' he found himself saying. 'My aunt died, do you see. Suddenly. And I had to compose the uh, "eulogy" for her funeral.'

'Your aunt where? In England?'

'No. She lives in...' This was not the verb Rodney wanted. 'She was in uh, Connecticut. It was all very awkward. I took the train to, to Connecticut, do you see. Now normally I'd have put up with Auntie Jean, but her, her son was there, with his family, and I...'

When he wasn't talking, which wasn't often, Pharsin had a stunned look. As if he couldn't believe he was listening to a voice other than his own. Rodney's agonizing tale had brought them out on to Thirteenth Street. In the middle distance the Empire State seemed to sway for a moment, and was then restiffened by its stress equations.

'...and *that* train was cancelled too. So with one thing and another I've had my hands full all week.'

Pharsin's expression had softened to something more quizzical, even indulgent. He said, 'I see it. I see what you're doing here, Rod. You're digging yourself into a situation. You *want* to read my novel. But it's like you left it so long you can only see it coming back the other way.' Pharsin tapped his temple. 'I understand the mind. I know the mind. Last year I took a lot of—'

He paused as if to listen. Rodney was expecting the next word to be *Prozac*. But Pharsin went on quickly,

'—psychology courses and I know how we do this, how we set these traps for ourselves and walk right into them. I understand. Rod?'

'Yes, Pharsin?'

'You're going to read my book next week. Isn't that right?'

'Pharsin, I will.'

'One more thing. You got to imagine that novel is written in my blood. In my blood, Rod. It's all there. Everything I am is in that—'

Rodney tuned out for a while and listened to Manhattan. Listened to Manhattan, playing its concerto for horn.

'—the trauma and the wounds. Written in my *blood*, Rod. Written in my blood.'

That night (it was Sunday, and Rock was out of town) Rodney faced a void of inactivity. He was so at a loss that for the first time ever he contemplated digging out his typescript of *The Sound of the Words, the Sound of the Words*. But there turned out to be a

Martin Amis

reasonably diverting documentary about synchronized swimmers on TV. And he managed to kill the rest of the evening by washing his hair and rolling around in twenty-dollar bills.

'I see her in an Abyssinian setting. Or Ancient Ethiopia. She's a Nefertiti. Or one of the Candaces. Here'll do. Actually I think it's a gay place but they don't seem to mind me coming here.'

No irony was intended or understood by this last remark, and Rock followed Rodney unsmilingly down the steps.

Rock's older brother Inigo had known Rodney at Eton; and in his schooldays Rodney had apparently been famed for his lending library of glamour magazines and his prolific onanism. So Rock sensed no sexual ambiguity in his friend. But others did. For instance, it had never occurred to any of his sitters' husbands that Rodney was straight. And Rodney himself had entertained inevitable doubts on this score, in the past, in London, lying on his side and apologetically stroking the back of yet another unslain giantess of the gentry.

They ordered their Highballs. The clientele was all-male but also middle-aged (woollen, paunchy), and Rodney received no more than his usual deal of stares.

He said, 'This'll amuse you. The first time we uh, "hid the salami"... No. The first time I *revealed* the salami—I felt a real pleb. A real cur. Like an Untouchable.'

'How so?'

'I'm a Cavalier.'

'Me too.'

'Of course. We're English. But over here they're all Roundheads. It's posh to be a Roundhead here. Only the hicks and Okies are Cavaliers.' Rodney well remembered Mrs Vredevoort, wife to the construction grandee: how, when at last she had found the salami (the salami having been located and identified), she gave a little mew of surprised distaste, and immediately came up for air. 'Ours look like joints. As opposed to cigarettes. Which is what they're used to. I bet they're all Roundheads in Africa.'

'But there's not much difference, is there, when you've got the horn.'

'Exactly! That's *exactly* it. Anyway, mine didn't seem to mind.

224

She didn't say anything.'

'She *never* says anything.'

'True,' said Rodney. 'You know, there's just one thing she won't let me do. No, nothing like that. She won't let me *paint* her. Or even photograph her.'

'Superstitious.'

'And I feel if I could just paint her...'

'All slime,' said Rock, 'and no paint. A reversal of your usual set-up.'

'Balls. I did pretty well with the wives. All slime and no speech. That's what's really weird.'

'Come out to the house this weekend. It's finished now.'

'Ooh. That does sound like a good idea.'

Love without words. A caveman could do it. And it sounded like something that Picasso or Beckett might have pulled off. But Sir Rodney Peel? He had never shown any sign of pretending to such masterful purity. More scavenger than predator, in matters of the heart, Rodney was the first on the scene after the big cats had eaten their fill. He liked his women freshly jilted. His lips knew the sweet tang of liquefying mascara; his eyes knew the webby rivulets it formed on the blotting paper of a powdered cheek. He was an old hand at the consoling caress. Rhythmically he would smooth the sideswell of the breast, murmuring *there there*... It suited him. Sexual expectation, in such circumstances, was generally low. In such circumstances, impotence could almost be taken as a gallantry.

Love without voices. Usually she came around half past two. Flushed and blotchy from his shower, wearing his long blue robe, Rodney would be lying on the chaise longue, trying to skim a magazine or else just dumbly waiting. Sometimes he went and stuck his head out of the window and tried to glimpse her as she glided under the ginkgo trees; once he saw her out there in the middle of the street, sharply questioning the driver of the cab from which she had slid. When he heard her keys in the locks, he felt, beneath his robe, the ceremony of painless circumcision.

A smile was all she wanted by way of greeting. Humbly he looked on as she walked the room, her head dipped over her folded arms. She had arrived at his place; but it took time for her to get around to him in her thoughts. Then she would move towards the two lacquered screens that bowered the bed. She undressed matter-of-factly, laying her clothes on the chair (as if ready for school). Around now a switch would be thrown in Rodney's head, immersing him in greater gravity. His ears were trained inwards only, and he listened to the muscles creaking in the root of his tongue.

There *was* something primitive about it—about what followed. Not least in the startling elevations engineered by his blood. But she was one thing and he was the other. Rodney Peel had come to Africa. Her body seemed preternatural in its alternations of the soft and the hard; and her skin, unlike his own, did not reflect the light but absorbed it, confidently annexing its powers. As for her scent, it seemed to Rodney to be of a higher proof, or just more concentrated. And his thoughts went further—to her volcanic breasts, her zebra-ripping teeth! Sun-helmeted and canvas-shoed (and settling down to his task of tribute), Sir Rodney parts the lianas and the sweating fronds and sees... Actually it reminded him of a barbecue at Rock's place in Quogue, when he pierced the charred surface of the beef and saw that the flesh was still very rare.

Afterwards she rested. She never slept. Quite often, and increasingly cravenly, he would point to his easel or his brushes; but she always swiped a finger through the air and turned away. And once, early on, when he sat on the bed with his cocked sketch-pad, she wrenched it from his grasp with an awful severity in her snuff-coloured eyes. With real strength, too—a strength he knew all about. Still, she had created or revealed something in him, and he thought it might be Talent. Rodney's loft contained no internal walls, so he was allowed to watch her as she used the bathroom or made the milky tea she liked. She had the overdeveloped upward-surging calf muscles of a dancer. All her movements showed the mechanical security and high definition of intense technique. Rodney thought about it: of course she was an artist. A non-businesswoman under thirty-five living in Manhattan? Of course she was an artist. A dancer. Maybe a *singer*. The performing arts, without question. But which one?

She never slept. She drank her tea, and rested, sighing sometimes and powerfully yawning, but she never slept. Her thoughtfulness seemed centralized and assiduous, as if she were following an argument taking place on the near side of her eyes. Rodney worried about interrupting this argument when he later returned to the bed, but her body always fully admitted him to its heat. He often imagined, as he squirmed and bounced above her, that the first word he would ever hear her say would be the forename of another man... All the same, what they did and made together had nothing to do with art. No play: sheer earnest. It felt like honest work.

'Hey. Hey! Ain't no damn use you sneaking out like that. Have you read my novel yet?'

'*Yes,*' said Rodney.

Rodney said Yes, not because it was true or anything like that, but to make a change from saying No. It was an impulse thing. And Rodney was surprised it worked so well.

Pharsin stepped back. For several seconds he wore a plugged expression. Then with his brow softly working he bent and lowered his head. Rodney almost reached up a hand to stroke the black filings of Pharsin's hair.

'So, man. What did you think?'

It was gently said. What a welcome change this makes, thought Rodney (putting all that unpleasantness behind him): these chaps are perfectly sweet and reasonable, when tactfully handled. He laughed, saying,

'Ho no, my friend. With a novel like that...with a *writer* like that, I'm not going to stand here in a doorway as if I'm talking about the weather. Oh no.'

'But you saying it measures up?'

'*Oh* no. Pharsin, don't try and do this! You my friend are going to come up to my studio. One day very soon. We're going to take the phone uh, "off the hook", put a log on the fire, and open a bottle of good red wine. A claret, I rather think—a nice sharp Morgon. *Then* we'll talk.'

'When?' said Pharsin, with familiar vigilance.

'Actually there's a good reason why we can't do it this weekend.'

'What's that?'

'I'm *re*reading it.'

'...I applaud your rigour. Such works seldom render up their secrets on a first absorption.'

'Exactly so.'

'As I've said, Rod, a great deal hinges on your critique. It's been suggested to me that I'm not cut out for fiction, and I'm impatient for a second response. I'm at a stage in my life where... You got a minute to hear this?'

Half an hour later Rodney said, 'Of course. On second thoughts, perhaps we'd be better off with something thicker—like a Margaux. We'll have some Stilton. And black olives...'

On parting, the two men performed an old ritual (now long disused): a series of street-guy handshakes. Rodney, as ever, looked like someone slowly and painfully learning how to play Paper, Scissors, Stone.

It was a gallery opening near Tompkins Square Park—an occasion sponsored by a new brand of vodka, and marked by a nostalgic deluge of Martinis. Rod and Rock had established themselves near the caterers' table. Sexually at peace, and additionally numbed by cocaine, Rodney was temporarily under the impression that everybody loved him. Now he bantered with the barman, affecting interest in the lot of barmen everywhere. Though invariably polite to servants, Rodney never differentiated them. Failing to see, for example, that this waiter was definitely an actor who had waited way too long.

'I have reached a bold conclusion,' he said, swinging round on Rock. 'All my troubles with women come from...from words. From speech.'

And there was something in this. Surprisingly, for such a fragile and ingratiating presence, Rodney, over the years, had had his face slapped practically out of alignment, so often had his patter gone awry. He was a flatterer—by profession. He believed in flattery and was always trying to deploy it. But something went wrong with the words: they came out, as his mother would say, just a bit *off*. If conversation was an art, then Rodney was no artist. He created ratty atmospheres around himself. 'Put a sock in it, Rodney,' they would say. 'Oh shut up, Rodney, do.' And the fat beak of his upper lip, after framing its latest unwelcome bauble, would stoically self-transect. Prose wasn't any better. His scented notes routinely caused year-long *froideurs*: 'non-speaks', as in 'She and I are now on non-speaks.' Non-speaks: that's how they should have *started*...

'Silence,' he went on, 'was the only reason I got anywhere with the wives. You can't speak while you paint.'

'I thought women liked the kind of rot you talk.'

'Me too. But they don't. I always seem to say the wrong thing.'

A while ago, as an experiment, Rodney had reopened his flirtations with two of the wives: Mrs Globerman, wife to the telecommunications tycoon, and Mrs Overbye, wife to the airline boss. The idea was to see if his new puissance was transferable and could be tried out elsewhere. Both efforts were failures—impossibilities. The things he said and the things they said. The things they all said. It seemed far stranger than silence. With these women Rodney had felt the utter superfluity of human speech. So the rain held off. So tell me about your week. So how have you been? Oh, you know: so-so. So-and-so said this and so-and-so said that. So tired. So soon? And so on and so on.

'You and your bleck girl seem to be made for each other.'

'We do. We are. Capital cocktails, these. Blimey, though. Bit strong, aren't they? Feeling rather tight. It's loosening my tongue. Rock, can I ask you something? Why do I *know* it's going to end in tears? Why do I feel all this anxiety? And all this guilt?'

'Because you're getting something for nothing. Yet again.'

Rodney's eyes widened. He thought about the first time: the fraudulent feeling, when he watched her undress. As if he had reached his objective not by normal means (flattery, false promises, lies) but by something worse: black magic, or betrayal. For a moment he had the strange suspicion that she was his cousin, and they were playing doctors.

'Because you've bucked the work ethic. Yet again. Oh. I'm seeing Jaguar tomorrow. Have you done something with that money yet?'

'Yes,' said Rodney. He *had* done something with that money, if you counted counting it and rolling around in it and spending a lot of it on cocaine.

'I'll check with Jagula. I mean Jaguar. Whew, that last one just

Martin Amis

hit me.' Rock went on in a smudged voice, 'I sometimes feel like a trader in slaves. A white-slaver. Onna butlers. Anna nannies. Maybe that's what's worrying you. It's just because she's bleck.'

Rodney said suddenly, 'Blick? No.'

Could that be it? No. No, because he had always felt that she was a woman who carried freedom around with her. On her person. Somewhere in the jaws it seemed to lurk.

Soon afterwards he started to find the bruises.

Nothing florid or fulminant. Just a different kind of dark beneath the dark. The hip, the shoulder, the upper arm. On noticing a new one, Rodney would arrest his movements and attempt to meet her eye—but he never achieved this, and, having faltered, went back to what he was doing before; and afterwards he didn't smile at her in praise and gratitude, as he usually did, turning instead to the stain on the wall, oval and the colour of nicotine, where his head had rested these many months.

He thought he knew something about women and silence. There they would sit before him, the wives, engaged in self-conscious small talk as he made his preliminary sketches—as he situated the human posture against the jut and rake of the chair, the wall cabinet, the low table. Artists of course crave silence. They wish their sitters dead, stilled: a bowl of apples, a wineglass, a cold fish. But the sitter is alive, and must talk, perhaps sensing that speech is needed to bring colour and indignation to the throat, the cheeks, the eyes. And the painter chats back with his skeleton staff of words until the moment comes when he is incapable of vocalization: when, in short, he is getting the head. Even Rodney knew this moment of deafened concentration (it felt like Talent). And the sensitive sitter would come to note such moments, maintaining a pious hush until her next thrice-hourly intermission. Her breather, when it was OK for her to be alive again.

He thought he knew something about women and silence. But this? Rodney slipped from the bed and, in his blue robe, set about the preparation of English Breakfast Tea. He watched her through the gap between the two screens: the pillow clutched to her breast like a baby. And always she was following the argument inside her own head. The bruise on her shoulder, tinged with betel or cinnabar,

230

looked artificially applied—caste mark, warpaint. Rodney assessed it with a professional eye. It was no accident that he worked in oil. Oil was absolutely right. His brush, he realized, was not an artist's wand so much as a cosmeticist's tweezer. Oil, in his hands, was the elixir of youth. It would be different with her, he felt. Because everything else was different with her. But he would never dare broach it now.

For an instant she loomed over him and then moved past, to the shower. Rodney had never supposed that he was her single—or even her principal—erotic interest. How could he own *her*? He thought of a scene in a huge American novel he had read, years back, where a young man comes of age, pleasantly, in a Chicago bordello. And it went something like, He had used what others used. So what? That's what cities are.

On the other hand he suddenly knew what he wanted to say to her. Three words: a verb flanked by two personal pronouns.

'Hey. *Hey.*'
No black shape—no roller or mugger, no prison-yard rapist, no Hutu warrior, no incensed Maroon on the blazing cane fields of Saint Domingue—could be as fearful to Rodney, now, as the man who occasionally guarded his building: namely Pharsin. Rodney's weekends were entirely devoted to avoiding him: four of the last five had been spent in Quogue. He had even made a couple of phone calls about the possibility of moving. There was apparently a place in midtown, quite near Rock's offices...

'Ah, Pharsin. There you are.'

Rodney turned, physically wincing, but only from the rain. He was afraid of Pharsin, and generally well attuned to threat. But his anguish here was almost wholly social.

'What's the latest, Rod?'

'Yes, it's high time we uh, "broke bread". I find myself leaning towards a Chambertin-Clos de Bezel and a swampy Camembert.'

'I keep hearing about these goddamn wines you got. But I'm thinking these are the exact same hoops we were going through before. What do I got to do, Rod? It's not just me who's hurting—it's everyone around me. I never thought a man could do this to me.

I never thought a man could reduce me to this.'

It was raining. Raining on the terrible city, with people suffering through it and giving voice to their pain, groaning, swearing, babbling. In New York, if you had no one to talk to or shout at, then there was always yourself: always yourself. As Rodney debarked his umbrella he noticed the way the raindrops fell from the lobes of Pharsin's childishly small ears.

'Friday at five.'

'That's in stone?'

'On my mother's life. Hock and smoked salmon might be more the thing. Or some Gewürztraminer. Or what about some Trockenbeerenauslese, with Turkish Delight?'

'Friday at five.'

'Busy week?' said Rock on Thursday evening. They were drinking in a bar they usually went to only very late at night: Jimmy's. Although he had been there perhaps a dozen times, it turned out that Rodney had no idea where it was. 'Where *is* Jimmy's?' he asked, as Rock guided him there. The place looked different, in the happy hour.

'Not really,' Rodney answered. 'But you know how it is in New York. You've got nothing on and you think, I know: I'll stay home and read a book. Then the next thing you know…there's an opening or something. And then you're bawling your head off across some restaurant.'

'Got anything on tonight? There's a freebie at some punk club in Brooklyn. I've got all-you-can-drink coupons. It doesn't start for hours and it'll be a bugger to get to.'

'Oh all right,' said Rodney.

The next day he left for Quogue rather earlier than usual. He rose at noon and, held upright only by the strata of dried come in his pyjamas, made tea. He took a fifty-minute shower. He performed surprisingly creditably during his tryst (she seemed relieved that afternoon, but expeditious) and he practically joined her in the elevator. To the weekday janitoriat he entrusted a long note for Pharsin about his aunt's exhumation and reburial in another plot; by way of a PS he switched their date to the same time on Monday.

Only when the Jitney was idling outside that cinema on its stop near the airport did Rodney question the packing choices in his garment bag: the three new magazines, along with his standard weekend kit.

Just gone one on Monday afternoon.

He was sitting at the kitchen table and reading—in preparation for his task—the back of a cereal packet. Lifting his head and blinking, he thought of the corpulent Victorian novels he had gaped his way through at university, the *Middlemarche*s and *Bleak House*s: they had taken him at least a month each. Still, he had never contemplated spending more than about half an hour with *The Sound of the Words, the Sound of the Words*. He was just beginning to reread the back of the cereal packet when he heard the keys in the door.

Her appearance almost shocked him into speech. What had happened was this. The argument which for months had been taking place inside her head, illegibly, was now written on the outside. For all to see. Her eyes steadily invited him to register this change: the nether lip all smudged and split, and the right cheekbone loudly marked, as if swiped with a hot daub of rouge. The thing that was wrong had now been stated, not by her but by the thing that was wrong.

Aghast, he tottered towards her. And found himself leniently received. He kissed her neck, her jaw, and, with circumspection, her mouth—but then all circumspection was lost. Fearfully and ardently, and for the last time, Sir Rodney Peel stoked the tarry blood of Eve.

Afterwards she did something she'd never done before. She didn't speak. No. She slept.

Rodney got to work, and quite noisily.

He dragged his easel across the floor, shifted the screens, and rattled around with his brushes. There was no sense of tiptoe in his body or his mind: her sleep seemed elementally sure, like hibernation. He pulled off the cover. She was lying on her side, the upper knee raised, one hand beneath the pillow and the other placed flat between her thighs. First get the head, he thought. Then get the neck. Then get the body.

'Artists are waiters!' he said. Waiting for the right thing in the right place at the right time. And with that he said goodbye to his discursive mind—until the painting was about done and somebody seemed to be banging on his door.

And Rodney spoke. In a childishly lucid voice he said, 'Oh dear. That will be Pharsin.'

She was looking up at him over her shoulder. And she spoke too. What she said was obliterating; but it wasn't the content—it was the style. Heard by him before only on English high streets, in supermarket checkout bays, in cauldrons of dry-cleaning. Maybe, too, in the squawk of the minicab switchboard, endured from the back seat, late at night. She said, 'Eez me yusband.'

'OPEN THIS FUCKING DOOR RIGHT NOW.'
Rodney would later describe the events that followed as 'something of a blur'. But in fact these events were clear. It was good that he was feeling so talented. And enormous chemicals were igniting his brain.

'YOU GOT ONE MINUTE. THEN I RIP THIS DOOR OFF THE FUCKING WALL. SIXTY. FIFTY-NINE. FIFTY-EIGHT.'

In an ideal world Rodney would have liked rather more than a minute to read *The Sound of the Words, the Sound of the Words.* But before he could read it he first had to *find* it.

Mrs Pharsin Courier having been shushed, and sealed off behind the twin screens, Rodney went and thrashed around in the double-doored closet (FIFTY-ONE), then bent himself under the piano (FORTY-FIVE), then wriggled about among the low shelves and shadows of the kitchen (THIRTY-FOUR). On the half-minute mark he paused to take stock—and to hoist a lumpy brown rug over the gap between the screens, noticing, as he did so, a suspicious wedge in the heap of death-grey newspapers silting up the corner beyond the bed. Rodney pounced (THIRTEEN): A Novel by Pharsin J. Courier (NINE, EIGHT). Skilfully he flipped it on to the table (SIX, FIVE), read half a phrase from page one ('Around noon Cissie thought she'd') and, as he rose to answer the door (THREE, TWO), half a phrase from page 1,123 ('seemed that way to Cissie'). And that was all he had time for.

'Ah, Pharsin. You respond to our cries of "Author! Author!" Step forward, sir, and be recognized. Now. If you'll just sit yourself there, I'll just...

'Now I'm not a writer,' said Rodney sternly, laying before Pharsin a glass of flat Pepsi. And a saucer with most of a Graham Cracker on it. Heartier and more various fare could have been plucked from the surface of Rodney's burred blue robe. 'I'm a painter, a visual artist. But as you have written elsewhere there is a certain...affinity between the arts. Now. The *first* time I read your book I was quite overwhelmed by this cascade of visual images. These things you describe—I felt I could reach out and touch them, smell them, taste them. Only on a second reading and, may I say, a third uh, "perusal" did I see that these images were, in fact, connected. In very intricate ways.'

Admiringly hefting the typescript in his hands, Rodney gave Pharsin a candid stare. So far so good. Pharsin's wrath, while still manifest, had reached some trance-like register. Rodney knew enough about novels to know that they all *tried* to do something like that: to connect image with theme. Cautiously he continued with his own variations, feeling the spasms of unused muscles: his lits, his crits. Yes, he could still swim in that pool. He could still ride that old bike.

'...shaping the whole composition. I could step back from the fretwork, the mouldings, the beadings, the uh, flutings and so on. I could step back from the gargoyles and see the whole cathedral.'

It looked for a moment as if Pharsin was going to ask a question about this cathedral: what it looked like or where it stood. So with a woozy roll of his head Rodney proceeded,

'And where did you find those *characters*? Quite incredible. I mean—take Cissie, for instance. How did you dream her up?'

'You like Cissie?'

'Cissie? Oh, Cissie! Cissie... By the time I was finished I felt I'd never known *anyone* as intimately as I knew her.' As he talked he started riffling fondly through the pages. 'Her thoughts. Her hopes and dreams. Her doubts. Her fears. I *know* Cissie. Like you'd know a sister. Or a lover.'

Rodney looked up. Pharsin's face was a screen of tears. Thoroughly emboldened, Rodney hunched himself forward and leafed through the text.

'That bit...that bit where she...when Cissie—'

'When she comes to the States?'

'Yes. When she comes to America.'

'The thing with Immigration?'

'Yes. Now *that scene*... Incredible. But so true! And then, after that—I'm trying to find it—the bit when she...'

'When she meets the guy?'

'Yes. The guy: now there's another character. And there's that great scene when they... Here it is. No. When they...'

'At the rent tribunal?'

'Oh now that scene. Can you believe that?'

'The judge?'

'Please,' said Rodney. 'Don't get me started on the judge.'

And so, for forty-five minutes, always a beat late, he somehow sang along with a song he didn't know. It seemed like scurvy work, of course; and it was strangely shaming to see Pharsin's face awaken out of hunger into vivid varieties of animation and delight (as at the chessboard, Rodney felt dwarfed by a superior force of life). It was scurvy work, but it was *easy*. He wondered why he hadn't done it months ago. Then Pharsin said,

'Enough. Forget the laughter, the characters, the images. What's *The Sound of the Words, the Sound of the Words* actually *saying*, Rod?'

'*The Sound of the Words, the Sound of the Words?*'

'What's it *saying*?'

'What's it saying? Well, it's a love story. It's about love in the modern world. How love gets hard to do.'

'But what's it *saying*?'

Ten seconds passed. And Rodney thought *fuck it* and said, 'It's about race. It's about the agony of the African-American male. It's about the need, the compulsion, to express that agony.'

Pharsin slowly reached out a hand towards him. Once more tears shone in the bloodbaths of his eyes.

'Thanks, Rod.'

'It's been a pleasure, Pharsin. Hello, is that the time? Shouldn't you be uh...?'

Until that moment Pharsin had seemed insensible of his surroundings. But now he jerked himself upright and began to move around the room with purposeful curiosity, one arm folded, the other crooked, a forefinger tapping on his chin, pausing to inspect a knick-knack here, a doodad there. Rodney wasn't thinking about his other guest (who, he assumed, would still be wedged behind the bed). He was thinking of her simulacrum: her portrait, arrayed on its stand, in blazing crime. Redigesting a mouthful of vomit, Rodney watched as Pharsin loped up to the easel and paused.

The black shape on the white sheet. The beauty and power of the rump and haunches. The sleeping face, half-averted. Rodney, out of sheer habit, had salved and healed her bruises. That was probably a good idea, he thought.

'This a real person pose for this?' Pharsin turned, artist to artist, and added, 'Or you take it from a book.'

'A book?'

'Yeah, like a magazine?'

'Yes. From a magazine.'

'Know who this kind of reminds me of? Cassie. My wife Cassie.' Pharsin smiled ticklishly as he followed the resemblance for another second or two. Then he rejected it. 'Maybe ten years ago. And she *never* had an ass like that in all her born days. Well, Rod. I want you to know what this last hour has meant to me. There was a man crying out in the dark here. You my friend have answered that cry. You've given me what I wanted: a hearing. I sent that novel to every registered publisher and agent in the city. All I got was a bunch of printed slips. Know what I think? They didn't read it. They didn't even *read* it, Rod.'

'That's a terrible thing, Pharsin. A terrible thing. Oh, by the way. You once told me that your wife was an artist. What kind is she?'

Then for a second their eyes met: horribly. And in Pharsin's face you could see the ageless and awful eureka of every stooge and sap and cinch. He said,

'You read my book and you're asking me what Cassie *does*?'

But it came to Rodney and he said, 'I know what *Cissie* does. In the book. I was just wondering how close you were sticking to life. I know what Cissie does.'

Pharsin's voice had Rodney by the lapels. It said, 'What?'

And he told him: 'Mime.'

With Pharsin caged and dropping in the elevator, and all loaded up with his typescript like a bearer, Rodney's head remained limp and bent, hangdog with relief. Even the strengthening conviction—not yet entire, needing more thought—that he, Rodney, had no talent: this brought relief. He let his head hang there a little longer, before he faced the music of human speech.

She said, 'You fucking done it now.'

He said, 'Oh dear. Have I said the wrong thing?'

'All a slight nightmare, really. She couldn't leave, do you see, because Pharsin was on the door. So she rather let me have it.' Rodney was no stranger to the experience of being denounced from dawn to dusk; but he wasn't used to accents such as hers. 'A terrible way for things to end. Our first night together and it was all talk and no sex. And such talk. She was *livid*.'

'What about? I wish those people would go away.'

Cocktails alfresco in Rockefeller Plaza: Amber Dreams under a cold blue sky. The square was punctuated by people dressed as mannequins and posing as statues. Just standing there with painted smiles.

'Oh God, don't ask,' said Rodney—for her grievances had been legion. 'She knew someone or something had been driving him nuts. She didn't know it was me. He'd never been violent before. It was me. *I* put those marks on her.'

'Oh come on. It's in their culture.'

Rodney coughed and said, 'Oh yeah. And she said, "He'll write another one now." She'd been moonlighting for two years. As a waitress. To support him. And she could tell I hadn't read it. By my voice.'

Rock looked on, frowning, as Rodney imitated her imitating him. It sounded something like: Ooh, ah say, wort simplay dezzling imagereh. Rodney said,

'She thought I was sneering at him. Him being bleck, do you see.'

'Yes, well, they can be quite chippy about that over here. Do you think his novel might have been *good*?'

'No one will ever know. But I do know this. She won't have to support him while he writes the second one.'

'Why not?'

'Because she stole my money.'

'Oh you *tit*. How many times did I tell you? Jesus Christ, what a silly old tart you are.'

'I know. I know. Waitress? If you please? Two Amber Dreams. No. *Four* Amber Dreams.'

'Are you telling me you just left it lying around?'

'In the middle of the night I... Wait. When I first met her, in the bar, do you see, I offered her five hundred dollars. No, as a sitter's fee. So I reckoned I owed her that. Went and got it out for her. Thought she was sleeping.'

'Oh you *tit*.'

'She did leave me the five hundred. Ah. Thank you most awfully.'

And on her way to the door she paused in front of the easel and whispered a single word (stressed as a menacing and devastating spondee): 'Wan*ker*.' And that was the end of that, he thought. That was the end of that.

Rock said, 'Were they in it together, do you think?'

'No no. No. It was all pure...coincidence.'

'Why aren't you angrier?'

'I don't know.'

Pharsin he never saw again. But he did see Pharsin's wife, once, nearly two years later, in London Town.

Rodney was consuming a tragic tea of crustless sandwiches in a dark café near Victoria Station. He had just left the Pimlico offices of the design magazine he worked part-time for, and was girding himself to catch a train for Sussex, where he would be met at the station by a childless divorcee in a Range Rover. He no longer wore a ponytail. And he no longer used his title. That sort of thing didn't seem to play very well in England any more. Besides, for a while Rodney had become very interested in his family tree; and this was his puny protest. The scars had deepened around his eyes. But not much else had changed.

Weatherless Victoria, and a café in the old style. Coffee served in leaky steel pots, and children eating Banana Splits and Knickerbocker Glories and other confections the colour of traffic lights. In this place the waitresses were waitresses by caste, contemplating no artistic destiny. Outside, the city dedicated itself to the notion of mobility, fleets of buses and taxis, herds of cars, and then the trains.

She was several tables away, facing him, with her slender eyebrows raised and locked in enquiry. Rodney glanced, blinked, smiled. Then it was dumbshow all over again. May I? Well if you. No I'll just...

'Well well. It *is* a small world, isn't it.'

'...So you're not going to murder me? You're not going to slag me off?'

'What? Oh no. No no. No.'

'...So you're back here now.'

'Yes. And you, you're...'

'Me mum died.'

'Oh, I'm so sorry. So you're just here for the...'

'For the funeral and that, yeah...'

She said that her mother had been very old and had had a good life. Rodney's mother was also very old and had had a good life, at least on paper. But she wasn't dead. On the contrary she was, as the saying had it, 'very much alive'. He was back with his mother. There was nothing he could do about that. He had to talk to her a lot but everything he said enraged her. Better to seal up your lips, he thought. Mum's the word. Seal up your lips, and give no words but—mum. She said,

'I can't believe you're being so sweet about the money. Have you got loads more?'

'No. What? Sweet? No no. I was upset at first, of course. But I... What did you do with it in the end?'

'I told him I *found* it. In a cab. It's New York, right?' She shrugged and said, 'Went upstate and got a place in the Poconos. We were there twenty-two months. It was handsome. Look. A boy. Julius. Not quite one.'

As he considered the photograph Rodney was visited by a

conventional sentiment: the gift of life! And stronger, according to his experience, in the black than in all the other planetary colours. 'Can he talk yet? When do they talk?' And he pressed on, 'Our code of silence. What was that—sort of a game?'

'You were a Sir. And me with my accent.'

The implication being that he wouldn't have wanted her if she'd talked like she talked. And it was true. He looked at her. Her shape and texture sent the same message to his eyes and his mind. But the message stopped there. It no longer travelled down his spine. Sad and baffling, but perfectly true. 'Well I'm not a Sir any more,' he said, and he almost added 'either'. 'Did uh—?'

'It was nice though, wasn't it. Restful. Uncomplicated.'

'Yes, it was very nice.' Rodney felt close to tears. He said, 'Did uh, Pharsin continue with his...?'

'He got it out of his system. Let's put it like that. He's himself again now.'

She spoke with relief, even with pride. It had not escaped Rodney's plodding scrutiny that her face and her long bare arms were quite free of contusion. Violence: it's in their culture, Rock had said. And Rodney now asked himself, Their culture? Well we had something to say about that...

'He's back doing the chess,' she said. 'Doing OK. It's up with the economy.'

Rodney wanted to say, 'Chess is a high calling'—which he believed. But he was afraid it might be taken amiss. All he could think to offer was the following: 'Well. A fool and his money are soon parted.'

'That's what they say.'

'Take it as...' He searched for the right word. Would 'reparations' answer? He said, 'Still doing the mime?'

'Doing well. We tour now. How about you? Still doing the painting?'

'Got fed up with it. Don't know why really.'

Although Rodney was not looking forward to his rendezvous in Sussex, he was looking forward to the drinks he would have on the train to prepare himself for it. He turned to the window. His upper lip did its thing: slowly folding into two. He said,

Martin Amis

'So the rain held off.'
'Yeah. It's been nice.'
'Thought it looked like rain earlier.'
'Me too. Thought it was going to piss down.'
'But it held off.'
'Yeah,' she said. 'It held off.'   □

GRANTA

COMING TO AMERICA
Hans Magnus Enzensberger

Hans Magnus Enzensberger

As a child in Germany I knew next to nothing about America. It was for me a continent of pure fantasy, populated by cowboys and Red Indians, perhaps with a few gangsters thrown in, though what these unshaven figures were up to was far from clear to me.

One of the salient facts of life in Nazi Germany was that you simply could not leave the place. To travel abroad was a privilege not available to ordinary people. In this respect, the Germany of the late Thirties was like the Soviet Union: a self-contained, claustrophobic space, which offered to my elders only one way of escape: invading and plundering their European neighbours.

I remember wondering whether America was real. It sounded like a figment, like something out of a children's book. Every now and then our vacuous newspapers tried to convince their readers that the United States was run by plutocrats. These were pictured with big cigars in their mouths and wearing top hats. It was not easy to believe that such people really existed. They looked like the equally implausible Jews whose caricatures appeared on the bulletin board of my elementary school. Nobody had ever seen anybody remotely resembling them in real life.

When Hitler declared war on the United States, I was probably too busy passing a Latin translation test to take notice. Because of the war, my family had moved to a village in Bavaria. To go to school was a nuisance. Every day at five in the morning we had to take the train to a town which boasted a *gymnasium*. In late 1944, the railroad tracks were bombed and all travel was suspended. This meant that we had to walk about seven miles to school and back, a daily trip which before long became very tiresome.

On this road I had my first direct contact with America, an experience which settled any doubt about its existence. On a bright autumn day, a fighter plane suddenly roared down on us. We were three fifteen-year-old kids and had very good reflexes, so we immediately took cover in the ditch at the side of the road. I remember clearly the little clouds of dust rising in front of me where the bullets hit the ground, and only a fraction of a second afterwards the hammering of a machine-gun. It was a near miss. When the plane had passed us, we looked up and saw it glitter in the sky. I think it was a Mustang. We could even distinguish the star on its wings and the pilot in his cockpit. In any case, the plane made a U-turn and came back to us, but since we did not offer a good target, it swept by without another volley. When it was gone, we leaped up and danced on the road. Strangely enough, it was an altogether exhilarating experience.

Half a year later, I was called upon to defend Germany. I was handed a greenish uniform made of scratchy cellulose, a gun and a bazooka. The Allies had long since crossed the Rhine. Together with a group of thirty other kids I was stationed at a trunk road about twenty miles from our village. We were supposed to save the Reich, which consisted of a vast heap of rubble, by shooting at the approaching American tanks. Under the circumstances I did not see much point in pretending to be a hero. I prepared myself carefully, taking along a good map and a hoard of civilian clothes which I tucked away at a few strategically chosen locations. It was a risky business, since there were a lot of people who had a mind to shoot you: on the one hand the advancing Allied armies, and on the other hand our own officers, who were eager to execute deserters.

The choice of the right moment was therefore decisive. As soon as I heard the first Sherman tank rumbling in the distance, I ducked and took to my heels. In a nearby forest I found my little cache, shed my uniform and became a civilian again.

I walked the whole night, and when I arrived at my village early in the morning, I saw them coming: an endless procession of armoured vehicles, artillery, trucks and jeeps. The men looked like visitors from outer space. They were well-fed, their khaki trousers were clean and neat, and their attitude was supremely insouciant. With a casual nod to the gaping peasants, they jumped from their cars and proceeded to light a bonfire in the village square. Some of them were black giants, and they were chewing a substance unknown in our part of the world tasting of peppermint. As soon as they had settled down round the fire, they began, to my utter astonishment, to read what looked to me like children's books. Overcome by curiosity, I began to talk to them in my rudimentary schoolboy's English. They laughed and handed me my first comic book.

It turned out that I was the only person in the village who had some slight command of the language, and within a week or so I was established as their more or less official interpreter. Only very much later did I realize that they had acted against their regulations. On the very first day of occupation, they ignored military discipline and began to fraternize with the enemy.

I had a wonderful time. As long as I could remember, there had always been someone to boss me around, shouting orders: teachers, janitors, party bosses and sergeants. Overnight, all these authorities had vanished. It was a huge relief. Of course, there was something called the Military Government, but this was an abstraction, an invisible entity far away in cities beyond our reach. All civilian road and rail traffic had ceased long ago. German newspapers did not exist. I was lucky, since I could glean fascinating bits of information from the pages of the army news-sheet, a daily called the *Stars and Stripes*. It was clear that there existed an immense outside world unknown to me, and its name was America.

In due course I made two other discoveries. One day, Captain McCann, our local commander, handed me a parcel the size and shape of a brick. It was wrapped in greaseproof paper, which gave no clue as to what it might contain. When I opened it, I found a tightly packed plethora of intriguing objects: first of all, a small can, to the bottom of which was attached an ingenious opener. Inside, I discovered an unfamiliar sort of pressed meat called Spam. Next came an aluminium foil with a brown bitter powder in it which went by the equally mysterious name, Nescafé. There were also individually packed cubes of sugar, a bag of powdered milk, a supply of aspirin, a tin of sweet pineapple, matches, paper handkerchiefs, toilet paper, and, most intriguing of all, a condom and a tube of antibiotic ointment for the prevention and cure of venereal disease.

All these things were organized and put together in the most thoughtful manner. The whole contraption was called a C-Ration. It contained everything a soldier far away from home might need, not excluding what in my eyes seemed to be the most extravagant luxuries. It was clear to me that a nation capable of such foresight was invincible.

My next surprise was even more overwhelming. Captain McCann had set up his headquarters in a large farmhouse at the end of the village. I used to hang around his office, and one day I noticed in a corner a huge box full of books. Somebody on the other side of the Atlantic had thought of the intellectual needs of the GI and supplied the American Expeditionary Forces with a cornucopia of world literature, absolutely free of charge. Help yourself, said Captain McCann.

Starved of reading matter, I could hardly restrain myself. I came home loaded with paperbacks. My hoard was a wild mixture of thrillers and classics, pulp fiction and philosophy. I wallowed in Somerset Maugham and Hemingway, Louis Bromfield and Thoreau. I remember a fat grey volume put together by an earnest American academic called Louis Untermeyer. His anthology of modern American poetry opened vistas to my fertile mind. Someone in Washington must have decided that the troops were eager to read William Carlos Williams, T. S. Eliot, Marianne Moore and Wallace Stevens, though Ezra Pound, I believe, was off-limits for the Army. I am not sure that many GIs shared these enthusiasms, but the whole operation was a sign of generosity and yet another proof of American superiority.

At the bottom of the heap I even found a few books by German authors: *Arch of Triumph* by Erich Maria Remarque, a best-seller long since forgotten, *The Magic Mountain* by Thomas Mann, and *The Trial*, written by someone I had never heard of, Franz Kafka. They all made for heady reading, even in English. After the long cultural blackout of Nazi Germany, world literature, shipped by the ton from the United States and handed out for free, was an unforgettable source of illumination in the bleak and depressing climate of post-war Germany.

After a few years, my country returned to an uneasy sort of normality. Reams of worthless old banknotes were traded in for a new currency printed in the US. Empty shop windows filled up, almost overnight, as if by miracle, with shoes, sausages, screwdrivers and apples. In a frenzy of reconstruction roofs were mended, streets cleared of rubble, railway tracks repaired. At the same time, and with the same amazing speed, millions of Nazis disappeared from sight. Most of them had instantly turned into demure democrats, blithely pursuing their careers in government, business, education, law and medicine. Nobody wanted to hear about what were politely called

Hans Magnus Enzensberger

'Germany's darkest years'.

Within a very short time, the western part of the country had become an American protectorate. True, there were also British and French troops around, but everybody knew that the true winner of the war was the United States. To consider America a 'young nation' is a well-worn European cliché. In the event, the alleged adolescent became the guardian of a decrepit and worn-out Germany. The US took on the difficult job of re-socializing our part of the world. This was not, of course, an act of sheer benevolence. Germany's future was determined by the beginning of the Cold War. Never was a defeated nation offered more generous terms, and never were such terms less deserved.

Despite the Allies' feeble efforts at deNazification, there was something murky about our recovery. Many Germans harboured silent resentment about what they saw as a disaster rather than a liberation. Amnesia was a common affliction, and the old authoritarian frame of mind was still very much in evidence.

Many people of my generation hankered for America, a place where such hang-ups did not seem to exist. In our imagination, it was a paradise of jazz, of civil liberties and easygoing morals.

As a student at one of our antique universities, I one day found in my mailbox a letter from Washington inviting me to undertake a six-week tour of the United States. How I came to be a candidate for the Fulbright exchange programme I cannot say, but it certainly felt like a passport to utopia. I was given a plane ticket and a small allowance. The itinerary was up to me, but the Washington office offered to put me in touch with any institution I wished to visit.

Since I could not afford a car, I decided to buy a Greyhound pass valid for travel throughout the US. I walked the clapboard settlements of the Mississippi delta, talked to plasma physicists and movie producers and spent a lot of time at forlorn bus depots and in motels resembling flophouses. The lack of money provided me with certain insights into the American class system. The Greyhound bus served a clientele of sailors without ships, demobilized GIs, prostitutes and a variety of other losers.

I found everybody from government officials to the last tramp incredibly easy to talk to, forthcoming and helpful. The only hitch was when I boarded a bus in Alabama and took a seat at the back. I was politely told by an old black lady that I had to sit in front. Later on at the bus stop I ended up on a bench with a sign that said FOR WHITES ONLY. The vast country I had set out to discover seemed exotic beyond my wildest dreams. Very often I felt lost, like a person in a Hopper painting. The natives seemed gregarious enough, more so than most Europeans, and yet I was struck by a pervasive aura of loneliness.

Another baffling aspect was the weird discrepancy between image and reality. At the time, Europe was still an underdeveloped region in terms of advertising and public relations. In America, the promises made by ads and neon signs seemed to be wide of the mark. The most wretched fast-food joint on the wrong side of the tracks would proudly proclaim that only here could you relish 'Arthur's world-famous meatballs'. Similarly fantastic claims were made on behalf of shaving creams, motels, nightspots and even entire states. Nobody appeared to be bothered by the unbridgeable gap between promise and reality. It took me a lot of time and effort to learn the grammar of representation which prevailed in this outlandish civilization.

And when I finally came to Hollywood, another shock awaited me. I was given free tickets to a live television show. For a German student in 1953, this was a sensational attraction. I had never seen a stand-up comedian in action, and I daresay that most of his punchlines were lost on me. But what really filled me with apprehension were two signs which every now and then flashed their message to the audience, asking us to laugh or to applaud. Both of these instructions were dutifully followed. Even now, when this arrangement has become commonplace all over the civilized world, it remains a riddle of obedience which I have never been able to solve.

And thus, when I returned home, envied by my fellow students, I had to confess that my first American venture had been a glorious failure—that I could admire this far-flung land of promise, worry about it, dream about it, but that to understand it was beyond me.

□

LETTERS
to the editor

Sex on the Pier

I have subscribed to *Granta* for many years. I have been stimulated by it, challenged by it, amused, occasionally repelled but always interested. Copies of *Granta* lie around our house and have often been the subject of discussion. We have four children under ten and they have often looked at the photographs or asked about the cover and up until now I have never felt the need to censor anything. Unfortunately, issue 61 is now shut away in my desk because I do not wish my children to be exposed to Michael Ackerman's explicitly sexual photograph: Recreation Pier at Christopher Street. I am quite happy to accept that I may benefit by being challenged by ageing sexuality, homosexuality, public sexuality or whatever else but I do not consider that it is necessary for young children to be confronted by such images before they are ready.

Perhaps the editorial staff of *Granta* live a 'cool' childfree existence—but you must realize that your wonderful magazine is dropping through the letterboxes of a huge variety of households in Britain. We do not expect to have to censor it before allowing it on our bookshelves.

Rosie Russell, The Weaver's House, Knockfarrel, Dingwall, Ross-shire IV15

I am returning pages 191–192 of your recent—and very excellent—edition of *Granta*. I found the inclusion of the pornographic and voyeuristic photo of the New York wharf to be out of character for your fine magazine.

A number of things troubled me about the inclusion of the image. The first was that the description of the uses of these areas—'the pleasure piers'—was so lacking of context that it was meaningless. It appears as a set-up—either as a forum to describe homosexual interaction as wanton and free of inhibition and values of privacy, or as a shame tactic (look at what those dirty people do!). The second troublesome aspect was the decision to portray the New York waterfront with such a clear and biased treatment. Is this the current usage of *all* these piers? Clearly not. But Ackerman chooses to identify a singular and limited example as if to demonstrate his artistic 'independence' and 'creativity'. The core of your edition was not about the diversity of people—thank God for it—but about its universal equalizer— the sea. Everything that was presented in the edition was superb—but what of the photograph? Some requisite gay quota? Sexuality, like gender and ethnic diversity, *can* be left out of a discussion, periodical, essay, edition etc. These things separate us—identify and categorize us—as peoples. What binds us, what makes us all the same (at least for a moment) are those universal connections—like the sea. Was there no gay writer to attend the issue? What was the artistic meaning of

250

LETTERS

the set of photographs? Why the coyness? Editorial discretion? Artistic independence? Freedom of speech? Sly humor? Or whispered Puritanism? Look at those dirty men—tee-hee, tee-hee...
Alex D. Keuper, Foothill Road, Santa Barbara, California

I wish to make manifest my disagreement with your publication of a photograph of nude homosexuals engaged in what should be a private sexual act (Recreation Pier at Christopher Street/*Granta* 61). Exactly what you had in mind by deciding on publication of such material defies and mystifies one's imagination; was titillation for your readers the purpose behind it? That is doubtful, since your two would-be porno stars appear more like pathetic street dogs licking old wounds than anything else.

It is truly a pity to see your excellent magazine of great storytelling taking a sad turn for the worse by depicting what is probably an illegal public show of the gay lifestyle as something perfectly natural and casual. What are your heterosexual readers going to expect next in the interest of equally fair exposure? Madonna giving head to her child's father outside some church steps? Just what is *Granta*'s intent in depicting that kind of crude sexual behaviour? Perhaps you have now outgrown plain literary endeavour, and wish to tackle a new, more commercially viable publishing genre?

If that is what *Granta* is going to be like in the future, I will consider cancelling

my subscription to your magazine. Other than that, I humbly ask that you stop pushing a homoerotic line, or any other type of crude erotica, within the pages of what I thought would always be the best storytelling magazine in the English language.
Frank Aguilera, Woodrail Drive, Webster, Texas

As a regular and appreciative subscriber to *Granta*, I took out five subscriptions to the publication as Christmas presents for friends and family. A couple of recipients have made adverse comment about the photograph on page 192 of the 61 issue in the chapter 'Taking the Air'. You will notice that one of the gentlemen on the pier is taking in a little more than air. It's undoubtedly a good photograph, but maybe foreground fellatio was going a bit far for *Granta*?
Nicholas Gray, Chapter House Ltd, Bothwell Street, Glasgow

Editor's note

Michael Ackerman's photograph prompted about thirty letters in all, none of them applauding publication of the scene at Christopher Street pier.

Perhaps I should explain how it came to be published. Late last year, Ackerman, a good young photographer from New York, came to the *Granta* office in London with his portfolio. We were preparing the issue on the sea. He had several pictures of the New York waterfront. The one of the pier at

LETTERS

Christopher Street was among several that were strange and memorable (or shocking). A week or so later, while reading a new study of the port of New York (*The New York Waterfront*, edited by Kevin Bone, The Monacelli Press, 1997), I came across the history of such 'recreational' piers and some photographs of them earlier this century. To match Ackerman's with an earlier picture seemed to me an interesting exercise in photographic contrasts—the old and simple business of 'then' and 'now'. I understood that some people might draw moral conclusions from it, 'decadence' for some, 'liberation' for others, but that it seemed to me would be up to them. All I knew was that the two pictures placed together made me think about how we behaved in public then and now, and about how we took pictures and of what, then and now. I then made the usual (always fallible) editorial assumption that if it interested me it would interest others. I knew the risk of offence, but I didn't (and don't) think that the picture was pornographic; and it wasn't posed. Anyone passing by the pier at Christopher Street can witness similar scenes, at least when the weather is fine. Yes, there was something disturbing (and perhaps also comic and humane) about this picture, and, yes, that is a good part of the reason we published it. But it is never easy to know what falls inside or outside the line of this changing thing called public acceptability, the line between surprise and revulsion, partic-

ularly in depictions of sex. And I think that *Granta* has published more disturbing pictures than this over the past twenty years, of cruelty and violence, which did not attract the same opprobrium.

I apologize to those readers who were offended and assure them that there was no catchpenny, attention-seeking motive on *Granta*'s part.

Impaled Alive

The recent sad loss of Martha Gellhorn prompted me to reread her memorable piece '*Ohne Mich*: Why I shall never return to Germany' which appeared in *Granta* 42. This time around I noticed a polemic contribution at the end of the volume by a Bosnian Muslim writer, Nedžad Ibrišimović. On page 251, Ibrišimović purports to quote a lengthy and graphic passage by the masterly Ivo Andrić, where some Serbs cold-heartedly impale a Muslim on an oak staff ensuring a long, lingering death.

The impaling scene comes from Andrić's novel, *The Bridge over the Drina*, but Ibrišimović in his *Granta* piece has shamelessly reversed the roles of the participants. In Andrić's novel the victim is a local Serb and his torturers gypsies acting under the cruel orders of the Turkish tyrant in charge of the town. Ibrišimović has also felt entitled to move the event forward several hundred years to World War II presumably to enhance the relevance to today's conflict in the Balkans.

LETTERS

Andrić is a Nobel Prize winner, and Ibrišimović's deliberate corruption of his work is a shameful example of propagandism. May I impress upon you the importance of correcting such a matter even at this late stage and even though you were not editor at the time. The barbaric custom of impalation so powerfully described was, as a matter of historical fact, practised by the Ottoman Turks against the non-Muslim indigenous population during their 500-year occupation of the Balkans, including Bosnia and Serbia. The method was considered barbarous and cruel even in an age when execution was commonplace. That a nation's ancestors should have suffered such things is bad enough without that suffering being cynically manipulated to turn the world against their descendants.

Brian Pocock
Melrose Gardens, London W6

Nedžad Ibrišimović replies from Sarajevo:

In the summer of 1992 I wrote a novel with the title *A Book of Adem Kahriman Written by Nedžad Ibrišimović the Bosnian*. The book was published at the end of 1992 both in English and Bosnian by Svjetlost Sarajevo. The book was written under incredibly hard circumstances: the constant shelling of the completely besieged town of Sarajevo. Part of the book was published in *Granta* that same winter.

In my novel I took a description of a man being impaled from *The Bridge over the Drina* by Ivo Andrić and I did not hide the fact that he wrote this and not I. But I replaced Radisav from Unište, a character of Andrić's literary imagination, with a real person, Mustafa Dovadžija, who was born on 8 October 1921, in Sarajevo, and killed at the beginning of May 1942 in the most cruel way. The atrocity was committed by Serb-Chetniks under the command of one Sava Derikonja (source: *Sarajevo u revoluciji*/Sarajevo in the Revolution, vol. II, page 436, Sarajevo, 1977). Mustafa Dovadžija was impaled at the age of twenty-one. (Rodoljub Čolaković, *Zapisi iz oslobodilačkog rata*/Notes from the Liberation War, vol. III, page 145, Sarajevo, 1950).

I also replaced the three gypsies in Andrić's novel with three Serb-Chetniks. I do not consider any of this to be embarrassing for me or for *Granta*. The impaling scene from Andrić's novel is well known by readers of Bosnian, European and indeed world literature, and I think my use of this scene has a literary justification. Ivo Andrić had to use a source for his information on the act of impaling. And here is one.

In 'Sarajevski list'/Sarajevo Paper No. 127 from May 1915 a supplement was published with the title 'An Example of the French Barbarity—the Martyr Death of Sulejman el Halebija'. In the book by Ljubo Jandrić, *Sa Ivom Andrićem*/With Ivo Andrić, 1968–1975, SKZ Beograd, 1977, page 88, Jandrić wrote:

LETTERS

"'I am sure that you have read about that," I reminded Andrić, "how Sulejman el Halebija, the assassin of General Kleber, the Governor of Egypt, was tortured. Did it have an impact on you?" "Yes, I have read it, of course," he said.' So, from the literary point of view, if Ivo Andrić can replace Sulejman el Halebija with Radisav from Unište in his novel, why cannot I replace Radisav from Unište with Mustafa Dovadžija from Sarajevo in my own?

Editor's note

Brian Pocock's letter is the most recent in a steady drip of readers' complaints about Nedžad Ibrišimović's piece since its publication almost six years ago. An explanation is long overdue.

Ivo Andrić was born in Bosnia, then a protectorate of Austria's Habsburg empire, in 1892. His parents were Catholic Croats and he grew up in Bosnia's mixed society of Catholics, Orthodox Christians and Muslims. He was an early campaigner for the creation of Yugoslavia and joined its diplomatic service when the new state was founded after the First World War. His diplomatic career ended after the Germans occupied Yugoslavia in 1941, when Andrić retired to his home in Belgrade to write. He won the Nobel Prize for Literature in 1961. The prize committee cited the 'epic force' of his best-known novel, *The Bridge over the Drina*, which had been first published in Serbo-Croat in 1945 and in English translation in 1959. The novel

spans several centuries, from the sixteenth to the twentieth, and tracks the rise and fall of Ottoman civilization in the Balkans. The bridge of the novel's title was real—that is, it existed outside fiction. It was built by an Ottoman grand vizier in the sixteenth century at Višegrad, where Andrić grew up, and its subsequent history is the thread of Andrić's book. Andrić died in 1975, before Communist Yugoslavia broke up into the separate states of Bosnia, Serbia, Croatia and Slovenia. On the evidence of this novel and of his biography, he was not a Serbian or Croatian nationalist or chauvinist; he believed that Yugoslavia's religious, cultural and linguistic pluralism was impossible to untangle and needed to be made to work. Opinion in Bosnia, however, has turned against him and he has been denounced as anti-Muslim and, therefore, anti-Bosnian.

In *The Bridge over the Drina*, it is a Christian peasant, Radisav, who opposes the building of the bridge; and the bridge's Turkish (and Muslim) overseer who orders his torture and impaling. The cruelty of this scene is vivid, detailed and shocking. Nedžad Ibrišimović, in the extract from his novel published in *Granta*, reproduces Andrić's prose sentence by sentence, but (as he writes above) changes the time of the incident from an unspecified date in the late sixteenth century to 2 May 1942; now the torturers are Christian (Serb Chetniks) and the victim a Muslim. In Andrić, the tortured man cries out that

LETTERS

he hopes the Turks 'die like dogs'. In Ibrišimović, the tortured man cries out that he hopes the Chetniks 'die like dogs'. In *Granta*, about 800 words of this scene are preceded by the sentence: 'This is how Ivo Andrić, our Nobel Prize winner, described it.'

It is difficult to see how this bald untruth can be excused, even if (as Ibrišimović argues, without proof) Andrić began this unpleasant game of religious tit-for-tat by changing a real Muslim victim of impaling into a fictional Christian one; or even if the intention is subversively 'ironic'. We apologize to our readers and to the reputation of Andrić for

publishing a distorted version of his writing; for suggesting by its presentation that Ibrišimović's piece was non-fiction rather than fiction; and, in this instance, for failing to be sufficiently aware of the slippery and dangerous repercussions of the Balkan conflict on literature.

Reader's letters are welcome. We reserve the right to abridge them.
Write to: Editor's Letters
Granta, 2–3 Hanover Yard
Noel Road
London
N1 8BE

Granta's new website will be launched on 15 October 1998.

It will feature the latest information on the magazine, back issues and Granta Books; excerpts, author profiles and special offers—with, as ever, additional discounts available to our subscribers. There will also be a letters page and, to come soon, an on-line photo essay.

The website is for you—Granta's readers—and we welcome your comments and suggestions.

Design by Artlogic   GRANTA   www.granta.com

NOTES ON CONTRIBUTORS

Martin Amis's forthcoming collection of short stories, *Heavy Water*, will be published by Jonathan Cape in Britain and by Crown in the US.

Paul Auster's 'Mr Bones' is from a novel-in-progress, *Timbuktu*, to be published by Henry Holt in the US and Faber in the UK.

John Barth is the author of nine novels and two collections of non-fiction. His collection of short stories, *On With the Story*, was published by Little, Brown in 1996.

T. Coraghessan Boyle's most recent novel, *Riven Rock*, was published this year by Bloomsbury in Britain and Penguin in the US. Granta Books has just reissued *The Collected Stories*. His new collection will be published by Penguin in the US.

Gary Enns lives in the San Joaquin Valley of California. 'The Ventriloquist' is his first published story. He is writing more.

Hans Magnus Enzensberger's new collection of essays, *Zig Zag*, will be published later this year by The New Press.

Gordon Grice's book, *The Red Hourglass: Lives of the Predators*, was published by Delacorte in the US, and will be published by Penguin UK.

Michael Ignatieff's latest book is *Warrior's Honour*, published by Chatto & Windus in Britain and Henry Holt in the US. He is completing a biography of Isaiah Berlin. He lives in London.

Anwar Iqbal is a journalist who lives and works in Pakistan.

Jackie Kay was born in Edinburgh and grew up in Glasgow. She has published two volumes of poetry. Her first novel, *Trumpet*, is published by Picador in Britain and Pantheon in the US.

Deborah Levy has published five novels and two books of poetry. Her most recent novel, *Billy and the Girl*, is published by Bloomsbury in Britain and Dalkey Archive Press in the US.

Hilary Mantel's latest novel, *The Giant, O'Brien*, is published by Fourth Estate in Britain and Henry Holt in the US.

Simon Norfolk spent almost four years photographing the sites of mass killings and memorials to genocide throughout the world. His book *For Most of It I Have No Words* will be published by Dewi Lewis Publishing. He is a freelance photographer based in London.

Joyce Carol Oates is the author of twenty-seven novels and numerous collections of stories, poetry and plays. Her new novel, *Man Crazy*, will be published by Virago in Britain and Dutton in the US. She is the Roger S. Berlind Distinguished Professor of Humanities at Princeton University.

Sam Toperoff produces and writes documentaries for a public television station in New York. His novel, *Jimmy Dean Prepares*, was published last year by Granta Books.